D0935454

Due

The
Campus
Ministry

The Campus Ministry

GEORGE L. EARNSHAW

Verlyn L. Barker • Richard R. Broholm • Robert E. Davis

Robert H. Eads • Margaret Flory • Milton C. Froyd

Charles F. Kemp • LeRoy S. Loats • A. Stanley MacNair

Glen O. Martin • William B. Rogers

C. Frederick Stoerker • Myron M. Teske

LIBRARY
UNITED THEOLOGICAL SEMINARY
of the
Twin Cities

THE JUDSON PRESS
Valley Forge

THE
CAMPUS
MINISTRY

Copyright © 1964

The Judson Press
Valley Forge, Pa.

All rights in this book are reserved. No part of the text may be reproduced in any manner without permission in writing from the publisher, except in the case of brief quotations included in a review of the book in a magazine or newspaper.

Chapters 2 and 8 were published in the July, 1964, issue of the magazine *Foundations*, in cooperation with the Judson Press.

Except where indicated otherwise, the Bible quotations in this volume are in accordance with the Revised Standard Version of the Bible, copyright 1946 and 1952 by the Division of Christian Education of the National Council of the Churches of Christ in the United States of America, and are used by permission.

Library of Congress Catalog Card No. 64-15798

PRINTED IN THE U.S.A.

Contents

To compare you in words
I hesitate.
But my exuberance compels me
To celebrate
Your inspiration.
So to you, dear Claire, I dedicate
This volume.

G.L.E.

Preface

AMERICA IS BECOMING the home of a highly technological society, more and more dependent upon a complexity of data, theory, and intricate machines. To keep our nation's bewildering maze of business growing steadily from year to year requires many additional thousands of engineers, scientists, and highly skilled technicians. Commerce and industry, in light of this fact, place large monetary subsidies in the hands of college administrators. Further budgetary support comes from the government for research, much of which is for the military.

The former general secretary of the National Student Christian Federation, Herluf Jensen, has posed the disturbing "university question" by asking whether the institutions of higher learning in a democracy can remain sufficiently free to be concerned about arts and letters ("the humanities") or whether they will gradually succumb to becoming mere training schools for robot-type men.

With the tremendous growth of American universities as they continue to live and operate on secularistic principles, it becomes the primary task of the campus ministry to help Christians discover afresh how "to be" the *laos* (the people) of God.

This book is a cooperative attempt to give to those living and working on today's college campuses an overview of what the church's mission is and how it is being implemented. It is hoped

9

that it will prove helpful to campus ministers and pastors of college-town churches as they minister in academic communities, as well as to seminary students and pastors contemplating a move in this direction. Actually, the increasing number of commuter schools and junior colleges places almost every Protestant congregation in a position of ministering to students. In addition, the chapters herein presented are geared to give insight to anyone who wants to be informed on this subject, such as campus foundation board members, faculty, administrators, college students, parents of students, and pastors of the students' home-town churches.

Chapter One attempts to define — in broad fashion — the scope of higher education and the church's concern with it. Frequently in the past, many campus religious groups have operated without a well-formulated theological rationale, and program weaknesses have resulted. This chapter therefore sets down some definite biblical assumptions and theological presuppositions from which come guidelines for a relevant campus ministry.

In Chapter Two, Milton Froyd tackles the task of stripping off the layers of secondary issues to reach the fundamental problem facing Christian higher education: "Whether [the] institutions of higher learning are going to remain free to serve their own distinctive function as agents of God in the world or whether they are to become, wittingly or unwittingly, agents of the culture. . . ." He astutely analyzes the problem by concluding that the university is a "symbol of a new kind of lostness in the world. There was a time when the lost soul was symbolized in the derelict on skid row, and salvation was symbolized in the succor offered to man in his weakness, helplessness, failure. But in our day . . . we are most likely to encounter the lost soul not in his weakness but in his strength. . . ." If we are to speak to this condition, Froyd adds, it must be in words backed up by a deep and penetrating understanding of the condition of men in the university.

Chapter Three deals with the problem of "town and gown." Robert E. Davis shows, with clarifying insight, that "the college town is not always the utopia that it would seem to be at first glance." He assesses the cleavages which sometimes occur between the conflicting interests of the college and the college town. He goes beneath the surface to show why, in certain instances, college administrations and townsfolk are at sword's point with one another. Out of his penetrating analysis come some concrete, positive suggestions as to how the lack of community can be overcome. He says it is in this area that the churches can fulfill their redemptive role.

"A Brief History of Student Christian Movements" is the title of Chapter Four. In this essay the author, Robert H. Eads, endeavors to give the reader a historical perspective on the present work on college campuses. He goes back to the "haystack prayer meeting" near Williams college in 1806, traces the Student Volunteer Movement under the direction of men like John R. Mott, and tells of the contribution of the student Y's. Also covered briefly is the history of the National Student Christian Federation and its parent organization, the World Student Christian Federation. Eads sums up his chapter in the following words: ". . . the present worldwide explosion of student populations, as well as the amazing mobility of students in every direction across the world, injects a new dimension into the ministry related to all campuses. . . . The new understanding of the *laos* [people] of God is demanding of the church a depth of renewal far exceeding the changes engendered by the Reformation."

Chapter Five is entitled "Campus Culture." In it, Glen O. Martin describes how the traditions of the school, the social and economic class, and the religious orientation all influence the student culture. Where a student lives, his class and extracurricular experiences play a major role in determining the characteristic features of student life. Martin says, "Those who assume that campus ministry can take the form of one big happy family in which faculty, administration, and students sit down together before the fire to talk about religion are only slightly more naïve than those who believe that faculty and administration can be brought together in one culture." He goes on to report that the church, in order to develop an effective campus ministry, must first understand the campus in all its complexities and "find ways to be significantly relevant in its various structures and subcultures."

The first five essays here presented are thus attempts to analyze philosophically, historically, and sociologically the fundamental problems which the Christian pastor, teacher, and student must face and understand in order to participate intelligently and re-demptively in the campus milieu.

Myron M. Teske surveys the "Creative and Experimental Ways of Ministering to the College Mind" in Chapter Six. He looks at today's campuses and sees "a complex, anxious-yet-confident, mush-rooming, sprawling, giddy-with-growth community." Of this sky-rocketing phenomenon it is increasingly being asked whether the church can find either personnel or money to keep pace. To aug-ment its mission, various creative experiments in campus ministry have been and are being tried. Many are described and evaluated in some detail in this chapter, such as the residential and disciplined Faith and Life communities; the Christian Faith and Higher Edu-cation Institute; study groups organized along professional disci-plines such as law, medicine, and science; joint study conferences where more than one denominational group participates; drama and theater groups sponsored by campus Christian groups; and joint sponsorship of lectures by various denominational groups with the university.

Chapter Seven describes the philosophy, work, and mission of the Faculty Christian Fellowship as it relates to the campus min-istry. Its executive director, William B. Rogers, states that, since the university's vocation is study, the church should form its pri-mary strategy at this level. He writes, "The professor is obviously a key figure in any consideration of the university's vocation," and comes to the conclusion that a Christian faculty movement must be directed to "a high level of intellectual integrity and scholar-ship." The Faculty Christian Fellowship for ten years, he adds, has concerned itself with "affirming Christian purposes in ways in-digenous to the campus and the university's vocation" by means of discipline-research groups, study guides, and conferences.

Chapter Eight is a description of the art of preaching to an aca-demic community. Its author, A. Stanley MacNair, drives "four pegs of principle" into the wall and hangs on them his admonitions for revelance and clarity. They are: (1) to preach and not to lec-ture, (2) to proclaim the gospel, (3) to preach to a specific congre-gation, and (4) to preach to the whole of that congregation. He writes: "We do not proclaim one gospel for the learned and an-other for the unlearned, one way to Christ for the Ph.D. and another for the day laborer. . . ." Although there is need for being well versed, humble, and accurate, the most important facet of persuasive preaching, says MacNair, is the sounding of a "declarative, positive note."

There is hardly a campus in the United States that does not have many foreign students intermingling with Americans. What do we do about these foreign students? Is there a Protestant strategy to guide us in ministering to them? This is the subject of Chapter Nine. This section of the book is authored by Margaret Flory who is the secretary for student world relations of the United Presbyterian Church. In a very thorough manner she runs the gamut of problems which students from abroad face, such as language, finances, and customs alien to American culture. She alerts the reader to the expectations which foreign students have toward us. While it is true that a ministry to foreign students is needed and can have some important spiritual overtones to those involved, it is also true that "internationalization is indeed a two-way process." She quotes a leader of the World Council of Churches, Dr. Paul Löffler, as saying that "if Christ's mission is to the whole world, our ministry is not for students but with students in the university world. . . . Obviously, the 'foreign student' will have problems of his own which demand special pastoral care."

"Travel, Study, and Service as Related to the Campus Ministry" is the subject of Chapter Ten. C. Frederick Stoerker states his conviction that "faith is validated through experience . . . the mission of the church must be carried on outside its institutional walls . . . education in many dimensions occurs only as the members of [the academic] community 'find' themselves outside it." This essay addresses itself to specific programmed aspects of the "outside" experience. Stoerker reminds the reader that "the study seminar, the field trip, the weekend consultation or conference, are as important to the campus ministry as worship. In fact, in terms of those outside the fellowship, they may be more important!"

One of the central tasks of the campus minister is counseling. Charles F. Kemp outlines this phase of his work in Chapter Eleven. After giving a brief history of the field, he delineates the proper sphere of pastoral counseling as opposed to vocational and educational guidance. He writes: "The religious worker must recognize his limitations and work with those who have skills and resources he does not have." He urges a closer tie-in with the university counselor. The heart of his chapter is summarized in a practical illustration which brings most of the main principles of counseling into focus.

Chapter Twelve is an attempt to show there is a major difference between state-supported education at the university level and that given at the primary and secondary levels. This essay, written by the editor, tries to clarify the constitutional issues of religion and public higher education and further to show that state universities have much more freedom in contributing to the religious life of the students than is generally understood — as long as the principles of voluntarism and equity are followed. Because of the important part which religion has played in Western civilization, this essay urges that, in the form of primary content courses, it be included in the curricula of all the state universities.

One of the most central aspects of Christianity is found in the term, "evangelism." Chapter Thirteen, written by Richard R. Broholm, deals with this as it applies to the campus. In forthright language the author refers to the product of the second half of the nineteenth century as an "emerging new man" who is both "postreligious and postmoral." In order to communicate the Christian faith to this new man, Broholm says we not only must understand the biblical revelation but must also have an awareness of the culture out of which the new man comes. He speaks of the failure of many conventional evangelistic methods on campus, the "ghetto nature" of much of our present ministry, and the need for theological wholeness. He identifies decision not in glib phrases but in deeper commitments which enable certain things to happen. He speaks of a "tent ministry" allowing us to be more mobile, a closer tie-up between worship and work, a courage and faith which allows new expressions of form and outreach. He says, "Thus the church must more and more become a church *within* the campus community rather than a church *alongside* the campus community."

"The United Campus Christian Fellowship" is the topic for Chapter Fourteen. Verlyn L. Barker, the author, says that the subject can be viewed from two perspectives: (1) as a union of several Christian movements; and (2) as a response by the participants "to the changing scene within the nation's colleges and universities as well as to the new currents of theological understanding found within the contemporary church." After describing the changing college scene externally and internally, Barker turns his descriptive spotlight on the changing context in which the church's mission is cast. He writes that there are now signs such as a new theological language and an emerging climate for dialogue plus "a growing emphasis upon the mission of the church directed in the world, an emphasis which, to some degree, has shifted the church's focus to a concern for the world in which the church has its life rather than on itself." The UCCF is an expression of the ecumenical church. It is "dedicated to the hope that other communions will find it possible to 'own the covenant.' " In fulfilling this hope it may require radical changes, but "ingrained deeply within the very formulation is its dedication not first to traditions and structures, but to mission."

Chapter Fifteen is entitled "The Church Alive in the University." In it LeRoy S. Loats carried out the assignment of describing a variety of campus ministries. In a sense, his was the most difficult of all the assignments, because it is the fruit, the practical, tangible programming. The author shares with the readers, in a sense of forthright honesty, the experimental character of many forms of ministry which are theologically and biblically oriented. These show that the witness of the ministry "is exercised not apart from, but within, the structured life of the university. . . . Where once they had gathered for mere refreshment and fellowship, they now conceived of gathering for being equipped for their ministry as students and faculty in the university. What had once been a chummy group who enjoyed each other, now resembled a task force gathering to be fed and forgiven and sent forth to labor and live authentically in the world."

I am grateful to the many people who have helped in the production of this very exciting volume on the ministry to the college campus. Gratitude must be acknowledged to Robert H. Eads, my "father in the faith," who in conjunction with M. Parker Burroughs, was responsible for the "germ idea" for this whole venture. Special thanks is due to Robert N. Zearfoss, my colleague at the First Baptist Church of Evanston, Illinois, for the kindness and patient encouragement which he gave me; also to A.T.L. Armstrong and David Peters, my associates in the United Campus Christian Fellowship at Northwestern University, for their help in discussing the philosophy of campus ministry. The counsel of Edward C. Starr, curator of the American Baptist Historical Society, has also been highly valued. I have had immeasurable help in typing from Miss Katherine Beadle and Mrs. Virginia Batts Charley.

To Frank Hoadley and the editorial staff of the Judson Press I owe a debt of gratitude for many personal considerations over and beyond the call of duty. To all I say:

> Thanks be to God, who gives us the victory through our Lord Jesus Christ. Therefore, my beloved brethren, be steadfast, immovable, always abounding in the work of the Lord, knowing that in the Lord your labor is not in vain (1 Corinthians 15:57-58).

GEORGE L. EARNSHAW

GEORGE L. EARNSHAW

1: A General Philosophy
for a Relevant Campus Ministry

IT WOULD APPEAR, AT FIRST GLANCE, somewhat audacious on the part
of any one individual to attempt to put down a philosophical
statement that would be pertinent to *all* who work or minister in
the shadows of a college campus. This is especially so when we
know full well that we are living in a pluralistic society that represents all shades of theological and philosophical presuppositions.

In producing a book of this kind we have two purposes. One is
to reflect honestly and candidly the best thinking of Protestant
leadership in the contemporary campus ministry; and a second is
to attempt subtly but nonetheless effectively to influence the future
thinking and action of those who will be laboring for Christ in the
vineyards of the university community.

Therefore, it will be the purpose of this introductory chapter to
outline — in rather bold strokes — the total scope and particularity
of the mission of those who are commissioned to bring the gospel
to persons involved in higher education.

The first question to be briefly answered is: What is the *scope*

Formerly the Baptist chaplain at Northwestern University, George L. Earnshaw has also held the position of midwestern director of the department
of campus Christian life of the American Baptist Convention's Board of
Education and Publication. He is currently pastor of the First Baptist Church,
Syracuse, N.Y.

of education? More and more the educational leaders are coming to an agreement that, if education is to escape the provincialism and fragmentation of specialization, it must reflect a larger concept of the total-life enterprise. Taken as a whole, education seeks to accomplish two main objectives: (1) to help persons fulfill the unique, particular functions of the complete life which is their potential, and (2) to fit them so far as it can for those common spheres which, as citizens and heirs of a joint culture, they will share with others.

The problems of the modern American university are found in the context of two areas, academic specialization and vocational freedom, both of which are considered indispensable values that have been won and preserved at great sacrifice and vigilance. The student comes to the university with the broadly defined purpose of "obtaining an education," and he is given a free reign in a wondrous and bewildering world of facts and courses. The university, under the policy of disinterested devotion to truth (neutrality), takes no responsibility for monitoring the student's morals or manipulating his mind. What actually happens, as recent studies have shown, is that students find in their years at college little help in the shaping of a relevant philosophy of life; and so when graduation comes they go out into the world to their chosen profession with the same moral and spiritual values which they brought or (and this is worse) they fall victim to those ubiquitous pressures of a business society which subtly surround them when they leave.

The church's concern in and with higher education stems from the fundamental conviction that God is the ultimate ground of Truth to which every aspect of human truth and knowledge is related. Though there are many fragments of knowledge and manifold strands of truth, the church has consistently claimed that the ultimate meaning and purpose of these is seen in a framework of Christian truth. This means that students are much more than mere intellects to be filled with facts. They are, rather, whole beings composed of heart, mind, soul, and will. This understanding has motivated the church to be concerned with the whole man as it is concerned with the whole truth. This also has impelled many Christian educators to say that education is vapid and fragmentary unless it is connected to some overarching purpose, and further that students are uneducated unless they manifest in their lives some deep, personal commitment.

All this has led the churches to become present to colleges and universities in order to listen and learn, to preach and teach, to counsel and support, and to "make the reality of Christian community visible within the university, to bring the whole scholarly enterprise under the devoted scrutiny of Christian faith and Christian truth, and to assert both by word and life the claim of Christ to the service of all men's minds . . . and to define and advance the work of scholarship, Christianly understood as the veritable work of God." [1]

The campus ministries of the churches are present to the universities (including church-related schools), but must stand in no official controlling relationship with them, lest they inadvertently stifle the character of liberal learning. General practice has it that they will relate to the university in a voluntary, semi-official manner.

Frequently in the past, many religious groups have operated without a well-formulated theological rationale which often resulted in a wasting of effort and frustration on the part of the staff and an embarrassment (not to say irritation) to the university administration. Much of their motivation was a pragmatic desire to "keep the students safe for the churches" and protect them from the "liberalizing" tendencies of the world of learning. Many of the means that were employed involved a cafeteria of activities served up in a quasi-religious environment. This position was poignantly illustrated by the casual but penetrating remarks of a famous English churchman who, after visiting and observing many of our American college campuses, stated:

> America has far more full-time students' chaplains, whether appointed by the Y.M.C.A. or the churches, in universities of all kinds than any other country in the world. Yet, while a surprising number of these gentlemen show, to the astonished admiration of European visitors, a virtuosity in devising spontaneous entertainments equal to that of the great Danny Kaye himself, their intellectual responsibilities appear to sit very lightly upon their shoulders. With a few shining exceptions,

[1] Alexander Miller, *Faith and Learning* (New York: Association Press, 1960), pp. 152-153.

their purpose in the university appears to be to run a bigger and better young people's group than in the church back home.[2]

These caustic remarks show only too plainly that the experimental attempts at "student programming" often become mere activistic and socially-oriented affairs unless they are solidly undergirded by sound and well-thought-out theological supports.

What is the campus ministry? It is that special work of the church of Jesus Christ which takes place in the particular vocational community of the university campus. The campus minister is called to confront the academic community with the good news, the gospel of God. He seeks to gather the *laos* (the people of God) together in a task of equipping (training) the "saints for the work of ministry" (Ephesians 4:12), which is evangelism, reconciliation, and witness. The campus ministry becomes involved in the academic community in order to help students, faculty members, and administrators to obtain a Christian education. This means that, in the special context of higher education, a Christian is helped to see all truth and values in relationship to the biblical truth of Jesus Christ and is thereby freed to live as a whole person and to participate responsibly in the world of *academia*. For the undergraduate student it means not only a sanctification of his studies, but active involvement in witnessing to the truths of the gospel in the affairs of dormitory and fraternity life, campus politics, and all other extracurricular activities.

As our institutions of higher learning increase in size and take unto themselves many of the characteristics of small cities, it becomes increasingly the task of the Christian community to discover anew how to *be* the people of God.

CHANGING CONCEPTS OF A CAMPUS MINISTRY

At the outset it is important that those in the universities as well as those in the churches should recognize several important concepts which have undergone (or are in the process of undergoing) some basic rethinking and reshaping in the past several decades.

The first of these is found in the term, "student work." Many

[2] Daniel Jenkins, "The Crisis in the University," *Christianity and Crisis,* Dec. 12, 1949 (IX:21) , p. 166.

of the denominations had departments of student work which co-ordinated the activities of those who were assigned to work on the various campuses. While it is true that students represent the numerical majority of those on college campuses, they are only one segment of the total academic community.[3] Today, most religious bodies recognize that the thrust of their ministry is toward the entire community, encompassing faculty, students (undergraduate and graduate), administrators, and all who labor for the university. This all-inclusive aspect of the ministry is caught up in the term "campus ministry," which is preferred to "student work." This recognizes the wholeness of the community and in practical ways offsets the fragmentation and isolation that is inherent in the academic structures. It also dramatically points out that all who labor in the vineyard of the university have need of the witness and pastoral care of the church of Jesus Christ.

The second concept that has changed (which is akin to the first) is the term applied to the "professional" in this area of the church's ministry. Since the denominations operated from departments of college and university work, those who labored in the academic area were referred to as "student workers." Today in most circles they are called "campus ministers."[4] On the surface this appears to be nothing more than a changing of title or an upgrading of the office, but in reality it is a witness to the renewed understanding of the church and its mission to the world (and in this context to the academic world). It means in fact that the main task of the campus minister is not to engage in mere "religious activity," but to take the lead in the gathering and scattering of God's flock. He is to communicate with his constituency by preaching, teaching, counseling, and all other means available to his office, the unique task and function of God's people in the world.

The third function that is changing is the appearance of a broad, honest ecumenical spirit. This has taken many forms, including the agreement of four of the major Protestant denominations to engage in a common mission and strategy in their campus minis-

[3] It has been estimated that by 1970 there will be somewhere between 7 to 10 million students on American campuses (*Presbyterian Life*, April 15, 1961, p. 9).

[4] The campus worker is called by many titles: chaplain, pastor, director, secretary, and minister. Minister is preferable to this writer.

try, and a cooperative approach by the various groups in shared ministries, united service projects, joint teaching endeavors, and interfaith activities. Many thoughtful observers of the contemporary scene are saying that the time of sectarian duplication and competition must come to an end if the "body of Christ" is ever to be one as Christ has ordained it. The world of the university is different from that of our towns and cities in that it does not have denominational institutions as an integral part of its social structures. Critics of the old sectarian approach are saying that to carry out the work of the church denominationally within the context of higher education merely imposes another division upon an already fragmented community as well as being an "offense to Christ." A recent study conducted under the auspices of the Danforth Foundation in California adds its weight to the growing indifference on the part of students concerning the denominational approach to campus religious work. The study concludes:

> A clear presentation of Christianity requires some kind of united Christian approach to the campus. Above the clamor of a host of competing Protestant organizations, each intent on keeping its own program promoted, its own students stimulated, its own meetings provided with speakers, no clear voice is likely to be heard even if such a voice were directly addressed to the academic community. If the Christian enterprise on campus is contained in a plethora of confusing and competing small organizations, it will spend its force within itself and never reach out to the significant issues of our time.[5]

BIBLICAL ASSUMPTIONS AND THEOLOGICAL PRESUPPOSITIONS

One of the important aspects of any philosophical statement is that of the underlying biblical assumptions and theological presuppositions. There is a story told of a man who was taking a Civil Service examination for the position of postman. One of the questions on the exam was, "How far is the earth from the sun?" The man wrote, "It is so far away that it won't make any difference to my delivering mail on Main Street." Too many people today on the college campus feel that theological questions about God or about sin and salvation are far beyond the practical affairs "on Main Street," but it is not so! How one acts and orders one's life

[5] M. K. Skaff, ed., *Perspectives on a College Church* (New York: Association Press, 1961) , p. 20.

depend on one's beliefs. The New Testament says, "We . . . believe, and so we speak" (2 Corinthians 4:13). The following premises for a relevant campus ministry are an attempt to spell them out in brief, succinct fashion. They are meant as guidelines to help focus our ministry.

For Protestants these basic affirmations of the Christian faith are found in God's Word which is contained in the Bible:

1. God is the creator and sustainer of this world

"In the beginning God created the heavens and the earth" (Genesis 1:1). This was the insight of the Old Testament prophets (Amos 5:8; Ezekiel 37:1-6; Jeremiah 10:12; and Isaiah 42:5-7), and this also was the teaching found in many of the Psalms (100:3; 90:1-2; 139; etc.). The New Testament continued this theme as seen in the following two quotes taken from many: "For from him and through him and to him are all things. To him be glory forever" (Romans 11:36); ". . . for thou didst create all things, and by thy will they existed and were created" (Revelation 4:11b).

2. God loves the people who dwell in the world and beams his creative love toward them

"The earth is the Lord's and the fulness thereof, the world and those who dwell therein" (Psalm 24:1). This is seen poignantly in the story which Jesus told about the Prodigal Son (Luke 15) and graphically in John 3:16, "God so loved the world that he gave his only Son. . . ."

3. Man is created in the image of God

Man, whom God has created, is endowed with intelligence, emotion, and will. From the beginning man was designated by God to have dominion over the world and to "fill the earth and subdue it" (Genesis 1:28). As man stood in the garden, God looked at his creation and "behold, it was very good" (1:31).

4. Man has marred the image

Man has denied the destiny for which he was created. He has tried to become intellectually autonomous and to usurp the throne of God. He has consistently chased after false gods. Such is the story of Israel. Hosea, speaking for all of the Old Testament prophets, likens God's people to his own faithless wife, Gomer. They have "played the harlot." Man is a sinner, and in this sinful state he finds himself at enmity with God (Romans 1:18; 3:23; 1 John 1:5-10). The fundamental issue for religion in higher education can be stated thusly: "Is, or is not, man able to save himself?" The answer of this writer is emphatically "No," because man's inordinate self-interest perverts his reason and leads him to rationalize his wants. Because man is finite (limited) he needs a god. The question is, *which* god? The Christian faith says that giving trust and allegiance to any lesser god than the God revealed by Jesus Christ is idolatry.

5. *God's will is man's salvation*

"God shows his love for us in that while we were yet sinners Christ died for us" (Romans 5:8). One of my lay friends put it: "In short, man wasn't a stinker, now is, but need not be forever!" The crux of the Christian faith is that God has acted supremely and decisively through Jesus Christ in such a way that man can be restored to full fellowship with God. "The wages of sin is death, but the free gift of God is eternal life in Christ Jesus our Lord" (Romans 6:23). "There is therefore now no condemnation for those who are in Christ Jesus" (Romans 8:1). This is the gospel, the good news. Man can be returned to God in his created essence as a child of God through his acceptance of Jesus Christ as Lord and Savior.

6. *Man's life is ordered around Jesus Christ*

The reorientation of a forgiven sinner's life is centered in the conviction that Christ *is* "the way, and the truth, and the life" (John 14:6). This loyalty shapes the Christian's *Weltanschauung* or world-view. Through faith in God as revealed in Christ, he acknowledges that God is in complete control of the world including its natural, historical, and personal events (Romans 8:28). The faith that man is known by God and destined to be with him for eternity, frees man from anxiety over doubt and fear, and eliminates the threat of meaninglessness. Thus the person of Christ is central in the life of the Christian.

7. Man is justified by faith for his task of ministry in the world

Although man is freed from purposelessness and despair thanks to God's redeeming love in Jesus Christ, he is still involved in the struggle for sanctification (Romans 7:14-24). In the university, God calls man to live out his mission in the academic world and to abound in the work of the Lord. In 1 Corinthians 15:57-58, it is plainly stated that man's steadfastness is conditioned upon God's victory over sin which Christ has already accomplished. Knowing that he shares in this victory as he has taken Christ's spirit into his life (Romans 6:1-5), he can fearlessly enter into any phase of study, research, or campus activity knowing that no matter what the outcome, his labor is never in vain.

8. Man is saved to serve his neighbor

"You shall love your neighbor as yourself" (Matthew 22:39). Modern psychology teaches that a person's inability to relate to his neighbor in a loving manner can only be cured by his being on the receiving end of someone else's love. When man accepts and receives God's love, it comes into his life, heals (unifies), and makes him whole, therefore enabling him to be lovingly outgoing (1 John 4:19). Theologically speaking, God's nature demands perfection (Matthew 5:48). The spirit of imperfect (finite) man cannot be united to the Holy (infinite) Spirit. However, when the spirit of Christ is brought into a life and is able to indwell a believer, Christ's holiness seeps through his being like penicillin. God then sees him not as he is (corrupt and sinful), but as he is in the process of becoming — like Christ, who is perfect. This new center of love is what casts out all fear (fear of rejection, death, judgment) and allows man to be free to respond creatively to his neighbor without any destructive elements of guilt and anxiety.

9. The church, the society of forgiven sinners, is called to witness

Christ is the head, and all believers in the gospel are his body (Ephesians 1:22). This new kind of community (ecclesia) was called into being by God for the renewal of the saints for their mission in the world (Matthew 28:19-20; Acts 1:8). Just as Jesus called his disciples in order that he might send them forth (Luke 10:1; John 12:26), God calls believers for his church so that they may become the instruments for his mission to the world. First and foremost, the church's task is evangelistic and missionary. God in Christ has reconciled the world unto himself (2 Cor. 5:19-21), and it is the task of the church to tell the world of this marvelous gift that has been wrought for them to — "declare the wonderful deeds of him who called you out of darkness into his marvelous light" (1 Peter 2:9). Furthermore, the church is to concern itself with the total scope of God's creation. It is to implement, wherever it can, plans and programs which will insure the prevailing of God's purposes for his creation. Christians should therefore be deeply involved with national and international politics, for it is in these power structures that justice and good can come to God's children.

The church (people of God) will periodically need to gather for worship and study. Under no circumstances, however, must the gathered church be thought of as a haven of refuge from the world. It must be nourished and strengthened for its mission. Jesus sounds the battle cry: "As thou didst send me into the world, so I have sent them into thy world . . ." (John 17:18).

10. *The clergy are pastors to a servant people*

The ministry of the church to the world is performed by the people of God *(laos)* (1 Peter 2:9-10). The obligation for ministry cannot be separated from God's calling of his people. This ministry cannot under any circumstances be delegated. It is for all.

In the midst of his people, God calls certain individuals with specialized knowledge and gifts, to be set aside (ordained) as pastors and teachers for the purpose of equipping their fellow-believers in order that they might be more discerning and better prepared for the work of ministry to which they have been called. The ordained clergymen, then, is essentially a pastor to a servant people whose task is to carry the gospel to the world. Whatever helps him in this task is a part of his legitimate function; whatever takes him away from this end is not a part of his work. Campus ministers must ponder, hard and long, this statement!

DIRECTIVES FOR CAMPUS MINISTRY

From a general understanding of the context in which campus ministry takes place, plus the insights of the foregoing biblical and theological truths, we have now reached the place where some specific directives can be enunciated. They are, of necessity, broad enough in scope and general enough in outline to apply equally to the many different forms and expressions of ministry found on the American college scene. Further, their order of appearance does not indicate their order of importance.

1. *Evangelism is the major task of campus ministry*

The totality of God's people in the university community is called to bear witness to Jesus Christ as Lord of all areas of campus life. Each Christian, as part of the people of God, is a "missionary." He is sent by Christ into the world of the dorm, the classroom, the laboratory — wherever he finds himself — to be a witness to the "good news" of the gospel. He is to proclaim by word and deed that, amidst the complexities of partial truth and fragments of knowledge, there is a wholeness of life in which all truth coheres. This truth of God, which overarches and binds together all truth, gives status and dignity as it personally embraces each individual. When asked, "how does one know?" the church individually and corporately points in faith to an event in history: The Omnipotent Upholder of the universe condescendingly appeared among men as a man, Jesus Christ. He lived the life of God in human form and "humbled himself and became obedient unto death, even death on a cross" (Philippians 2:8). Furthermore, in humility when asked, a Christian believer witnesses to his own experience of finding meaning and deep fellowship in the love of God as mediated through the gathering of his people. Thus he offers to share it with others.

In gratitude for the love which has claimed the believer, he will want to share this joy. This sharing will usually take the form of a deep concern for the well-being of a roommate or neighbor. The open acceptance and support of an acquaintance in trouble often opens the door to the sharing of experience and faith. The "giving of a cup of cold water" to one in need is often one of the most powerful nonverbal ways of sharing one's faith. McCoy and McCarter put it this way:

> Seen in this light, service merges into proclamation, proclamation into community, and community into fulfilling the neighbor's need. These

are aspects of Christian witness pointing to the infinite variety of patterns which faithfulness to our Lord may take. When we welcome persons of different race into our church for supper, discussion, and worship, are we proclaiming the universal Lordship of Jesus Christ, witnessing through Christian community, or seeking to carry out God's will in improved race relations? We might well be doing all three if we do it in His name.[6]

The campus minister's task in all this is to call into self-conscious being the various cells of the body of Christ, the church. He gathers them into face-to-face relationships for study, worship, and edification. He counsels with his flock, giving them encouragement and direction. It is important that the believers are brought together periodically to be renewed by the Spirit and to be reminded of their primary mission — evangelism!

2. *The campus ministry should challenge those in the university to take seriously their vocational responsibilities*

Vocation *(vocare)* in the biblical sense means a "calling" by God to a life of fellowship and service in the church. God does not call a man specifically to be a doctor, an engineer, or a schoolteacher, except in the sense that he expects all men to be good stewards of the abilities with which they are entrusted. He does call doctors, engineers, and schoolteachers to participate responsibly in his church (1 Corinthians 12:28). Campus ministry must declare the Reformation doctrine of the priesthood of all believers, which implies that work of all kinds (including that of the mind) is an offering acceptable to God. The people of God must be helped to see that "this is our Father's world" and that they must take it seriously and live in it as unto God.

Serious confrontation within the Christian community ought to take place with reference to one's secular work. Individual students should be challenged to reexamine the all-too-prevalent idea that a college education is merely a means for more security or a higher salary after college. Continuous dialogue in the church ought to take place as to the fitness of individuals for their chosen profession. Although the guidance staff of the university is best qualified to give aptitude tests and provide technical counseling,

[6] Charles S. McCoy and Neely D. McCarter, *The Gospel on Campus* (Richmond: John Knox Press, 1959), p. 53. Used by permission.

the open and frank atmosphere of the *ecclesia* can supplement this effectively with a permissiveness in which trusted judgment can reaffirm or question the choice of an individual's occupation. If a student feels that his capacities and aptitudes are leading him to become a scientist, then he should be stimulated to become the best scientist possible. He needs strengthening and undergirding from the Christian fellowship to explore all of the ramifications that his elected profession implies and to relate it to the Christian world-view.

Faculty members also need to be challenged by the church to reexamine periodically their role in terms of their mission. They, too, need to know that there is a loving support available when in the light of their commitment they center their activities on the needs of undergraduates instead of the more prestige-laden research projects.

For the student, college life is not merely preparation for vocation; at the same time, it *is* vocation. The campus ministry has the responsibility of confronting those in the college with the Christian meaning of time (2 Corinthians 6:1-2). What God has done for man in Christ has made man's future secure (for it is in God's hands) and this security, in turn, has freed the Christian believer to live fully and creatively in the present moment. Students, faculty, and administrators must be stimulated by the power of the gospel to achieve academic excellence in all that they do. Christian vocation can mean no less than the use of the mind for the glory of God!

The campus minister must set the prime example. In his personal life he should develop disciplined habits of study, meditation, and worship. Only from the spiritual overflow can he minister effectively. In addition, he should attempt to do all he can to keep in touch with the thought-patterns and modes of expression common to various academic specializations in the university. Because he is generally not a specialist in any one subject field (other than biblical theology), he must sharpen his mental faculties in the arts, physical and social sciences, and other academic disciplines by attending lectures, having frequent conversations with faculty members, and reading. In this way, he will be better prepared to enter intelligently into meaningful dialogue with those he ministers unto in the university community. By his personal example he can be a living witness to the biblical injunction that says, "So . . . whatever you do, do all to the glory of God" (1 Corinthians 10:31).

3. *The campus ministry should provide a pastoral function for God's people in the academic community*

In the gigantic complex of mass educational plants and the impersonal commuter colleges of today, people get lost. There is, due to the specialization and compartmentalization of the modern universities, an increasing social distance of faculty to students, faculty to faculty, and administration to all others. In these unique educational cities there are power squeezes where students get "caught in the middle." There are always those out-group persons who are not acceptable to the more sophisticated fraternity and sorority crowd. There are the academic near-failures, the rejected lovers, the confused, the dazed, the insecure, and the homesick individuals. To a myriad of people with problems, the gospel of love and forgiveness is needed. Tantamount to proclaiming the "good news" to an intellectual community is a deep, honest concern for people and their problems. The people of God can do no less than their Master, who said to a weary people: "Come to me, all who labor and are heavy-laden, and I will give you rest" (Matthew 11:28).

Many problems are unique to the college campus. There are the tremendous social and intellectual adjustments which most entering freshmen must make. There are adjustments of dorm living, of study routine, of extracurricular organizations, of dating, and many more. To meet these new students and to help them in finding their place and mission is the pastoral function of the *laos*. The members of the community of faith in their daily contacts must be the vehicles for God's continuous expression of love, sympathy, and outgoing concern.

The campus minister is the key to much of the pastoral activity. He is called to the academic community to work with the *laos*. He equips them for their task of worship, study, and service. He counsels with individual members of the fellowship, helping them to see their task as ministry. He visits the sick, gives encouragement to the discouraged, acceptance to the unacceptable, "comforts the afflicted, and afflicts the comfortable" so that isolated Christians can self-consciously become full participating members of God's church. He must inculcate in the *ecclesia* the words of Jesus: "Whoever would be great among you must be your servants . . ." (Mark 10:43) .

4. *The campus ministry must accept the necessity of experimentation and research*

The communication of the "good news" (evangelism), as has been pointed out, is the primary concern of the campus ministry. Although the truth contained in the gospel is unchanging, the thought forms and the media of communication must always be changing if the people of God are to witness in a relevant way to the world of the academic community. Sometimes the church has become bogged down with old forms and language, and has actually at times mistaken the symbols that are used for the truth to which they are supposed to point. As Richard Broholm has said:

> We become enamored of the forms and engage in a kind of ancestor worship, declaring that what was good enough for our parents is good enough for us. Let us never forget what was relevant and meaningful for them is most likely not what will be relevant and meaningful to our generation. . . . If we are to effectively communicate the biblical expression of the "good news" to today's students, then we must seek to discover contemporary symbols and images which express the truth of the gospel in the twentieth century in the same way in which the biblical symbols expressed or conveyed the message of those in the first century. This is not a call for a new translation set in modern lingo, but rather a call for re-symbolization.[7]

On the other hand, we must not throw out old patterns merely because they are old. One of the unique aspects of campus ministry is its freedom and fluidity. Because of its setting and the age of its constituency, it is not bound by tradition. Unhampered by rigid institutional structures, it offers the *laos* a context out of which many exciting and new patterns of churchmanship can be explored. For instance, Sunday night suppers may or may not be relevant to any given situation, even though in the past they have been the main program emphases of the campus Christian community. It may be time for something different.

[7] Quoted from a sermon preached at the First Baptist Church, Madison, Wisconsin. Used by permission.

Campus ministry ought to be mobile and flexible so as to be able to deal with the changing patterns of the complex modern campus.

5. *Campus ministry must be responsibly related both to the church and to the university*

The lines of responsibility for campus ministry extend in two directions: (1) to the church and (2) to the university. Individuals converge on the university from many different geographic areas, coming from many local churches. The campus minister is a representative of the various churches from which the students come. He is employed collectively by them for a particular work in the university as minister and missionary. He is the called servant of God whose mission it is to gather the *laos*, help prepare them for their part in God's mission, and creatively participate with them in doing God's work.

In this sense, he owes a responsibility to the churches. The campus minister should take advantage of all opportunities to interpret the university and its contributions to those people of God who have their life apart from the world of *academia*. There may be strategic times when members of the campus religious community can get away from their studies to do deputation work if this can be arranged without doing violence to important academic tasks. Such absences must be handled judiciously. Another means of interpretation includes reports and articles written by the campus minister for conferences, conventions, and synod meetings.

The other side of this same coin is the responsibility of campus ministry toward the university. The members of the community of faith need to recognize that the university is one of the institutions ordained of God for the edification of men's minds and the transmission of their cultural heritage. It must never be thought of as a threat to faith. Rather, the responsibility of the people of God is to undergird the order which God has ordained and to help it function properly.

In its study of biblical theology, the campus ministry should come to the conviction that, although ordained by God for an important divine purpose, the university is still subject to the judgment of God whenever it tries to usurp divine prerogatives. In addition to supporting and undergirding the proper function of the university, the community of faith has the responsibility of criticizing the university *in love*. Whenever the administration fails to police its admission policies properly, and discrimination is discovered — whenever an overemphasis on athletics begins to eclipse the activities of the classroom — whenever academic freedom is threatened — or whenever any other incident causes the legitimate interests of learning to be bypassed, then the campus ministry needs to speak a word of judgment! Never are these judgments passed in pious isolation, but rather they are offered within the community of learning itself by committed members who are also God's people.

In all this, the campus minister stands in a place of mediation. He must be sensitive to both directions and, in a sense, is held accountable by both. In the last analysis, however — and this is his uniqueness — the campus minister must answer ultimately to God (Acts 5:27-32). The Rev. James V. Davison, who ministers to students at Iowa City, Iowa, sums it up by saying:

> Whatever his involvement and relationship with the life of the whole university, the campus minister must keep constantly in mind that personal acceptance or even Christian apologetics is not his primary goal. He, with the rest of the Body of Christ on the campus, works for the continuing transformation of both human life and the institution, that each may more faithfully fulfill what it is called to be: the one, a man, and a man of faith in relation with his Creator; the other, an academic community in which knowledge is transmitted, truth searched for and examined, skills developed and taught, all to the benefit of mankind and the glory of God.[8]

6. The campus ministry must periodically gather to perceive clearly its task of mission

"And they devoted themselves to the apostles' teaching and fellowship, to the breaking of bread and the prayers" (Acts 2:42).

God's people on campus are called to be salt (Matthew 5:13). The task at hand is to preserve and flavor the academic community with the saltiness of the gospel. The job cannot be accomplished if the *laos* remain isolated in the shaker. Periodically, however, it is mandatory that they come apart from their campus activities

[8] Quoted from an unpublished study paper prepared for the Committee of Local Staff, Commission on Higher Education, National Council of Churches, meeting at Lake Geneva, Wisconsin.

for study and worship. The gathering of God's people is a means of preserving the church for its intended function: witnessing to the world. From this periodic gathering comes renewal. The corporate study of God's Word in relation to the world allows the *laos* to sharpen the focus on their mission. It is against this backdrop that the whole educational pursuit takes on meaning.

Taking advantage of the natural tendency of the college community toward study, the campus ministry should develop a creative boldness in presenting to its members a systematic program of theological and biblical studies. Gone forever (we hope) are the days when campus groups had for their study emphases an *ad hoc* program of assorted topics which added up to nothing short of theological chaos. Instead, as the late Alexander Miller suggested, the campus ministry will do well to devise and develop a curriculum of study that would extend over a four-year period of time, covering the Bible, systematic theology, Christian ethics, and Christ and culture. One of the unique opportunities of the teaching function of campus ministry is that of offering to neophyte believers not only a systematic approach to the Christian heritage, but also a permissive atmosphere in which they can frankly raise ultimate questions without being embarrassed about offending official Christendom!

Worship is nourished and enriched by study. The two are both halves of the whole. In study, the *laos* discovers and renews, through vicarious encounters with the Old Testament and New Testament stories, its sense of God's activity throughout history in relationship to his people. In worship, the members self-consciously reenact the story of salvation and, with the quickening of God's Spirit, discover who they are and to what they have been called. In worship each senses his being a part of the "society of forgiven sinners." As he confesses, "It is no longer I who live, but Christ who lives in me . . ." (Galatians 2:20), he is exhibiting the radical kind of humility which breaks down the barriers that separate mankind.

For those in the academic world, the acknowledgment of God's sovereignty through worship diminishes the danger of arrogance and creates an atmosphere where persons of widely differing backgrounds and academic specialties can find a common ground for community. As they participate in the sacraments, human relations become purified and strengthened, and the call to become servants of the Living God becomes clear. As the campus fellowship meets for worship, there is experienced a mysterious ingathering of the Holy Spirit. Amid the company of the committed, there comes to the lowliest of students and the wisest of Ph.D's, a calm repose and a wisdom greater than all the wisdom of the wise. Through this periodic retreat from the world to study and worship, the *laos* of God is equipped and fortified to go out into the world with a deliberate and unapologetic witness, filled with the power and Spirit of God.

"And when they had prayed, the place in which they were gathered together was shaken; and they were all filled with the Holy Spirit and spoke the word of God with boldness" (Acts 4:31).

MILTON C. FROYD

2: The Church, the University, and the Culture

HIGHER EDUCATION IN OUR DAY FACES MANY PROBLEMS — swelling student population, lack of adequate housing, faculty shortage, and (perhaps most dominant of all) mounting costs. But here we shall deal with one matter which many of us are convinced is more critical — perhaps the word should have been *threatening* — than any of these. This is the problem of higher education being transformed into an agent of our culture.

Perhaps the church-related institution senses the problem with peculiar urgency because of the claim of such institutions to distinctiveness of purpose. But their problem is not theirs alone; it is encountered in the whole scheme of higher education, wherever the church has a stake in the education of her youth.

The issue can be stated most clearly in terms of the church-related institutions of higher education, however, and we might do so in this way: Whether these institutions of higher learning are going to remain free to serve their own distinctive function as agents of God in the world or whether they are to become, wittingly

Since 1949, Milton C. Froyd has been connected with Colgate Rochester Divinity School where he is now dean and professor of pastoral theology. Together with Hugh Hartshorne, he wrote the important book, **Theological Education in the Northern Baptist Convention.**

or unwittingly, agents of the culture (that is, of the standards, values, and goals of the society about us) — this in the judgment of many is the number one problem facing Christian higher education in our time. Among state and independent schools the problem might be stated in secular terms, but at bottom the issue is the same. Somehow, in some workable measure at least, we are probably going to lick the pressing problems of enrollment, housing, faculty, and finance, although doing so will not be easy. But there is little, if anything, to indicate that we are ready to cope with the great cultural issue that threatens to transform institutions of higher education on every level, no matter how effective educationally they might become, into something other than that for which ultimately they were designed.

It is important that we keep in mind the nature of this problem if we are to take seriously the church's witness in the academic community.

THIS IS NOT A NEW PROBLEM

Seen in primitive cultures

What we are talking about is not necessarily a new problem. We can look back and see one form of it among primitive cultures. If a function of education is to transmit the wisdom and experience of one generation to another, then primitive cultures had a carefully designed form of education.

The primary principle governing the purpose of this education was the reproduction of type. Primitive societies lived in a precarious environment where existence was dependent upon the survival of the group. In the struggle against heat and cold, hunger and disease, hostile tribes and prowling beasts, the solitary individual was defenseless and as such a liability to the group. The all-important factor in this struggle against the elements was not the freedom of the individual but the solidarity of the group.

The main feature of primitive education, therefore, was this element of group welfare and security in the family, the clan, and the tribe. Those things that were considered essential to the solidarity and survival of the group were regarded as important for the young to know, and it was in this kind of wisdom that they were rigorously instructed. The end of all instruction was thus conformity to the goals of the group; deviation from the values and standards of the group was looked upon as the greatest of all offenses. Any questioning of these values and standards was regarded as a threat to this group solidarity, and such deviation, in word or deed, was handled with ruthless severity.

Primitive education, therefore, was conservative in nature. Unable to risk the new and unfamiliar, primitive society rested its security upon the tried and tested experience of the past. The interests of the individual were necessarily subordinated to the solidarity of the group, and so the goal of primitive education became the reproduction of type. Here in its barest, most primitive form is education as an agent of culture, whose only object of existence was to serve the dominant concerns of that culture.

Seen in another form in Greek culture

We can see another form of this problem among the ancient Greeks, who sounded a new note in reference to the object of education. If the dominant characteristic of primitive education was the reproduction of type, then the dominant characteristic of Greek education in its highest expression was growth *beyond* type. Here was a wholly new invention in educational thinking. To be sure, Greek education was tied up with Greek culture — but, at its best, it was not to be conceived as the tool of that culture. On the one hand, it had the job of transmitting the wisdom and experience which had been bound up in the Greek heritage. On the other hand, it also had to be free to do the job of criticizing that heritage, baring its foundations, disclosing its weaknesses, exposing its shams and immoralities, and pointing to better, freer, more meaningful ways of life for both the individual and society. What was important was not merely the reproduction of type, but the improvement of type, growth beyond type.

Now the reason the Greeks could introduce this notion into education was that they had arrived at the ability to engage in conceptual thinking. They were able to abstract experience, put it into conceptual form, generalize it, speculate about it. The ability to do this — which now is so commonplace among us — developed through a long and tortuous process, and in western culture came to flower among the Greeks. It was with the arrival of this ability that men found it possible to become free in some measure from the experience of their surrounding culture, to reflect upon it, criticize it, and, most astonishing of all, improve upon it.

Here, in fact, is where we find the birth of the liberal arts. To the Greeks the prime object of education was to free, to liberate the individual from bondage in the culture. The object of this liberation was not to isolate him from the culture, but to enable him to return in a more responsible relation to it — this meant as a free and responsible citizen. The arts or disciplines that contributed to this liberation of mind and spirit were known as the liberating or liberal arts. In the golden age of Greek culture these liberal arts came to be fixed at seven in number: the Trivium, composed of grammar, dialectic, and rhetoric; and the Quadrivium, composed of music, arithmetic, geometry, and astronomy. These, recognized as the ancestors of our arts and sciences, became lodged so deeply in the curriculum of western higher education that for more than 1500 years, right up through medieval times, they remained relatively unchanged.

But, even among the Greeks, this notion of education as a freeing, liberating agent was a dangerous one. The idea of education as an agent for the preservation and transmission of the culture and at the same time as an agent for the criticism and renewal of that culture sounded excellent in theory. But just as soon as men took it seriously, vested interests in the culture became alarmed, or even outraged. They wanted conformity to type — that was the safe thing. But deviation from the type, criticism of the type — that was the dangerous thing. It was a threat to the security of things as they were; it undermined the group's stability, which was rooted in old, accustomed ways. So the thing to do was to obey the impulse of primitive societies in the face of such threat, and get rid of the offending deviant. Thus Socrates was put to death. And, not infrequently in the course of history, others like him were ostracized, exiled, imprisoned, stoned, and burned at the stake. There is something in the nature of things that demands conformity to existing type and is afraid of that which is different. The struggle of education to liberate man from bondage to his surrounding culture has been a glorious and a heartbreaking venture.

The early church had to face it

It was inevitable that the Christian church, early in its existence, should be hit with this problem. For several generations the church was not much concerned about education. Christians lived under the imminent expectation of Christ's return and, with this event, a drawing-to-a-close of all earthly preoccupations. The Greek concept of higher education had by this time penetrated deeply into all cultures surrounding the Mediterranean, including Roman, Jewish, and Egyptian. But this held little interest for the early Christians. Not only was it irrelevant to the temporary nature of this earthly existence but (because of the pagan nature of much of the learning itself, dealing as it did with pagan gods and myths with all of their immoralities) it was regarded as positively dangerous to the Christian faith.

But eventually the church had to come to terms with this issue of education, and it was pagan culture that forced the crisis. During the first two centuries of its existence, the church grew and spread. Its membership penetrated deep into the recesses of pagan society, even into the household of Caesar himself. As one generation succeeded another, it became increasingly clear that the highly provisional attitude of the church toward earthly existence was neither good nor wise. Life had to be lived, work had to be done, and families had to be reared — all of this in a world of pagan relationships. Some of the converts, whose previous training had been in the schools of Greek learning, soon saw that the Christian movement stood in danger of being overrun and debauched by the superior pagan learning about it unless Christianity found some way of meeting paganism on its own terms. Third-century Egypt, Athens, and Rome were seething with contentious cultures, philosophies, and beliefs. The atmosphere was rife with questions about God, immortality, morality, virtue, and duty. While some Christians continued to fight against pagan learning, others saw clearly that the Christian movement was not likely to survive, or could survive only as an enclave within a culture, unless it was equipped with the intellectual tools for dealing with its environment.

The pattern for this encounter was set out boldly by Origen, a church father, early in the third century. Origen was in charge of a school in Alexandria, Egypt, where children were taught the elements of Christian doctrine in preparation for baptism in defiance of an edict of a Roman Emperor which threatened all Christian converts with death. In A.D. 212 Origen made a trip to Rome, where he discovered how Christianity was being challenged by the best intelligence of the times. He returned to Alexandria convinced that Christianity must be able to affirm unequivocally its own claims in the face of this kind of threat. He was also convinced that Christian leadership could do this only by engaging in encounter with pagan culture on its own terms. For this reason he set about reorganizing his own school by introducing the seven liberal arts, thus incorporating the subject matter of ancient Greek learning into the heart of the Christian curriculum.

Thus, in the main, Origen shaped the response of the church toward the subject matter of pagan learning from that time to this. The liberating disciplines of such learning became as essential to the Christian as to the pagan. The basic disciplines that would go into the shaping of the mind of one were seen as no different from those needed by the other. These were the liberating arts, which must be understood and mastered — or the Christian, too, stood in danger of bondage to his culture, as many leaders of the early church clearly saw. Their insistence that the church face up to the meaning of this insight was clear-cut and decisive. The words of our Lord took on more vital meaning for them than ever: "You will know the truth, and the truth will make you free."

Although the path of acceptance of the liberal arts within the system of Christian learning was a stormy one, eventually such studies became basic to the whole later development of Christian higher education. Even during the middle ages, after the university system had become firmly lodged on the continent and in Britain, a liberal arts foundation was looked upon as indispensable preparation for theological or other professional studies. Back of this central place accorded the liberal arts within the system of Christian learning was the assumption that the free mind, the liberated, unbound, mature, autonomous spirit, was the best guarantee against assimilation into the culture.

This is the threat that has always hovered over the life of the church — domination by the standards, values, and goals of the culture. This process of assimilation into the culture is a subtle operation, which usually takes place when a people are least aware of what is going on. Militarily, Rome could conquer Greece, but, almost before anyone knew what had happened, Greece had culturally conquered Rome. In similar fashion following the days of Constantine, the church conquered the empire; but eventually it was the empire that conquered the church, established its values, shaped its standards, and determined its goals. The face of the church had come to look very much like the face of the Roman Empire itself.

It is a strange fact that, almost invariably during those periods when the church was most powerful and most respected and most prosperous, it was most vulnerable to the loss of its own true identity. The nature of the Christian faith is such that the church must have built into its very life a principle for its own constant criticism and reappraisal. A major function of higher learning from the beginning within the Christian tradition has been to give support to this principle.

THE PROBLEM TODAY HAS BECOME MORE ACUTE

The distinction we have been making up to this point is the distinction between education as a free and responsible servant of the culture and education as a captive agent of the culture. The former has always stood in danger of being subverted to the latter. In our day this danger is more acute than ever. The reason for this increased concern is clear.

Education responsible to the culture

On the one hand, higher education still has a responsible task to perform in relation to the culture. This is the task of faithfully transmitting the wisdom and stored experience of one generation to another. As this knowledge becomes more vast and complex, the job of transmitting it becomes more difficult and demanding. This is the phase of education that assures stability and continuity within a culture; it is bound up with a respect for history and tradition. Though it is called upon to serve the needs of the present, it cannot allow the claims of the present to obliterate the values and wisdom of the past.

But radical changes have taken place in the culture

But, on the other hand, radical, even violent, changes have taken place within the culture itself. These, in turn, have affected significantly the task of higher education. I am referring particularly to what has happened in modern times to the behavior-changing forces of our culture.

Not many generations ago, the major behavior-changing forces could be identified with the family, the church, the school, and the community. These involved intimate and primary relationships. Because they existed in more or less manageable units, these behavior-shaping forces were the dominant factors in forming the attitudes, standards, and practices of each succeeding generation.

But look at the revolution that has taken place in our modern culture in reference to the dominant behavior-changing forces that operate in our day! Much has been written in the past about the technological changes that have radically affected the outer arrangement of man's life. Only recently have studies been made to show how these changes have even more radically affected the *inner* arrangements of his life. Man's genius has released new behavior-changing forces in the culture — forces that are vast, powerful, all-encompassing, forces related to the mass media of communication, such as the press, radio, movies, television, advertising, and organized propaganda. These have become the powerful bearers of the dominant values of our culture. These are the new forces that tend to form the attitudes, create the wants, set the standards, and fix the goals for the oncoming generation, where once the family, the church, the school, and the community were influential.

Because these new agents are responsive to the prevailing standards of the culture, they tend to become agents for perpetuating these standards. This is a new phenomenon in culture. The technological and psychological character of the behavior-changing forces that are now dominant is something with which man has never had to reckon on this scale before.

Institutions of higher education are caught up in these changes

It is important to keep in mind that it is in this kind of environment that higher education is now expected to fulfill its role. So long as these institutions conceive of their function as strictly technical and professional, there is no problem, for here they serve dominant interests of the culture. But as soon as they try to take seriously their role in terms of social and liberal goals — liberal in the sense of liberating or freeing from bondage to the standards and values of the culture — the massive forces demanding standardization and cultural conformity begin to operate. Their power is illustrated by the predicament in which schools find themselves as they seek to do something about changing the values of college students. Value change has always been a stated objective of higher education, but despite everything colleges do to further this end — by curricular changes, new courses, different methods of instruction — studies such as those reported by Philip E. Jacob indicate that, by and large, the real forces that actually determine what happens to the basic values and attitudes of the student are outside the school. There is a cultural mold into which the students fit — there is probably less inclination to criticize that mold than ever before.

Educational institutions become captive to the culture in two ways. One is to capitulate to its demands, openly and without apology; in word and deed they become the bonded agents of the culture. The other is by becoming irrelevant to it. Verbally and even organizationally, the institution might affirm its independent role, but the affirmation is so lacking in clarity and conviction that, in the struggle for survival, the school becomes engulfed by the prevailing culture and is shaped unwittingly into a tool of its purpose.

Church-Related Schools and the Cultural Problem

We have been talking about how difficult it is for institutions of higher education to keep from falling captive to culture in our day. What we have been discussing applies to the field of higher education generally, but it strikes with peculiar force at the institutions of higher education that are sponsored by church bodies. The strange thing is that we usually find more anxiety over this issue, more forthright critical discussion of it, by state and independent institutions, so-called secular institutions, than by those operating under the aegis of the church. An examination of the current literature would disclose how broadly this condition is so.

The mission of the church related to the mission of the university

It can be said categorically that the mission of the whole educational enterprise, whether we like to put it this way or not, becomes bound up with the mission of the church in the world. Educational institutions are not the church, of course. Even though some of them are the creation of the church and have a special responsibility to it, they have functions which must not be confused with the functions of the church. Regardless of the nature of their origin and support, the integrity of the distinctive task of these institutions must be recognized, protected, and supported at all cost. Still, their ultimate mission is not separable from the essential mission of the church in the world (not identical with it, to be sure, but definitely not separable from it, either). And so, whether we are talking about the church-related college or the publicly supported university, we are talking about a concern in which the church has much at stake in the education of her youth. It is important, therefore, to remind ourselves again of the nature and mission of the church and the relation of these to the whole educational enterprise.

It is the mission of the church to serve God in the world, to give witness of his purpose for the world and his activity in the world. God made the world. He loves the world. It is in that world, with all of its evil and its good, that he set his people, the church. There is where the church belongs: It is in the realm of day-by-day relationships in the world — where men live and love, work and play, vote and pay their taxes — that the will of God is obeyed or disobeyed, where his name is honored or dishonored. This is where the church is meant to be seen, not as institution but as people — people who visibly demonstrate in word and deed, in their attitudes, loyalties, decisions, that they belong not ultimately to the world, but to God. We can establish new churches, swell our budgets, expand our sanctuaries, and minister to standing-room-only congregations; but unless all of this eventuates in a new kind of people in the world, people who are known and recognized as God's people by virtue of their ultimate obedience to him — unless this happens, the church has lost its mission.

Here, then, is where the mission of our institutions of higher learning also enters the picture. Certainly, these institutions have a responsibility for training in the arts of survival in the modern world — that is, in preparing people to earn a livelihood. Somebody has estimated the value of a college education at $100,000 in cold cash (that was a few years ago; since then, inflation has boosted the figures upward). But, important as is the task of providing each generation of youth with the technical and professional equipment to take their place in the kind of world in which we now live, this function is incidental to that of producing a special kind of man and woman. Education has always been related to its understanding of the kind of person it seeks to develop in a specific cultural setting, for cultures always tend to reflect their dominant concerns and goals in the institutions that train their young. To the Spartans it was the warrior; to the Romans, the good citizen; to the Greeks, the man of virtue and liberality; to the early Christians, the saintly man. The schools of Nazi Germany had one kind of image, those of prewar Japan another, and those of modern Russia still another. In our own day, social researchers and other analysts of our culture have given us a disturbing picture of the kind of image that dominates, by and large, America's colleges and universities. Church-related institutions or no, all are on the brink of becoming captive institutions, captive to goals they neither choose nor desire.

Let us bring this issue to focus, first, in terms of what it means for specifically church-related institutions of higher education and, second, in relation to the state of independent institutions of higher education in which the church's stake is no less direct but where its relationships institutionally are more marginal.

The issue this responsibility poses for church-related institutions

First, then, what picture of the students they seek to educate do our church-related institutions have in mind as they set about to fulfill their task, and upon what ground finally is that picture based?

This is a question which must be answered by all who seek to justify their existence as free, church-related educational enterprises. It is not enough to refer to catalog statements, point to the many courses in religion, require attendance at chapel, and hold up an elaborate program of campus religious activities, or even require a creedal subscription by faculty and trustees. An institution can have all of these and still be essentially an agent of the culture, an instrument for the support and perpetuation of that image which represents the dominant interests, values, and goals of the society of which it is a part. The reason for this is not that the institution's religious claims and professions have been defeated in open conflict with the culture; it is rather that they have been embraced by the culture. Thus they are either transformed into instruments of its support or (what is more likely) isolated into a kind of cultural ghetto where, away from the main currents of life, they are preoccupied with the purely private and personal concerns of life.

The image of the man we ask our institutions of higher education to keep in mind, therefore, is the image of the person who belongs to God — whose ultimate obedience is to God, and whose essential purpose in the world is to give witness to the fact of the new being he has become through faith in Jesus Christ, God's Son — this in what he says, yes, but even more potently in what he is and does. A style of life is involved in our affirmation concerning the priesthood of believers. This doctrine, rather than being a symbol of personal, individualistic piety (as we have usually made it), sets us in fact right in the midst of the fierce struggle of our whole culture for the hearts and minds of men — a struggle that ought always to characterize the relation between liberal learning and the surrounding culture.

We cannot ask our institutions to supplant the church in its evangelistic task, which is not their main job. If these institutions are not to be the tool of the culture, neither are they to become the tool of the church. We can and ought to look to them, however, to become the bastion of support for the image of man as a child of God. This role they can assume by remaining true to their liberating tradition and taking care lest they become hosts to the very culture they seek to criticize. In this task they will need every support. In the days to come, as their growingly critical financial need destines them to become more and more dependent for support from vested interests in the culture, whether individual or corporate, they will become increasingly in danger of serving the dominant concerns of those interests. The possibility is real that at this point our church-related institutions may stand in greater danger of being captured by the culture than the state-supported or the independent and privately-endowed institutions.

The issue in relation to the secular university

Second, the concern we have expressed in connection with our church-related institutions holds no less true, though of necessity it will have to be expressed in different form, than what is happening to our youth in the state and independent universities.

It is in relation to the secular university that the church becomes exposed to its most critical challenge. In the midst of this kind of environment, the issue of what it means to bear witness to the gospel is seen in its sharpest form. Much has been said and done in recent years about bearing witness to the gospel in the university community. We can point to ways in which the church has surrounded these communities with impressive forms of campus ministry; we can remind ourselves of our elaborate program and staff and buildings; we can point to significant achievement in penetrating the very citadels of secular instruction through the appointment of religiously motivated faculty members and the creation of strong departments of religion, even in state-controlled institutions. But, despite these achievements, the whole strategy of the church in relation to the secular university seems to be falling upon critical times. Perhaps nowhere are sensitive spirits in the life of the church undergoing more agony of soul than among those who are committed to ministering in this kind of environment.

Why is this so? It is primarily because in the world of the university the church confronts the new specter of modern culture in its most naked form. Here the church is compelled to face the fact of a new world taking shape, a world that is wise and strong and confident. Freed from any feeling of need to rely upon sources of wisdom and power outside itself, it draws upon its own resources of wisdom, scientific genius, and technological skill to fashion its own instruments of hope and salvation. Where once religion spoke to man in his ignorance, weakness, and dependence, it now attempts in this new world to speak to man in his wisdom, strength and competence — and its voice is either not heard or, if heard, not understood. This is a world in which there is not so much a rejection of religion as a crowding of it to the margin of its concern. We are suddenly awakening to the fact that something radical has happened in the world of the university: What was once central to its existence has become peripheral. The terrifying thing about what has taken place for those of us who are ministers in this kind of world is not that we feel rejected; it is that we are beginning to have the awful sense that, in terms of what we represent, we are not needed. We can still carry on our ministry, but more and more we have the feeling that this ministry is becoming farther and farther removed from the actual world of the university.

It is not that we believe that the world of the university has achieved a new kind of salvation. Rather, when we reflect upon it, we become aware that the university becomes a symbol of a new kind of lostness in the world. There was a time when the lost soul was symbolized in the derelict on skid row, and salvation was symbolized in the succor offered to man in his weakness, helplessness, failure. But in our day and in this kind of world we are most likely to encounter the lost soul not in his weakness but in his strength, not in his failure but in his achievements, not in his ignorance but in his wisdom, not in his helplessness but in his power.

Look at what has happened in his kind of world! We have become part of a generation that has produced more widespread literacy than any other generation known to man. We have more colleges and universities; more books, libraries, and laboratories; more resources for research and for technological and industrial advance — all in larger measure than any previous generation of history. But we are also part of a generation that has seen more wholesale destruction, more mass brutality, more widespread fear and hatefulness — all this also in larger measure than in any other generation of history. This is a new kind of lostness which we are encountering in the world. It comes not from the ignorant peoples of the earth, but from the wise; not from the weak, but from the strong; not from the most backward, but from the most advanced; not from those who have nothing, but from those who have everything.

The world of the university and its challenge to the church

The world of the university, therefore, becomes a dramatic symbol of what is happening in the larger world of man's existence. We are reminded that this is a world suddenly "come of age"; in the strength and wisdom and abandon of its new-found adulthood, it is a world that has broken from one after another of its earlier dependencies. Whereas we once lived in a world where we were constantly reminded of our dependence and our finitude because of the forces around us which we could not understand or control, we now live in a world where, through our scientific genius and inventive skill, we proceed without any conscious feeling of need for help from sources beyond ourselves. It is not that we of this generation don't believe in God — we do — but rather that God becomes removed farther and farther from the centers of our existence.

Yet the church is sent to this very world to give witness to the gospel. As Christians we can try to fight this kind of world, but when we do we lose our capacity to speak to it. This world must be understood on its own terms; it must be addressed at the center of its strength, for this is where man is really lost and is most in need of the gospel. Here is a new kind of lostness, with which we are not accustomed to dealing. In our day it is not in the areas of ignorance, fear, and weakness that man's problem is most acute; rather it is where his wisdom is at its highest, his strength at its greatest, his confidence at its proudest — these are the areas in which his lostness becomes most tragic. What happens to our ministry in the specialized area of the academic community in the days immediately at hand may well shape the whole ministry of the church to the world, in terms of its relevance or irrelevance to the real needs of that world, in the years that lie ahead.

ROBERT E. DAVIS

3: The Problem
of Town and Gown

> Liberty is this little college that is I don't know how many
> hundred years old in the woods of old Pennsylvania. . . . The
> college was right outside the two-bit town of Olive Hill, where
> they had a cafeteria and a movie and a roller rink and a hotel and
> stores and all kinds of exciting things, such as the mop-handle
> factory.
> They hated us in Olive Hill.[1]

THE MINISTRY OF A CHURCH IN A COLLEGE TOWN can be an exciting
ministry. If the town is relatively small, almost every facet of its
life is affected by the presence of the college. There is frequently a
vitality and progressive spirit in such a town that offers the potential for a dynamic ministry. There are also certain cultural benefits
which the college brings to the community which make a college
town a delightful place to live and raise a family.

However, the college town is not always the utopia that it would
seem to be at first glance. Occasionally, the progressive spirits of the

[1] Marshall Terry, Jr., *Old Liberty* (New York: The Viking Press, 1961) , pp. 5-6.

Robert E. Davis has been associated with the field of campus ministry since
1945, serving at Amherst College, State University College of Education
(Fredonia, N.Y.), University of Nebraska, and as western regional director
for the department of campus Christian life of the American Baptist Board
of Education and Publication. Currently, he is the executive director of the
Division of Christian Higher Education of the same board.

college become too progressive for some of the more stable personalities of the community, and the youthful enthusiasm of the students becomes an irritant to the quieter elements of the community. Gradually the lines are formed, with those related to the college lining up on one side, and those representing other elements of the community on the other. When this cleavage occurs, and it does occur all too frequently, we have what has been described as the town-and-gown problem. It may be an almost subconscious undercurrent in the life of the community, one about which nobody speaks, yet which nobody can fail to sense. Or it may manifest itself in open hostility in the community, resulting in hard-fought, bitter campaigns in local elections, harassment of local merchants by college students, and harassment of students by local authorities.

Who is responsible for such a condition? It would be unfair to lay the blame wholly on one side or the other. In most cases there are factors on both sides which create the conditions out of which the difficulties emerge. In many cases, the colleges are guilty of trying to create an "ivory tower" of scholarship and erudition which is cut off from the world of everyday affairs. This condition stems from the feeling that involvement in community activities on the part of students and faculty will result in less effective academic accomplishments in classroom and laboratory. It is a carry-over from the period in our history when most students "went away to college." They would leave home, take up residence in an academic community and live out four years that were largely wrapped up in activities on that campus. In recent years, and especially since World War II, there have been fewer campuses of this type. In spite of larger numbers of commuting students, some colleges have attempted to preserve the close-knit-community idea, and in so doing have set an artificial barrier between the college and the larger community.

In other cases, the colleges have been guilty of intellectual snobbery of the worst order. There can develop, among faculty and students alike, a lack of appreciation for the contributions that might be made by persons outside the academic community, and in time this lack of appreciation can become contempt. From this comes the next step; not only do these town folk become unable to contribute, but probably also unable to understand the things being said within the academic community. Communication therefore breaks down under the rationalization of not casting pearls before swine.

Certain more earthy reasons have created the problem in some situations. In order to keep a community beholden to the college, and to insure an adequate labor supply for non-academic jobs on the campus, some colleges have exerted pressure to keep any form of industry out of the community. To be sure, the reason for such action is never stated in such crass terms, but rather is couched in such a phrase as "We want to keep the cultural standards high." The lack of work opportunities in the community directly traceable to the college is bound to produce resentment among those who are forced to seek a livelihood outside the academic community.

But certainly not all of the blame for the town-and-gown problem can be laid at the feet of the colleges and universities. In many cases, the difficulties arise from a lack of understanding on the part of the townspeople as to the nature of the educational process and the role of the college. Since in 1950 only 7½% of the American population over 25 years of age had graduated from college, it is not surprising that colleges and college life would be a mystery to many people. Vague rumors about "radical" ideas being expressed on campus can become blown up into something that produces fears and suspicions in an atmosphere where there is no understanding of the fact that a college by its very nature must explore any ideas, however "radical," and must pursue every line of inquiry if it is to be true to its calling.

Nor is the town free of mercenary reasons for resentment of the college. Some town officials look with a covetous eye at valuable real estate that enjoys the tax-exempt status of a non-profit institution. They feel that the college, in such a favored role, is not pulling its weight on the oars, and so they begin to have some resentments.

There are also lesser reasons for tension: the competition which the young non-college men of the community feel from the college men in trying to win the hearts of the young ladies of the community, the feeling of merchants that faculty people do not represent a high-income market potential, the fact that any concentration of energetic young persons in one place for a long period of time is certain to produce periodic eruptions of one kind or another (especially in the spring!). All of these combine to produce tensions, misunderstandings, and occasional hostility.

The church in a college community is inevitably involved in such a clash, since it is called to serve both town and gown. Any sharp cleavages that exist in the town are almost certain to carry over into the life of the church, and have been known in some cases to be of prime importance when considering such matters as the composition of a board of trustees or a board of deacons. While some churches are content to be victimized by such a bifurcation, or even help to widen the gulf, others have seen in the situation the opportunity for a significant ministry of reconciliation. There are things that can be done by both the college and the town to bridge the gap, and the church may be the mediating agency in helping each to discover these things.

For example, the college might be urged to expand its services to the community through a town-and-gown cultural series of concerts and lectures. This needs to be done through a joint planning committee rather than being planned solely by the college and presented to the town, a procedure that could be mistaken by the people for a patronizing act. As a body concerned for both groups, the church in the community might take the lead in forming such a committee. The college may also offer community courses, not necessarily for college credit nor requiring regular college admissions standards, but dealing with issues that are of real concern to persons in the community and offering the insights of college personnel who have a contribution to make in this area. A university in Ohio has made many friends in the community through courses of this kind as a supplement to its regular curricular offerings.

If there is a strong feeling in the town that the college is a financial liability rather than an asset (because of tax-exempt status, the discouraging of industry in the town, and a comparatively low salary scale), a dramatic demonstration of the college's contribution to the town's economy can have a good effect. On a given occasion, accompanied by adequate publicity in the local press, some colleges have paid their entire payroll in silver dollars. The presence of the silver dollars in the cash registers of the community provide a tangible reminder of the economic value of the college to the community.

On the other side, suggestions might be offered to the town as to ways in which it may assist the college. One such way is by encouraging support of college activities such as plays, concerts, and lectures. Another area of cooperation involves the use of college faculty and research personnel in community projects. A town should not import an "expert" in some field from miles away, bypassing an equally competent person on the college faculty simply because he is a local resident. There is a temptation on the part of townspeople to think that they can't use Professor Jones as the professional consultant on their sociological study, because "everybody knows good old Charlie from the Rotary Club," forgetting that "good old Charlie" may be one of the nation's most competent sociologists. A judicious use of college personnel can do much to promote harmonious relationships, providing, of course, that this use shall not mean exploitation and that it is remembered that "the laborer is worthy of his hire."

The basic problem which underlies the town-and-gown problem is that of lack of community. Where it becomes obvious that there are two separate communities within the confines of one geographical area, the problem becomes intense. The solution lies in helping those in the two communities to find areas of common life. It is in this area that the church can fulfill its redemptive role, since the needs of men, seen in theological perspective, are the same whether they are part of an academic community or not. The church is engaged in a ministry that confronts all men with the fact of their humanity, together with the reality of redemption and the possibility of the new life in Christ. As men respond to the call of God in Jesus Christ, they fulfill their vocation in many ways, some within an academic community, but more often outside it. But the Christian vocation is essentially one vocation, and all men share in common their need of the redemptive love of God in Jesus Christ.

The ministry of the church of Jesus Christ is essentially one ministry — whether to plumbers, ditchdiggers, or faculty members. When we speak of "the ministry to the academic community" it is easy to fall into an error of thinking of the academic community as a "thing" or an "institution," whereas our ministry is always to persons. So the ministry of the church is not to the university or college as an institution, but to all the persons who make up the academic community — the students, faculty, administration, house-mothers, groundkeepers, and others.

Furthermore, in the Protestant tradition, we do not think simply in terms of a ministry "to" someone in the sense that a professional minister, who stands outside the everyday affairs and concerns of those to whom he ministers, brings something to those to whom he ministers. Rather, the concept of the ministry of the laity, known to the New Testament church but only recently rediscovered by the twentieth-century church, recognizes a ministry of persons to persons, in which the professional minister acts as a kind of catalytic agent, helping all of the members of the church to fulfill their ministry. The ministry of the laity cannot become an incestuous matter within particular esoteric groups, whether these groups be social, economic, racial, or occupational. The ministry of the church is a ministry *of* and *to* the whole church, and to the world.

While there may be certain specialized needs of particular groups which a church must recognize in its planning and its program, the emphasis given to a particular group should not be so overpowering as to crowd out the needs and concerns of other groups and individuals in the church. A church that is located in a college town dare not become so college-oriented that it neglects to minister to the needs of those outside the college community. The persons from the college can and should minister to the rest of the community, and those from the community can make a significant impact on the lives of those within the academic framework. One of the churches in Cambridge, Massachusetts, has found that small study groups that are not organized in the traditional patterns of students, senior citizens, or women, but rather *cut across* these artificial barriers, produce a significant encounter that is more enriching to the group members than that of the traditional, homogeneous groups.

A church that attempts to take on the colorations of the academic community of which it is a part may find its life as a church becoming an extension of the life of the college. There is always the danger that a college or university may become so absorbed in its internal problems that it fails to see the need to grapple with larger issues in the world. If the church is representative of the larger community, it can be effective as the conscience of the college, helping Christians to sense their responsibility for fulfilling their Christian vocation within the academic community. For example, few colleges today are grappling in a serious and significant way with the tremendous problems of war and peace, overpopulation, and the race issue; at best, these become the subject of occasional forays or skirmishes, but are seldom the object of research and study in depth. The church can be the stimulus challenging the college to rise above the temptation merely to prepare technologically competent people to do a job. The church can inspire the college to prepare persons of deep commitment, as they live in the world, to deal with the basic issues of our time in the light of the Christian ethic.

An essential part of the work of any contemporary Protestant church is the preaching ministry. This poses certain peculiar problems in the college-town church. Chapter 8 of this book deals with the problem of preaching to the academic community in greater depth than we shall do here, but some mention must be made of the problem that faces the preacher who tries to preach to both town and gown. In many ways the task of the college chaplain is easier, since he is preaching to a more homogeneous congregation. However, the problem is not insoluble. Part of the difficulty lies in an improper understanding of what is expected by the various parts of the congregation.

In the first place, it is quite inaccurate to assume that the plumber and hardware salesman are not capable of understanding theology or biblical exegesis, and that they must therefore be fed puerile Bible stories and harmless homilies that suggest the possibility that they should try to behave themselves between Sundays. The contemporary preacher, whether in a college town or elsewhere, is always faced with the challenge of presenting the gospel and profound Christian theology in terms that are understandable and relevant to the butcher, the baker, and the candlestick maker.

The second misconception is that students and faculty are looking for esoteric lectures presented in polysyllabic words dealing with themes that would have no interest to the man in the street. To be sure, the profound theological lecture has its place, but that place is in the university itself, and provision should be made for it in every college and university. But the preaching of the Word, the *Kerygma,* is not a lecture, and should not be so confused. The preaching service is not the occasion for the preacher to impress the faculty with his erudition. Faculty and students are persons who come to church to hear the redemptive word. They come believing that their souls may be fed, and to give them a lecture is to give them stones when they are crying for bread.

What kind of preaching is adequate to speak to both town and gown? In the first place, it need not be different in kind from that which *should* characterize all contemporary preaching. It should have sound biblical and theological content, have relevance for contemporary life, be couched in language that is understandable to all who hear, and be logical, coherent, and consistent with our knowledge of the world. Such preaching would be meaningful and helpful to all who heard it, whether from the academic community or the nonacademic walks of life. If preaching shows good preparation and intelligent ordering of content, it will satisfy the most articulate members of the congregation. Specialists in certain academic areas do not expect the minister to demonstrate competence in their disciplines, although they will undoubtedly welcome any illustrations drawn from those disciplines that are both timely and accurate. A minister of a college-town church recently used an illustration from the field of chemistry in which he referred to "the 92 elements," thus dating his own undergraduate chemistry course, and revealing the fact that he was completely unaware of developments of the most basic sort in that discipline since that time.

While faculty members will not expect the preacher to be competent in their fields, they do have every right to expect that he will be competent in his. They will expect preaching to reflect continuing study and intellectual growth, indicating an awareness of new trends in biblical studies, theology, Christian ethics, and Christian education. Preaching that seems to indicate that the minister has not cracked a book since his seminary days is not likely to command a respectful hearing in an academic community, nor should it be expected to do so anywhere.

A possible source of tension between town and gown may be felt if the church attempts to create within the church the kind of openness to criticism and inquiry to which persons within the academic community are accustomed. Nonacademic people may tend to see such openness as a threat to the preservation of the faith and may tend to discourage the asking of questions on the part of students. And yet, the failure to provide this kind of openness is almost certain to drive college young people away from the church, since they will tend to identify the church with anti-intellectualism. Actually, we are coming to the place where no church, in a college town or not, can afford to deprive young people of all ages of the privilege of exploring questions of all sorts that may be bothering them. Many young people are disillusioned with today's churches because of this lack of openness, and are asking their questions and exploring possible answers — in the coffee houses, not in the churches.

In addition to feeling a sense of openness in the church, students should be made to feel that they are a part of the community of faith as well as of the community of learning. Students are sensitive to the attitude, sometimes manifest in college-town churches, that the students are a necessary evil to be endured rather than persons to be known and loved. While this attitude is largely dependent upon the basic feelings of the church members, certain programs can be initiated in the church to improve the relationship.

One such program is the student membership plan. Actually, there are two such plans. The first of these is to provide a special student membership in the church, with all the rights and privileges of regular church membership, but with the stipulation that regular membership shall remain in the student's home church, and that upon the termination of his college career he shall be dropped from the special membership role of the college-town church. A variant of this plan grows out of the feeling that a "student membership" is a kind of *ersatz* membership, and that students need to learn real churchmanship as early as possible. Therefore, churches holding this position put on special membership drives in the fall to encourage students to move their regular membership from their home church to the college-town church. In both cases, the purpose is to give the student a sense of genuine identity with the church.

Another program that some churches have used to help integrate students into the life of the church is what has been called the "church parent" plan. In this program, couples in the college-town church "adopt" students for the school year, and make it a point to have them in their homes frequently throughout the year. Obviously, the plan works only as well as the ability of the "parents" to express genuine love and concern for their "children." Some churches have found this to be a very fruitful program, not only in terms of integrating the students into the church, but also of rendering a significant ministry to the students. In one case, an unmarried student at an eastern university became pregnant during the school year. It was significant that the first person to whom she turned for help was not the dean of women, the college chaplain, the pastor of the local church, nor the college counselor; it was her church "mother"! Before a church undertakes a "church parent" program, there should be considerable attention given to orienting the "parents" as to their role in relation to the students. Care must be taken that it does not degenerate into a program of smothering affection, or of interfering in the lives of students at the very time when they are seeking to be independent and to establish identity.

Another source of tension between town and gown lies with the minister himself, and the attitude of the church toward the amount of time that the minister spends with each group. It is not unusual for a "town" church to feel resentful of time spent on campus by a pastor. This is less likely to be the case if some of the other sources of tension have already been dealt with in a creative way. The church will then see that the campus is also a genuine part of the pastoral concern of the church, and that the time which the minister spends with the students, faculty, and administration is not time that should be "theirs." This particular problem is sufficiently serious that any pastor being called to a college-town church would be well-advised to agree upon a division of time before accepting such a call. Whether or not a local church pastor should take classes at the college or university may be a question fraught with some difficulties, but, in general, the practice should be looked upon with favor, since it serves to identify him in a genuine way with the academic community and will also tend to keep him intellectually alive. Similar positive values may attach to the question of whether or not a pastor should teach at the college or university. If he has the proper academic qualifications (if he didn't, he would be foolish to try to teach, and the college would be foolish to hire him!) this could be a mutually beneficial relationship between the church and the academic community.

Actually, the problem of town and gown is rapidly ceasing to be a problem. In part, this fact is due to the changed patterns of collegiate life since World War II. There are fewer distinctively college-town pastorates, simply because there are fewer distinctively college towns! Because of improved transportation, there are many students who commute daily as much as 60 miles. Many others drive much farther on weekends. The result is that colleges that were once isolated islands of learning, now have large numbers of commuting students living out large portions of their life detached from the college or university. At the same time, the percentage of high school graduates going on to college continues to rise, with the result that there are fewer "townies" around to feel resentful toward those who have had the privilege of education that was denied them. Also, because more and more of our population are going to college, there will be less of an intellectual gap between town and gown.

But at the same time, while it is true that there will be fewer distinctively college-town pastorates, it is equally true that in another sense there will be more college-town pastorates. That is, while there are fewer of the traditional isolated college towns and, therefore, fewer college-town pastorates, many new kinds of colleges are springing up within close proximity of most of our population, so that in a real sense almost every church will be a college-town pastorate. A recent study in the Los Angeles area confirmed the fact that most of the churches of one denomination in that area had college people, both students and faculty, in the congregation. They were from a variety of institutions, and frequently did not know one another as members of an academic community, but they were present in churches that a few years ago would never have conceivably been called college-town churches. The U. S. Office of Education predicts that by 1980 there will be at least a junior college within 30 miles of every United States citizen.

This means that every church is going to be faced with the problem of ministering to the academic community. Every pastor will be faced with the problem of preaching to both college and non-college persons in his congregation. So, while the intensive problem in a few unique spots disappears, a more extensive one looms ahead.

ROBERT H. EADS

4: A Brief History
of Student Christian Movements

A PERSON FIRST CONFRONTING THE COMPLEXITIES of the campus ministries in the United States has a sense of bewilderment which can be fully appreciated by those who have invested their lives with students. It is not easy to simplify the telling of the story of the movement and structures that have grown through the years, but some things are clear. In the midst of the swirling cross-currents of history God has been constantly at work, and right in the middle of the stream is the student, perhaps confused, but almost always willing and eager to throw his full energies into whatever challenge is posed by his time.

Students have always taken the initiative in relation to their interests and organizations. Records from the oldest European universities, like Bologna in Italy or the Sorbonne in Paris, show that students through the centuries have often had great power and assumed unusual risks. There have been times when their radical initiative not only controlled curricula and faculty salaries in the universities but toppled governments and radically altered solid social structures.

Robert H. Eads was once the Baptist university pastor at Pennsylvania State University, and is now director of field education and assistant professor of religion in higher education at Colgate Rochester Divinity School.

Christian students have not infrequently been in the vanguard. In American colonial times active voluntary Student Christian groups formed almost as soon as the universities were chartered. In the 1690's Harvard seems to have had the first such group in America. Colonial education was designed in such a way that students might be "fitted for Publick employment both in Church & Civil State."[1] Most of the twenty-two colleges in existence in the New World before 1800 were founded by "pious and learned gentlemen" whose earnest Christian concerns led them personally to assume administrative responsibility for campus religious life. But the students themselves did not always see eye to eye with administration's interpretations or interests in religion. They took initiative themselves, and in the earliest times often met in secret — either to avoid strong faculty paternalism or to escape acid criticism of fellow students. In spite of a prevailing secularism that made the identifiably Christian groups something of a "remnant," there were sixteen of these twenty-two early American schools that had Christian groups meeting regularly.

Intellectual currents during the Enlightenment ran strong on these campuses, and the Christian minority at that time was in a sort of arena, as it often is today. In Williams College, for example, in the first five years of its history (1793-1798) only five of the ninety-three students dared profess their faith publicly. In the Dartmouth class of 1799 there was one professing Christian. But the turn of the century witnessed revolt and revival together. On the one hand, with the American Revolution over, materialistic and atheistic philosophies were popular and intemperance was commonplace; conventional moral standards were held lightly. On the other hand, religious revivals during this same period brought new religious societies in Harvard, Brown, Dartmouth, Bowdoin, Middlebury, Andover, and other schools. Unlike the secret religious societies of the past, the new groups functioned openly. Although most of them were devotional in nature at first, they soon broadened their concerns to include missionary zeal and social questions.

One memorable event from this period was the now famous "haystack prayer meeting" near the campus of Williams College in 1806.

---

[1] Yale University Charter, 1701. (*Bulletin of Yale University*, 1 November 1963, p. 100.)

A group of undergraduates, caught in a torrential rain, took refuge under a haystack and while waiting for the storm to pass they resolved in prayer to undertake a worldwide mission movement which had been the subject of long discussion among them. Their leader, Samuel J. Mills, guided them into organizing on September 7, 1808, the "Society of Brethren." Students offered themselves freely for overseas service. By correspondence and personal contact on an intercollegiate basis, widespread student support developed which led in no small way to the establishment two years later of the American Board of Commissioners for Foreign Missions (Congregational), the first American foreign mission agency. The movement thus begun led also rather directly to the formation a few years later of the student YMCA and YWCA, and much later to the Student Volunteer Movement. The immediate results, including the ordination of five missionaries in 1812 (Adoniram Judson, of Brown University; Samuel Knott, Jr., of Union College; Samuel Newell, of Harvard; and Gordon Hall and Luther Rice, both of Williams College) kindled a spark that brought light in many places. The beginnings of the American Bible Society, the American Educational Society, and the American Colonization Society are interwoven with this whole student thrust.

One of the most lasting influences of the Society of Brethren was the development of the technique of intercollegiate correspondence. Small and sometimes isolated student groups began to feel a dynamic identity with a world Christian mission. Information from the far corners of the earth was copied and shared by corresponding secretaries. The groups united in prayer revivals. Though they could not meet because of geographical separation, on June 17, 1815 they established the hour of nine o'clock as the time for "A Concert of Prayer," which eventually grew into the World Day of Prayer for Students. Home Mission endeavors sprang up as churches were founded on the frontier, and mission offerings were secured.

By 1850 student Christian groups tended to fall into four patterns: development of the devotional life, theological debating, mission study and correspondence, and study and action on ethical issues such as anti-slavery and temperance. In England the Young Men's Christian Association was established to provide living quarters, Christian teaching, and fellowship for young workers.

The YMCA movement spread rapidly and became a force on the American college campus, first at the University of Virginia (Charlottesville) in 1857 and almost immediately after that at the University of Michigan (Ann Arbor). The YMCA idea gathered up all of the previous student group emphases (devotional, theological, ethical, mission) in a package and gripped the young "lay apostles." Although the English movement was only for young men, on the campuses in America the young women were gladly incorporated from the start! Within a few years the fast-forming Christian Associations employed young Luther Wishard as a traveling secretary. He was continuously on the road, and by 1870 he had drawn delegates from forty colleges to the Louisville YMCA convention where a National Student "Y" was formally recognized as a part of the parent movement. In 1886 the National Intercollegiate YWCA was constituted.

Strong new currents of evangelical revival were moving in the student stream. The world vision of student groups was matched by local growth and intercollegiate contact. The time was ripe for tremendous new developments. From the beginning the student Christian movement had been interdenominational, international, and intercollegiate as the Y's served as the strong right arm of the churches on the campuses. In 1886 the first Intercollegiate Student Conference was held at Northfield, Massachusetts with the evangelist Dwight L. Moody as leader. Great expectations were clearly evident in the fact that the conference was planned to last for an entire month. Obviously only students of strong purpose would devote such a large portion of their valuable summer. Furthermore the conference was relatively unstructured; the only structure consisted of long periods for thought, conversation, and personal contact with the great evangelist.

A young law student, John R. Mott, of Cornell University, decided to attend the conference, and to walk all the way to its Massachusetts location from his campus at Ithaca, New York. Doubtless the economic factor entered into his decision, but he told his friends he wanted time to prepare himself alone. Later, when he had become "the most widely known man in the life of academia on five continents," and had been decorated by literally dozens of governments with their most coveted medals as a world Christian statesman, he spoke of this conference and the hours of thought and prayer as he walked to it as the most formative influence in his entire life.

It was at this conference that one hundred men volunteered for mission service overseas. Spontaneously the Student Volunteer Movement arose from this initial group experience. The "Mt. Hermon Hundred" (as they came to be known) spearheaded deputations to campuses in an unparalleled nationwide movement that electrified the student world. Students around the world felt the impact of these efforts, for between 1899 and 1914 more than 3,400 of the 4,500 missionaries who sailed from North America under Student Volunteer auspices came from the work of the student YM and YWCA's.

The conference pattern has become an established procedure in the American (and World) student Christian movements. The Student Volunteer Conferences have usually drawn more than 2,000 students, even up to the present time. The 1959 Quadrennial Conference at Christmastime in Athens, Ohio, brought together 3,600 students, of whom nearly 1,100 were from eighty different countries of the world.

The burst of vitality just before the turn of the century led directly to the formation of the World's Student Christian Federation in 1895 and the development of at least twenty-two national student Christian movements within two years. The leading spirit was John R. Mott, who had meanwhile been elected traveling secretary of the Intercollegiate YMCA in the United States and Canada. The Federation's work will be outlined later in this chapter.

Mott's influence was felt in many places during this period. By 1900 the student "Y" had developed 628 campus associations with almost 32,000 members and sixty-four full- or part-time secretaries. Twenty of the associations were housed in their own buildings, which became student centers of study and activity. Mott followed Moody in 1893 as director of the Northfield Conferences, which were now well established, setting a pattern for conference centers that developed on a regional basis under "Y" auspices all across the continent. He led in the strong evangelical emphasis, "To Win College Men to Christ," and with a strong team of co-workers introduced the "social gospel" emphasis that heightened the ethical aspects of evangelism. The Day of Prayer for Students was now seriously sponsored to unite the Christian students of the world. By 1908 the Bible study aspect of the student Christian movement, which had for twenty-five years been the basic undergirding factor of the program, reached a new climax in the 250 leadership training institutes held during a two-year period. Texts, study guides, and devotional books were specially published for the student movement, taking into account the tremendous development of biblical scholarship of that period. Today the publications of the Association Press still form the core of extensive literature beamed toward students. Theological students were integrated into the student movement through an Interseminary Movement, sponsored in its early years (beginning 1898) by the Student Committee of the YMCA. Work with foreign students was highlighted by the organization in 1911 of a Committee for Friendly Relations among Foreign Students. This came more than 23 years after Luther Wishard, the first traveling secretary of the "Y," had made a special point of inviting foreign students to the Northfield Conferences.

With the emergence of tax-supported universities, vast changes began to take place in American higher education. These universities had been greatly expanded after Lincoln signed the Morrill Land Grant Act in 1862 establishing Land Grant Colleges and putting practical instruction in such things as agriculture and engineering on a par with the liberal arts. Enrollments mushroomed, including thousands of Christian young people who might otherwise have gone to church-sponsored schools. These young men and women found the state colleges and universities appealing because of expanded curriculum offerings, economic advantages, and a variety of lesser reasons. The "Y" found it increasingly difficult to reach the vast number of students alone. At the same time the rise of Christian liberalism in theology, plus the growth of social action and sense of mission, often made the students critical of the churches from which they had come. The churches, in turn, feared that the best students were not being recruited at college for kingdom tasks as the churches saw them. The religious welfare of students had been virtually "handed over to the Y's," but now, to meet what was considered to be a numerical and spiritual need, the denominations began to set up their own "student foundations" and employed university pastors on many campuses. The first actual foundation was organized at the University of Illinois in 1907 although there had previously been considerable church-sponsored work based on careful studies. Soon all of the major Protestant denominations were deep in the work. Catholic and Jewish student groups likewise developed.[2]

As this movement of the churches to "follow their students to the campus" progressed, there was a growing need for financial undergirding and the selection of adequate leadership. Hence came the development of denominational boards of higher education. Whereas the "Y" program had most frequently and effectively laid stress on the leadership of the laity, the churches' selection of personnel tended to center on highly trained ordained people, called university pastors. In other ways, this new movement often followed the pattern of the "Y." The students were encouraged to become members of local churches and participate in them. Pastoral work included personal counseling in academic, vocational, marital, and religious areas. Recruitment for "full-time Christian service" was undertaken. Service in the local churches and through evangelistic and deputation teams was a key to keeping the student closely related to church life. Bible study, mission study, social action, and worship rounded out the program. Social and recreational activities were prominent. The university pastor's home became the student's "home away from home."

Tensions between the "Y's" and the churches seemed inevitable. The objectives of the university pastors were seen to be pastoral and conserving; the "Y" movements were seen to be critical of the churches at some points and moving into areas in an increasingly pluralistic society where some kind of syncretism seemed inevitable. The decade from 1900 to 1910 tended to be a time of opposition to church-sponsored student work from several directions. There were misgivings, misunderstandings, and sometimes opposition on the part of the Christian Associations; there were fears from some state universities that the work would engender sectarian rivalries; and

[2] Because there are definite works outlining the development of church-sponsored campus ministries, it is not our purpose here to do more than sketch the broad developments. For a fuller treatment see (for instance) Clarence P. Shedd, *The Church Follows Its Students* (London: Oxford University Press, 1938).

there were also fears in the denominational colleges that they would lose financial support. There was doubtless a gulf of misunderstanding caused by the subtle difference of perspective between the laity and the clergy. Those who had long been engaged in college work had two related concerns; would student initiative be overshadowed and lost? Would a proliferation of effort in churches "near the campus" weaken the united impact of Christians *on* the campus? Would a denominational emphasis vitiate an ecumenical thrust?

Many of these tensions still exist, but the very complexity of the problems facing all Christians after two world wars and a major depression, the new world into which we have been catapulted by modern technology and its attendant social changes, has kept us at the task of finding answers to our divisions.

The bewildering complexity of organizations within the student Christian movements in the United States demanded the attention of all, lest the very "machinery" brought into being as a means to accomplish Christian ends, become an end in itself. Throughout the 1920's several attempts were made to work out a more comprehensive coordination. In the 1930's three regional cooperative Student Christian Movements in the northeastern United States developed from this effort, along with a growing conscience about the "wheels within wheels." In 1934 the YMCA and YWCA student movements made common cause as the National Intercollegiate Christian Council, now known as the National Student Council of the YM and YWCA (NSCY). The churches likewise in 1944 evolved the United Student Christian Council, now a part of the National Student Christian Federation. The NSCF emerged in 1959 as one of the most significant developments in the life of the student Christian movement in America, combining three historic movements: the Student Volunteer Movement, the Interseminary Movement, and the United Student Christian Council. The call to the merger meeting at Oberlin, Ohio, in 1959 reflects the spirit:

> In order that the student Christian movements in the United States may more fully manifest oneness in Jesus Christ, Divine Lord and Saviour, and that they may more adequately serve to increase the vigor and integrity of the Church in the university, and that they may enter into the Christian mission throughout the world with greater obedience and imagination, the time has come to form an organization uniting

the life and work of the Interseminary Committee, the Student Volunteer Movement and the United Student Christian Council.

The work of the former Interseminary Movement (ISM) continues as a committee functioning within the National Student Christian Federation to promote, every three years, for its eight regional movements and the seminaries of Canada, a North American Conference; and in the interim period to bring about many smaller meetings of seminarians across theological, geographical, institutional, and denominational lines.

The work of the former Interseminary Movement for foreign missions now functions within the National Student Christian Federation as the Commission on World Mission. It is charged with three major responsibilities:

1) Interpretation on the work of the Church in the world in so-called missionary situations, 2) Enlistment or relating of persons to specific tasks in which the Church is engaged on "frontiers," 3) Provision of the means for strengthening, nurturing, increasing understanding, and preparation of those who expect to be working in these missionary situations. Through its work the Commission calls Christian students to study and rethink Christian mission today and its relation to the problems and issues of a revolutionary time, and seeks their commitment to specific Christian service in America and around the world, and relates them to denominational boards of foreign and home missions." [3]

The staff carries on extensive campus visits and interviews and continues the long-standing quadrennial Ecumenical Student Conferences.

The National Student Christian Federation thus combines the strength of the denominational movements and most of the historic concerns that have long marked the Student Christian Movement in the United States:

1) Intercollegiate ecumenical conferences on unity, mission, and witness in higher education; 2) Preparation and publication of Bible studies and study materials on contemporary problems; 3) Planning of regional Bible study conferences aimed primarily for the preparation of Bible study leaders; 4) Planning and administering voluntary service projects . . . ; 5) Holding consultations of specific concerns, as work with International students and interracial problems; 6) Repre-

[3] *Information Service* (New York: National Council of the Churches of Christ in the United States of America. Bureau of Research and Survey, May 13, 1961), p. 3. Used by permission.

sentation of student Christian movements in and to the churches,[4] government agencies, and certain national and international organizations, as World University Service, Committee for Friendly Relations among Foreign Students; and 7) Interpretation and fund-raising on behalf of WSCF [the World Student Christian Federation, of which it is now the United States member movement].[5]

Binding together the national movement in some 81 countries is the World Student Christian Federation.[6] We have observed earlier in this chapter how the birth of the modern mission movement in the United States was closely related to the dynamic life of the student Christian work. The WSCF was in a vital sense born out of the missionary movement. In 1895 representatives of the student Christian movements of Great Britain, Germany, Scandinavia, North America, and "the lands of foreign missions" met in Vadstena Castle, Sweden to unite student Christian movements throughout the world. The World Student Christian Federation purposes were simply but profoundly stated: "To lead students to become disciples of Jesus Christ as only Saviour and as God; to deepen the spiritual life of students; to enlist students in the work of extending the Kingdom of Christ throughout the world; to collect information regarding the religious condition of the students of all lands." The aims as now expressed are clearly put forth in the constitution as shown here:

[4] The denominational student movements now belonging to NSCF are as follows: Baptist Student Movement (BSM); Lutheran Student Association of America (LSAA); Methodist Student Movement (MSM); Westminster Fellowship Section of the Assembly's Youth Council, Presbyterian Church, U.S.; National Canterbury Association of the Protestant Episcopal Church; The United Campus Christian Fellowship (UCCF), which as of 1960 represents a merger of The Disciples Student Fellowship (DSF) of the Disciples of Christ Churches, the Student Fellowship Council of the Evangelical United Brethren Church, the United Student Fellowship (USF) of the United Church of Christ (Congregational Christian and Evangelical and Reformed Churches), and the Westminster Fellowship of the United Presbyterian Church, USA. In addition the National Council of the YMCA and the National Council of the YWCA are full members. The Baptist Student Union (BSU) of the Southern Baptist Convention is fraternally related.

[5] *Information Service, op. cit.,* p. 4.

[6] We are indebted to the staff of *Federation News* for material in this section used with special permission. In earlier years, the initials WSCF stood for World's Student Christian Federation, but the possessive form "World's" has now been simplified to "World."

The aims of the World Student Christian Federation in all its work among members of the academic community shall be:

1. To call them to faith in God—Father, Son, and Holy Spirit—according to the Scriptures, and to discipleship within the life and mission of the Church;
2. to help them to grow in the Christian life through prayer, study of the Bible, and participation in the worship and witness of the Church;
3. to help them to witness to Jesus Christ in the academic community;
4. to bring them into fellowship with one another in mutual service, and to support efforts to serve all students in their needs;
5. to help them to strive for peace and justice in and among the nations;
6. to help them work for the manifestation of the unity of the Church;
7. to help them to be servants and messengers of God's Kingdom in all the world.

The national movements have complete autonomy, yet they acknowledge interdependence and assume mutual obligations to one another. The role of the Federation has, therefore, been to inspire and advise its member movements, and to insure the strengthening of student initiative by establishing a program of training national leaders with a world perspective. From the beginning, the Federation was interconfessional. Meeting in Constantinople in 1911, the General Committee had its first contacts with the Orthodox world, and from this time on it was to be a truly ecumenical fellowship.

During the twenty-five years when he was General Secretary of the WSCF, Dr. John R. Mott traveled almost continuously, serving as teacher and "pastor" of national leaders, stimulating the evangelistic zeal of existing movements, and establishing new ones. With Ruth Rouse, the first women's secretary, he so built the Federation that at the outbreak of World War I there were member movements in sixteen countries and correspondents in many others. In 1920, when the first postwar General Committee met in Beatenberg, in Switzerland, they rediscovered their essential unity in spite of the wounds of war, years of isolation, and profound theological divisions. A European Student Relief program was started at that time, which continues today.

Henry-Louis Henriod, as the new General Secretary, headed a

new team under Mott's chairmanship, and headquarters were established at 13 Rue Calvin, Geneva, Switzerland where they remain today. As war continued to plague the world, the General Committee's meeting in Peking, China, in 1922 affirmed the Federation's concern for peace.

At the 1926 meeting in Nyborg Strand, Denmark, the ecumenical policy was clearly defined: The Federation "will welcome as members students of all confessions or no confession, and accept confessional groups which are willing to work within the framework of a national interconfessional movement." The Orthodox churches began to feel at home in the Federation work and interconfessional conversations took on a new dimension.

It was in 1928 that Francis P. Miller, an American, succeeded John R. Mott as chairman. W. A. Visser 't Hooft joined the staff to serve as General Secretary in 1932 and remain until 1938, when he began other ecumenical responsibilities in the emerging World Council of Churches. From that time to the present the Federation has continued a program of intensive study of the Bible, Christian doctrine, ecumenical questions, and the major political issues of the time (war and peace, disarmament, nationalism, communism, race, totalitarianism). "University Missions" confronted students on every continent with the relevance of the eternal truth of Jesus Christ in everyday life.

An historic meeting of the General Committee convened in 1938 at Bièvres, France, to which delegates came from China and Japan despite the fact their countries had been at war with each other for several years; also from Germany, where Hitler had just dissolved the Student Christian Movement; and from Czechoslovakia a few weeks before the German attack and the Munich crisis. But there was no one from war-torn Spain, where the young SCM had been outlawed. Robert Mackie of Scotland became General Secretary under the chairmanship of Visser 't Hooft at this time, only one year before the World War II "officially" began. During the war Mackie worked out of his Toronto, Canada, office opening new fields in Latin America, while Visser 't Hooft and Suzanne de Dietrich maintained the Federation office in Geneva. An almost miraculous spiritual unity was maintained among WSCF members in warring countries who remained united in their repudiation of national socialism and militarism. The story of Dietrich Bonhoeffer and many others remains a priceless heritage. World Student Relief (lasting until 1950) was a tremendous effort of the Federation.

In 1948 Philippe Maury, of France, became General Secretary, and Mackie remained as chairman. A period of geographical expansion was facilitated in the postwar period by the end of colonialism, by rapid growth of higher education everywhere, and by air travel. The number of countries represented by the Federation widened to 72, and regional staffs were appointed to help many national movements in postwar reconstruction, and through them to aid the so-called younger churches with trained leadership. Conferences were set up for Asia in Ceylon, for Latin America in Brazil, and for Africa in Ghana. A program of ecumenical assistance helped the SCM's with money and personnel, focusing again on the missionary and evangelical witness of the Federation.

At the General Committee session in Nasrapur, India, in 1953, the theme was "Witnessing in the University Communities," and D. T. Niles, one of the great evangelists of our time, became chairman of the Federation. Three years later in Tutzing, Germany, the General Committee took steps to maintain links with Christian students in countries where SCM's could not be organized for political or religious reasons, and with various movements like the Chinese and the *Evangelische Studentgemeinde* in the German Democratic Republic (East Germany), where world events forced isolation and special difficulties. The program of World Student Relief was succeeded by World University Service, and conversations were begun with the International Union of Students and with Jewish and Moslem students.

Central in the Federation's program of study, teaching, and action was a seven-year emphasis on the life and mission of the church, designed to help in rethinking the whole task of the church today and to help students find their place in it. So significant was this effort that it permeated every continent and was extended far beyond the original time established.

In 1960 the meeting at Salonika, Greece, called Valdo Galland, of Uruguay, as the new General Secretary. Thus the work in Latin America was bound closer into the Federation fellowship. Phillip Potter, of the West Indies, became its chairman.

RELATIONSHIPS

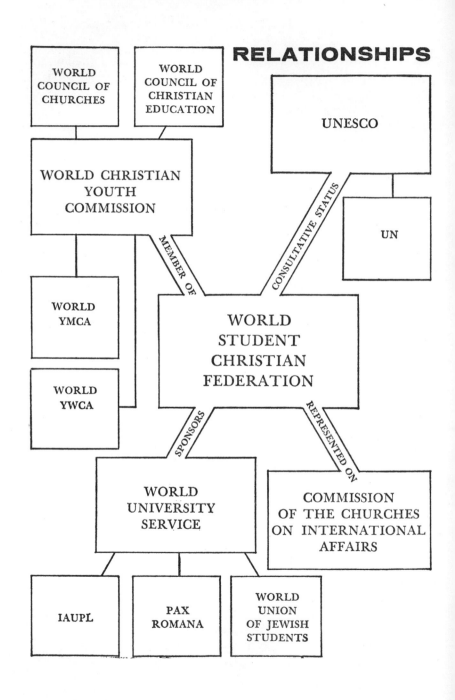

WORLD COUNCIL OF CHURCHES

WORLD COUNCIL OF CHRISTIAN EDUCATION

UNESCO

WORLD CHRISTIAN YOUTH COMMISSION

UN

WORLD YMCA

MEMBER OF

CONSULTATIVE STATUS

WORLD STUDENT CHRISTIAN FEDERATION

WORLD YWCA

SPONSORS

REPRESENTED ON

WORLD UNIVERSITY SERVICE

COMMISSION OF THE CHURCHES ON INTERNATIONAL AFFAIRS

IAUPL

PAX ROMANA

WORLD UNION OF JEWISH STUDENTS

The World's Student Christian Federation is truly an ecumenical community, bringing together student Christian movements from all parts of the world and from all church traditions. A majority of the member movements are independent and interdenominational SCM's. Some are student YM and YWCA's. In several countries there is a national council of movements, as in the United States, and they express not merely administrative unity but a profound sense of oneness in Christ.

Many Roman Catholic students, especially in Latin America, and Latin Europe, share in the active life of the SCM's. They have greatly helped the Federation to understand the ecumenical aspect of its missionary task. The experience of Latin American SCM's has led to the affirmation that the Federation and its movements are both responsible for bringing students to active membership in a particular church and morally bound not to impose on them membership in any particular denomination. The task of the SCM is one of pastoral counseling rather than of ecclesiastical proselyting.

Such relationships inevitably bring ecumenical tensions, but no one can realize the richness of the ecumenical encounter who has not first experienced the suffering of Christian division. Profound differences between representatives of "Protestant" and "Catholic" traditions, of orthodox, neo-orthodox, and liberal schools, divide local as well as international Christian communities. So-called "nontheological factors" cause further fragmentation. It has become apparent that unity is both a gift of God and something to be achieved painfully through common struggle with those with whom we disagree.

There are also divisions between the Federation and other student Christian organizations, including Pax Romana (which brings together Roman Catholic students and intellectuals) and the International Fellowship of Evangelical Students (made up of "conservative evangelical" groups which refuse to participate in the ecumenical movement).[7] In the conviction that Christians cannot ignore one another, but are mutually responsible for one another's

[7] There has been no description of the work of the Intervarsity Christian Fellowship because of its own decision not to participate in the "mainstream" of the SCM's; however, it should be noted that on many campuses in the United States and in other parts of the world it has entered into conversations and occasional cooperative participation.

faith, the Federation has welcomed and encouraged conversations and all possible kinds of cooperation between its members and these fellow-Christians. It is hoped that the day will come when full unity can be achieved among those who confess the name of Jesus Christ.

This historical sketch has of necessity been limited to the developments in the United States and their relationships with the WSCF. Even to mention the developments around the world of the national movements,[8] many of which are much older than those in the United States, would extend this chapter beyond manageable limits. It must be noted however that the present worldwide explosion of student populations, as well as the amazing mobility of students in every direction across the world, injects a dimension into the ministry related to all campuses in the world that is now calling for radical rethinking of the forms of ministry. The new understanding of the *laos* of God is demanding of the church a depth of renewal far exceeding the changes engendered by the Reformation.

[8] Although the number changes as the movement grows, the World Student Christian Federation listed movements as of June, 1963, as follows:

Affiliated Movements: Australia, Austria, Brazil, Burma, Canada, Ceylon, Chile, China, Czechoslovakia, Denmark, Finland, France, Germany, Ghana, Great Britain and Ireland, Hungary, India, Indonesia, Jamaica, Japan, Korea, Malaya, The Netherlands, New Zealand, Nigeria, Norway, Pakistan, Philippines, Puerto Rico, Sierra Leone, South Africa, Sweden, Switzerland, United States of America. (These comprise the voting members of the General Committee of WSCF.)

Associated Movements: Argentina, Basutoland, Belgium, Colombia, Dahomey, Greece, Italy, Ivory Coast, Madagascar, Portugal, Russian SCM outside Russia. (These comprise the non-voting delegates to the WSCF General Committee.)

Corresponding Movements: Bolivia, Cameroons, Chad, Congo Republic (ex-Belgian), Congo Republic (ex-French), Costa Rica, Dominican Republic, Ecuador, Ethiopia, Guatemala, Honduras, Gabon, Hong Kong, Iceland, Iran, Lebanon, Mexico, Nicaragua, Panama, Paraguay, Peru, Northern Rhodesia, Southern Rhodesia, Nyasaland, El Salvador, Senegal, Spain, Thailand, Togo, Uganda, United Arab Republic, Venezuela, Yugoslavia. (Representatives of these groups are welcome to attend the General Committee.)

GLEN O. MARTIN

5: Campus Culture

ANY ATTEMPT TO DESCRIBE A SINGLE CULTURE for the American college campus would result in a hopeless oversimplification. Nor is the problem solved by saying that every campus has its own culture, for even the most naïve observer can identify at least two distinct cultures on any campus — that of the students and that of the faculty and administration. Several studies of the current college scene refer to these as the student culture and the academic culture.

Each of them is far from a unity in itself. There are numerous subcultures in student life. Similarly, the academic culture is divided by differences in approach among the various disciplines or among the separate colleges in a university — to say nothing of the radical dichotomy which usually exists between the faculty and administration. Primary emphasis in this chapter will be on the student culture, but the academic culture must also receive some attention, both because it is a part of the total campus culture and because it has an important role to play as a partial determinant of the nature of student culture.

Furthermore, these cultures and subcultures are not stable even

Glen O. Martin has been director of the Wesley foundations at the University of Tennessee and at Hamline University in St. Paul, Minnesota. He is the current associate director of the department of college and university religious life of the Methodist Board of Education.

on a given campus but are rather in continual flux. There is considerable evidence that the rate of change itself is accelerating, so that a real danger exists that whatever parts of this chapter seek to be concrete and specific will be out of date to some extent before the book is printed. Some campuses, however, because of their relative isolation or because of basic policy decisions limiting maximum size and restricting admissions to a comparatively homogenous group, will show relative stability in campus culture.

The word "culture" has been variously used, but here it will be employed to denote in the most general terms the total way of life of the groups and subgroups being discussed, including their beliefs, attitudes, and values. A basic assumption is that every individual coming into a group brings certain beliefs, attitudes, and values, and thus contributes something to the culture of the group, but that for the most part he is more molded than molder in the group. A further assumption is that, with the proper kind of internal and external leadership, the continual changing of campus cultures can be more than random and capricious. This word of reassurance is needed here, lest the following pages leave the reader too discouraged to benefit from the concrete suggestions which will be offered as to how a campus ministry might be developed.

BACKGROUND FACTORS IN STUDENT CULTURE

Probably the most important single background factor in determining student culture on the American campus is that of the traditions of the school. Older schools will tend to have more of these in a relatively more stable student culture. In spite of such fads as panty raids, telephone booth stuffing, and rotation endurance tests in coin laundry drying tumblers, students are for the most part responsive to the traditional norms of the campus where they attend. The overwhelming reaction of all but the most sophisticated entering students at the average American college or university is one of bewilderment and confusion, followed by an earnest effort to fit in with the pattern unfolded to him by the established students and to a lesser extent by the faculty and administration. He wants to belong, and the upperclassmen are quick to outline for him the terms on which belonging is possible.

However, students do bring certain beliefs, attitudes, and values with them to college and — depending on the strength with which they cling to them and the depth with which these characteristics are rooted in their personalities — these will exert some influence on the campus culture and subcultures which they find on entering college.

Several students from the same secondary school entering a given college may bring certain elements of their earlier experiences with them and exert measurable influence on the campus, even though they do not live in the same units or belong to the same organizations. In most cases they will continue to associate with one another and find mutual reinforcement and support which enables them together to make a contribution even against the prevailing mores. For example, a group of students coming out of a prep school with a functioning honor system may challenge the easy acceptance of a pattern of cheating on examinations, and may even alter the behavior patterns of a significant number of their fellow students. It is harder for isolated individuals to accomplish such changes, but there is a tendency for dominant patterns of a culture to be transmitted by individuals crossing to a different culture, even when there is no direct contact between the two situations.

The social class of the entering student is another factor in the background of changes in student culture. The increasing emphasis in America on higher education for all, rather than for just a privileged few, has resulted in the enrollment of increasing numbers of persons whose previous social and cultural opportunities have been very limited. There is some correlation here with economic class, but the person of limited financial means is not necessarily socially impoverished, nor is wealth any guarantee of social sophistication. Very few colleges now include any criteria of social experience or background in the student selection process, and some time-honored traditions are having trouble surviving on the contemporary campus. Interestingly enough, some of these underprivileged students with real singleness of purpose academically are often able to embarrass their more sophisticated colleagues when it comes to scholastic record. They also add further to the complexities of campus culture and thus make their contributions to its changing pattern.

A fourth background factor is the religious orientation of the entering students. Persons bringing with them rather rigid theological or ethical systems to a campus where a non-committed or radically different point of view prevails are subject either to continuing frustration or to being forced into religious ghettos. If the individual with commitments to such rigid systems is able to find enough fellow-believers to whom he can turn for mutual support and understanding, he may survive the college experience without bitterness, but he is apt to be far less influential than the one who comes with a more open point of view and willingness to listen as well as speak. The Intervarsity Christian Fellowship and the Campus Crusade both tend far more often to be havens for persons with prior conservative theological orientation and commitment than the effective instruments of evangelism they consider themselves.

Many other factors could be singled out, but these should illustrate the complexity of background factors and the reality of the possibility for change, given the proper conditions.

THREE FOCI OF STUDENT CULTURES AND SUBCULTURES

There are three basic foci around which revolve dominant student cultures and subcultures on the American college campus scene. Every student will have at least a limited involvement in some aspect of each of these, and the subcultures of which he is a part will be determined primarily by what combination of these foci falls to his lot. There are certain elements of choice involved for every student in each category, but no student is completely free to choose without restraint in any of the categories. Consequently, the particular subcultures in which any given student finds himself will be a combination of his own choices and those which are forced upon him.

Place of residence

The first of these foci is the residential unit where the student lives. A given student may pass through several of these types of living units during his four-year college course, and all of them will leave some mark upon him. Needless to say, students are not all equally involved within the same given type of accommodation, nor are their experiences homogeneous. On most campuses having residential fraternity and sorority houses, these units play a major role in terms of influence if not in numbers. Several recent studies have suggested that such groups are declining in influence and importance, but few loyal alumni anywhere could be convinced of the accuracy of these findings, and on many campuses the decline — if there is to be one — has not yet begun. Often the Greek groups monopolize campus politics and serve both as the initiators and the conservers of campus traditions.

The persons who have held leadership roles in high-school-age church groups are likely to turn to fraternities and sororities as the prestige units on campus rather than making their leadership abilities available to denominational religious centers. Getting into the right fraternity or sorority becomes vitally important to the new student, and, once the goal of belonging to the right group has been achieved, only superficial involvement in other organizations on the basis of personal initiative may be possible. Greek groups frequently will almost totally monopolize the time of members through assigned involvements in other organizations, structured study halls, and in-group activities. Life outside the fraternity or sorority exists, but the terms by which the individual participates in it are rigidly defined by his primary group which demands absolute loyalty.

Those who reside in dormitories by choice or necessity are usually somewhat less regimented on a total basis; but, if the influence of fraternities and sororities is declining, then surely that of dormitory living units is increasing. Most of the newer dormitories now being built have elaborate facilities for social life and group activity built into living units of manageable size. Staff and facilities are provided for the development of in-group and intergroup programming, academic and social counseling, and self-government. House councils, once an instrument of discipline and rule-enforcement in women's dormitories, have now been broadened to include the full range of social and intellectual activities on many campuses, and have spread into men's dormitories as well. At Harvard College, the houses are almost complete academic institutions within themselves, including house master and tutors, as well as library, dining, recreational, and other common rooms. The development of coeducational dormitories at some schools has further enhanced their status. Dormitory group involvement in campus politics is also beginning on some campuses, although the Greek groups still retain a monopoly in this area on most.

Beyond this point, we are moving rapidly toward the periphery of campus life. However, the next most important category is that of the rooming house existing near the campus, with or without provision for board. Where several students live in a given house, it may develop a subculture of its own. Students often move to rooming houses because they feel lost in the dormitory or because they feel the dormitory makes too many demands on them for social involvement, but in either case they are expressing a desire to be part of a more intimate and less demanding group. Most freshman students prefer to live in the dormitories even when they are not required to do so, but as they become more firmly rooted in the academic and extracurricular life of the school they tend to depend less and less on their living unit for identification with the campus.

As this process of developing independence continues, the next move is into an apartment where two or three students may share costs and duties. Some of these apartment dwellers exist almost totally isolated from campus social life with the exception of individual dating experiences and involvements related to their academic and extracurricular group participation.

Students who are married when they come to the college campus, or who get married before graduation, stand at the outer edge of this apartment-dweller isolation. They do not even have the involvements of dating others on the campus, and frequently by the necessity for working are excluded from all but basic academic participation in the life of the college.

The most completely isolated insofar as the full experience of campus culture goes, however, are the commuting students who live at home and come to the campus only for classes. In a very real sense they never become a part of college life at all. Some of them retain their friendships and involvements of high school days, and others live a kind of frustrated hermit's existence. A few break out of the shell and become involved in the life of the campus but pay a heavy price either in terms of inadequate rest or lowered quality of academic work if the distance they have to commute requires them to invest a substantial amount of time in travel. When space has become available in a dormitory during the spring term, commuting students have sometimes taken advantage of this opportunity to have at least one term of on-campus living experience.

It is interesting to note that at least two experiments have been proposed providing for one night a week of campus residence for commuting students on a covenant-community basis. Both of these are under church sponsorship as campus ministry projects. In addition, several campus ministries have provided small dormitories or rooming houses in which resident faith-and-life communities could be developed. However, married students and commuting students, even though they appear to be relatively untouched by the value-transforming aspects of college life, are still the most neglected by the campus ministry.

In addition to the fact that each of the widely-varied living units is in some sense a subculture itself, each of them also makes some contribution to the character of the overall campus culture in any given college or university. No church which is truly committed to a significant campus ministry can afford not to be both informed and involved in relation to students in every campus living unit.

Academic relationships

The second focus around which student culture revolves is its primary point of contact with the academic culture, the classroom. Many studies of campus culture have omitted this focus entirely, as though it were assumed to be irrelevant or unimportant, but it can be a major determinant of the character of student culture. The classroom is the primary point at which the academic culture impinges upon and influences student culture, although the faculty and administration will be to some extent involved in determining the character of the other two foci.

Even though it may be argued that the most productive contacts between faculty and students occur outside the classroom through informal contacts and conversations, through counseling, and through advising extracurricular organizations, there is no doubt that the most frequent point of contact is in the classroom and that student culture is affected by this contact. Wherever else they may meet him, students are most eager to know what a given member of the faculty is like in the classroom. They want to know whether or not his lectures are interesting, what kind of tests he gives, how he grades, and whether there are any fringe benefits to be received from involvement in his courses. No one who has lived on a campus and observed how students will get into registration lines long before their normal rising hour, forge appointment cards, buy or sneak their way past monitors, and tell whopping lies about schedule conflicts — all in order to get into a given teacher's section before it fills up — can deny that these contacts are important. One of the most worthwhile services of the Harvard *Crimson* to this writer's college generation was its publication of a *Confidential Guide to Freshman Courses* through which the neophyte on campus was introduced to the personalities and advantages and disadvantages of all professors who taught freshmen courses.

Student culture will be strongly influenced by the academic standards of a given institution. A combination of deliberate and natural-selection processes results in a certain normal balance between the scholastic abilities of the students and the academic expectations of the faculty. There is not usually any written policy governing this balance, but it tends to be maintained by a kind of gentlemen's agreement. How important this balance is to student culture became apparent when the Russian space successes stimulated faculties all over the country to an effort to upgrade their institutions scholastically, particularly in the scientific disciplines. Any sudden tightening of the academic requirements without a corresponding tightening of admission policies results in substantial disruption of the level of student participation in extracurricular activities. The almost frantic attempt to raise academic standards following the Russian success with Sputnik I has forced many campus ministries to rethink carefully their nature and purpose. The end results of such a tightening may not necessarily be negative, but they are always substantially disruptive of existing patterns.

The style of teaching will also have a bearing on student culture. For example, some forms lend themselves more readily than others to cheating. Indeed, some teachers seem deliberately to be encouraging ordinary patterns of cheating by confining their teaching program to demands for rote learning of insignificant and essentially irrelevant bits of information. When no attempt is made to involve the students in a live learning situation, it is understandable if they seek short-cut methods of winning the game or defeating the system. Some campuses are alive intellectually, while others are dead. Where an undue emphasis is placed on grade achievement or on feeding back to the professor his pet theories which mean nothing to the students, the whole campus tends to become mechanical and lifeless. On such campuses, the newly-developed "teaching machines" may well replace a substantial part of the faculty. Such a replacement might actually improve the campus morale, since at least one does not expect a machine to be a person.

Another important factor is the prevailing philosophy or philosophies among the faculty, since professors will communicate their basic assumptions through the classroom to the students. Both Chad Walsh and Robert Hamill[1] in seeking to analyze campus culture have done so in terms of certain gods which seem to embody value systems of both students and faculty. In both books the heavy hand of basic philosophical assumptions by the faculty is in evidence in the analysis. Scientism does not grow out of a *misunderstanding* of what the faculty members are trying to say in their teaching program but out of *too careful and complete appropriation* of the value system implicit in the approach of the faculty members to the subject. Many of them are committed not only to the validity of the scientific method of observation, hypothesis, and verification (or rejection and repeat), but also to the further position that the only truth there is must be arrived at in this way. If students are materialistic and self-centered, it may just be that these values are being communicated to them through the classroom. On the other hand if they are uncommitted and uninvolved in the world, this posture also may mean that they are living out an ideal which has been held up to them by the faculty.

Another example of the way in which involvement in the classroom affects student culture is to be found in the content of the curriculum itself. Consciously or unconsciously, the faculty communicates a value system to the students by the courses which are included or excluded from the catalog and from the active teaching program. Even the titles and course descriptions communicate something to the students studying their college catalog. Of primary concern to the churches is the fact that so many colleges exclude courses in religion altogether, for one reason or another, often

[1] *Cf.* Chad Walsh, *Campus Gods on Trial* (New York: The Macmillan Co., 1962) and Robert H. Hamill, *Gods of the Campus* (Nashville: Abingdon Press, 1949).

without any realization of what this omission says to students. The fact that college administrators and faculty members have at least some subconscious realization of the problem posed by such an exclusion is made apparent by the way in which most college catalogs call attention to the strong religious program available through extracurricular activities or in surrounding churches. Most colleges wish to be thought of as having a religious atmosphere, even when the curriculum is completely devoid of any academic courses in religion. One wonders what kind of reaction the accrediting groups would have to a college which announced it was abolishing its literature courses altogether, but there were numerous literary societies on and around the campus in which the students were encouraged to participate, and that once every year there would be a literature emphasis week in which outstanding poets, playwrights, authors, and novelists were brought in to recite excerpts from their works and to laud the importance of literary activity. The exclusion of courses in religion from the curriculum does say something to the students, and the efforts of the churches in providing a supplemental instructional program through their campus ministries are not an adequate corrective. Nor is it enough for the church to get its word in edgewise by persuading individual faculty members to say a kind word for religion in the classroom or to permit an important speaker in religious emphasis week to have one hour of class. Every campus ministry should be committed to a strategy which has as its end the provision for courses in religion as a regular part of the curriculum of the college or university. This strategy should be in addition to providing a ministry to the faculty members as persons, which seeks to help them understand their work of teaching as a Christian vocation or lay ministry.

The "extracurricular" factor

The third focus is by far the most complex of the three, as well as being the most faithful indicator and perhaps the most influential causal factor in student culture. The usual title given to this focus is "extracurricular activities," and in the broadest sense this category includes everything which takes place outside the classroom. Many colleges recognize that the most valuable general cultural aspects of higher education come mainly from this source, and pour substantial sums of money and numbers of personnel into directing the program of extracurricular activities. One suspects that on a great many campuses the total amount of staff time invested in these activities will far exceed the amount invested in the actual teaching process. It is certainly true that many students invest far more time at this level than they do in preparation for and participation in the classroom experience.

There is such a multiplicity of opportunities on the average campus, and these are so invitingly advertised, that even good students must exercise substantial self-discipline in order to save enough time for structured academic life. There are always a number every year who do not meet their academic requirements because they are so busy getting a general education through the extracurricular route that they cannot maintain the necessary minimum grade average to continue in school.

In describing the complex of activities on one campus, Robert Hamill calls attention to the way in which students can be stretched beyond their limits by the myriad of organizations available to them.

> Wesleyan College in Connecticut found its pace so hectic that the Student Council appointed a committee to survey its thousand activities and to recommend the things that could be condensed, merged, or dropped to de-crowd the calendar. The committee members found their personal schedules so full and contradictory that they never found a time to meet![2]

One large segment of these activities really forms a bridge between the curricular and the extracurricular experience. The speech and drama faculty (often part of the English department) will sponsor oratorical contests, debating teams and clubs, drama groups, and even "little theaters" (which usually make use also of semi-professional talent from the community). Not all the students involved in these programs will be majors in this department, nor indeed will all of them even take courses for credit in the field. A "little theater" can consume a tremendous amount of student time in the production and advertising phases of the operation, and many students will also be involved on the basis of interest in prop gathering, scenery construction, painting, lighting, etc. On some

[2] Hamill, *op. cit.*, p. 26.

campuses considerable status is attached to leadership roles in debate or in drama.

Also related to English departments is the work made available as an extracurricular activity on many campuses in the field of newspaper writing, production, and distribution. Often a campus newspaper will play a significant role in criticizing and altering campus mores or in attempting to do so. Sometimes these attempts will create conflict and set one segment of the campus community against others, as, for example, at the University of Mississippi where the editor of the student newspaper was censored by the student government for publishing editorials which were critical of student involvement in the violence connected with the admission of a Negro to the university.

Some campuses also operate radio stations for either on-campus or community constituencies, and do most or all of the work connected with such an operation, including its technical phases as well as continuity writing, announcing, and general programming. Several campuses now have FM radio stations broadcasting cultural programs to the community, and a few have educational television outlets. All of these provide training opportunities for students and contribute to their sense of belonging and accomplishment, but all of them consume tremendous amounts of time which is not then available for use in other areas of activity.

Most music departments maintain several choral groups, a campus band, and sometimes even a symphony orchestra. Again training is made available through these extracurricular activities and a sense of group involvement is enhanced, but tremendous amounts of time are invested.

Those campuses having military units in the form of ROTC or other similar programs offer to the men students, at least, another challenging opportunity — or a seductive nuisance, depending on one's point of view. Some colleges, particularly land-grant schools, will require two years of basic military training of all able-bodied male students. Beyond the required-credit classroom structures is a vast organization appealing for student time and energy for military balls, rifle squads, drill programs, and advanced training opportunities. Any school with a full-fledged ROTC program can easily become the equivalent of a military academy for the student who seeks to take advantage of all the opportunities made available to him.

The whole structure of intercollegiate and intramural athletics is so complex as to defy description. Colleges playing major football schedules may make it impossible for a member of the varsity squad, no matter how brilliant he may be intellectually, to secure any kind of solid academic experience during his eligible years. Several of these fellows return to school following the expiration of their eligibility to complete their education, confessing frankly that intercollegiate athletics required almost all their time during the three years they participated. Basketball, baseball, track, hockey, and other sports are becoming major time consumers. Even though a limited number of persons are eligible to participate in intercollegiate athletics, most campuses have, and justifiably so, elaborate programs of intramural athletic events, involving women as well as men. Students living in fraternity and sorority houses are the largest group involved in intramural athletics on most campuses, but increasingly this involvement is spreading to the dormitory structure. These athletic programs are usually related indirectly to required physical education courses, and faculty time may be given to assist with the coaching and the administration of the program. There can be no doubt that students benefit greatly from these programs, but they must exercise some element of selectivity. The time the student spends in this activity cannot be used elsewhere.

In addition to these more highly publicized forms of activity available to students, almost every department and college sponsors some kind of extracurricular activity related to its work. There are French and German clubs, philosophy clubs, psychology clubs, home economics clubs, historical and literary societies, and so on *ad infinitum*.

Furthermore, there may be dozens or even hundreds of social clubs, political action groups, community service organizations, pep squads, religious organizations, etc., at work on a large campus. Fraternities and sororities are themselves social groups as well as living units. There are numerous honor societies more or less loosely related to academic or other achievement. Some of these are open to any student who is interested, while others are quite exclusive and very difficult to get into. There is also a certain amount of superstructure which appears to be necessary, as, for example, the Panhellenic Council which coordinates the sororities and the Inter-Fraternity Council which is the war council for the fraternities, to say nothing of the Inter-Faith Council which may seek to coordinate the religious life and activities of the various religious organizations.

As mentioned earlier, an elaborate structure for the guidance of these multiplied activities may be developed by the administration. This structure may be tied with the office of the dean of students, with the staff of a college union building, or with both. It is rarely any longer primarily in the hands of volunteers working overtime, but is a clearly defined and well-paid professional endeavor. Several campuses now employ a full-time coordinator of religious activities whose principal assignment is to bring some order out of the religious chaos on the campus. His job description does not ordinarily suggest that he should be involved in a ministry to the campus but rather that he should help to relate the groups seeking to promote religious activities on the campus and try to make some sense and reason out of their work. He is often also assigned some responsibility for limiting the scope of religious activities and for controlling those groups which are disruptive of the "more important aspects of campus life."

It should be noted that not all aspects of campus ministry as currently conceived by several of the churches are included in the "religious organizations" mentioned above. Some church leaders would no longer regard the student religious organizations as important at all, and a few are deliberately repudiating them and permitting or helping them to die. It is not the place of this chapter to discuss the forms which can or should be the vehicles of this emerging campus ministry, but they are exciting in scope and content.

The role of the college chaplain is ambiguous. It may vary in several indeterminate steps from that of a simple coordinator of religious activities to a full-fledged campus minister, depending on his own insights, his job description, and the openness of the academic and student cultures on the campus where he works.

The character of the student culture and subcultures will vary somewhat with the background experiences students bring with them to the campus, but they will be primarily a function of these

three foci—the living units, the classroom experiences, and the extracurricular activities. No two campuses will be exactly alike, nor will
any given campus continue year after year to evidence exactly the
same kind of student culture and complex of subcultures. On a few
campuses where it has really come alive, the student government
will comprise a fourth focus with considerable influence as a determinant of student culture, but on most campuses this is little more
than a political exercise or activity for the students. It gives them
some background experience in democratic procedures and political
maneuvering, but any influence it exerts on the student culture
comes largely from the use made of it by the academic culture in
communicating its patterns and concerns.

Let us now look briefly at the academic culture itself before turning to some concluding observations regarding contemporary student culture.

ACADEMIC CULTURE

The academic culture must clearly be divided into at least two
subcultures: the faculty and the administration. Those who assume
that campus ministry can take the form of one big happy family in
which faculty, administration, and students sit down together before
the fire to talk about religion are only slightly more naïve than
those who believe that faculty and administration can be brought
together in one culture. The goals and values of administration and
faculty are not the same, and only the wildest kind of abstraction
and distortion can make them sound like the same.

Charles S. McCoy takes note in a recent article on "The University and Its Culture" of the rapid growth of administration.

> No sector of the university has grown more rapidly over the past sixty
> years than administration. Whether by real need or through some
> curious application of Parkinson's Law, administrative personnel now
> outnumbers teaching faculty in American higher education by four to
> one! Of course this embraces a wide array of persons in the administra-
> tive sector. Included are the trustees, the president, and a growing
> group of vice-presidents, academic deans, deans of student personnel,
> associate deans, assistant deans, the registrar and admissions staff, the
> business office with the residence halls and eating facilities, the corps
> of secretaries, some of whom are the real centers of power, and the
> maintenance crew to keep the physical facilities in reasonably decent
> order against the invasions by faculty and students. Perhaps the

athletic department ought to be included too; for the faculty will not claim it and the players' status as students is often in doubt.[3]

There are three primary goals or concerns of college administrators: (1) that the college be a smooth-running organization with its various segments moving in peace with one another and functioning at peak efficiency, (2) that the college enjoy a high prestige or status rating in the community and over as broad a geographical area as possible, and (3) that there be enough funds to finance its current expenses and guarantee its continuing operation. Included in the concern for prestige or status is that of the proper accreditation by all the necessary bodies, the winning of football games, and the granting of a Phi Beta Kappa chapter, to mention only a few widely scattered illustrations. Concern for the actual quality of instruction and the extent of influence on the character of students who attend may in some cases be limited to such aspects as bear on the concern for prestige for status. One is left with the unhappy impression in many cases that college administrators would rather have a bad college with a good reputation than a good college with a bad reputation.

That the gulf between administration and faculty is deeper than the question of eligibility for AAUP membership was made clear to this writer when he proposed to a planning committee for a faculty fellowship that the deans and other administrative personnel be included in the membership. The emotional overtones in the immediate response were overwhelming, "If they come, the teaching faculty won't!" Actually, some of both finally did participate in the group, but there is no way of determining how many of the teaching faculty automatically excluded themselves on discovering that the administration was also permitted to come. The unabashed self-centeredness and desire for privacy which Jacob reports in his study of student values would apply to a great many faculty members as well. The primary concern seems to be with personal recognition and promotion, and the route to these for a faculty member is essentially privatistic. There are some whose concern for the prestige of the institution would exceed that of the administration, but these have never been in the majority.

[3] Charles S. McCoy, "The University and Its Culture," in Richard N. Bender, ed., *On the Work of the Ministry in University Communities* (Nashville: Board of Education, The Methodist Church, 1962) , pp. 35-36. Used by permission.

Dr. Charles S. McCoy has singled out four faculty subcultures which are described in his article on "The University and Its Culture."

> First, there is the *home guard*. Included here are the trusted older faculty, department heads, committee chairmen, the long-timers who carry the burden of community participation and local public relations. This group is most likely to be numbered among church members.
>
> Second, there are the *researchers*. These faculty members usually stay hidden away, take as little responsibility as possible with reference to counseling with students and faculty committees. They can be called hit-and-run teachers. Less likely to be active in community or church, this group probably includes the most "prestigious" and widely known scholars on campus.
>
> Third, there are the *tourists* among the faculty. Members of this subculture may spend more time away from campus than on it. They are off consulting for government or business, serving an agency abroad or on a Fulbright in a foreign university.
>
> Fourth, there are the *teachers* who love classroom contact, who willingly devote time and attention to the thankless job of instructing undergraduates. The smaller college will have more of this group proportionately. Students will remember them with affection, but seldom do they add to the academic prestige of their institution.[4]

It would not be fair to say that all faculty fit neatly into one or another of these categories, nor is there space in this chapter to go into detail concerning the origins and trends in faculty culture. However, because campus culture will be a composite of student culture and academic culture, it was felt necessary to include some brief discussion both of administration and faculty. Campus ministry is concerned with persons in the academic community at every level, but it would be naïve to assume that all levels can be dealt with together in one chummy fellowship. If a ministry is to be valid and relevant, it must be based on a careful analysis of the specific patterns of work, needs, and value systems of the major subcultures at which it is directed.

SOME CONCLUDING OBSERVATIONS

Much of what has been said is somewhat theoretical, because it is an abstraction from the real life of any particular campus. Every

[4] *Ibid.*, p. 40.

campus must be seen as in some sense unique, and every student is himself a unique person, both in terms of what he brings with him to the campus and in terms of his openness to change as a result of his college experience. There has been a plethora of studies in recent years dealing with student values and attitudes. Some of these studies have been more open to question than others, but none of them are beyond controversy and none have presented the whole story concerning the student mind. This fact should be clear to us when we note that, although a great many students have themselves written concerning the mind of the contemporary student, there is considerable divergence among these statements. Even two statements from the pen of the same student appearing just one year apart come to significantly different conclusions.

A recent statement in a pamphlet written by Philip E. Jacob takes a different viewpoint and claims "remarkable consistency" for these statements, summarizing them as follows:

> With remarkable consistency, current studies of student behavior and attitudes bring out four dominant interrelated dispositions: (1) an absorbing self-interestedness, directed essentially toward satisfying desires for material well-being, privacy within one's own male-oriented family domain, and relief from boredom; (2) group dependence, which causes students to bring personal conduct and standards into line with the expectations of groups to whom they turn for a sense of "belongingness" or look upon as vehicles to self-advancement; (3) social and political indifference and irresponsibility; and (4) an instrumental approach to reason and morality, which pulls both reason and the moral code into the service of preset personal goals rather than acknowledging them as guides to verity and controlling rules of conduct.[5]

After his statement is completed, Jacob goes on himself to point to the nature of some of the reservations which can easily be held about these studies, and suggests some of the reasons for doubting that they tell the whole story. The basic problem he sees is that these present a distillation from widespread analytical studies, in which the unique and creative aspects of student culture have been boiled away. In spite of administrative pressures against anything controversial, students are giving leadership to various movements in this country though perhaps not in as large numbers or as disorderly a fasion as in other nations. Students are involved in issues

---

[5] Philip E. Jacob, *Education for Social Responsibility* (Uncopyrighted pamphlet published by The American National Red Cross, May, 1961), p. 4.

of disarmament and world peace, racial and social justice, academic freedom, open lecterns on our campuses and in our communities, and other basic issues. They have attacked fascistic tactics, even on the part of congressional committees. They have brought about basic changes in policy regarding compulsory ROTC. Both students and faculty have been involved in sit-in demonstrations, have served time in jails because of their involvement, and have spoken openly of their convictions. Other students have attacked these involvements and stood for a far more conservative position. It is worth noting that, while there may be fewer resolutions of a radical nature being passed by contemporary campus groups than in past generations, there is certainly more direct involvement in demonstrations, even though the price is loss of status as a student through expulsion and of status as a citizen through prison sentences.

This is an exciting time to be alive on the contemporary campus, even if the bulk of the students and faculty seem to be self-centered and conformist, because there is a strong and creative minority which is breaking out of old patterns by showing a willingness to give themselves to causes worth living or dying for. The church which wishes to develop an effective campus ministry must first understand the campus in all of its complexities and find ways to be significantly relevant in its various structures and subcultures. Above all, however, it will need to be willing and able to stand on the frontier with the creative ones who are not willing to settle for comfort, ease, and plenty, nor for materialistic values and personal security, but who are in search of a worthy cause, of a commitment worth making. Even the sleepiest campus has such persons, just waiting for the right trumpet blast to call them to their task. A contemporary campus culture is complex and unstable, but this very characteristic opens the door not to a more fearful but to a more hopeful future.

6: Creative and Experimental Ways of Ministering to the College Mind

ROBERT KENT, A SENIOR IN THE LAW SCHOOL of a highly reputed midwestern university, is conversing with a campus minister. The minister, whose brother is a lawyer, has listened with avid interest to Robert's exciting and vital description of his summer experiences with a lawyer in St. Louis. He has been thinking to himself how much this student's very evident enthusiasm has helped him understand and appreciate his own brother's role as a lawyer.

In the course of the conversation, Robert raises a question concerning the role one's own experience plays in shaping his religious convictions, and the minister responds with a rather technical answer hastily remembered from his latest theological reading. At this point the student invites him over to his desk, directs his attention to a huge law book, and asks the minister whether what he sees on its pages makes any sense to him. Since the book has to do with federal income tax formulas, the minister admits that it seems complicated and, frankly, boring to him. Robert replies that

Myron M. Teske graduated cum laude from the University of Wisconsin and went on to get his B.D. degree at the Northwestern Lutheran Theological Seminary, Minneapolis. He has done extensive graduate work and was privileged to study on a grant from the Danforth Foundation's Campus Ministry Grant program. He is Lutheran campus pastor at the University of Wisconsin.

the minister's theologically technical response to his earlier question seemed similarly complicated and boring to him. "On the other hand," he says, "I can open this book to almost any page; and, when I read what's there, I can see just about my whole three years of law studies come into focus — almost everything I've learned about law is involved in looking at just one of these tables. When I look at something like that, it's not at all complicated. But if I opened one of your theology books to almost any page, I suspect I would find it as complicated and as boring as these law books seem to you."

We shall have occasion a number of times in the following pages to refer to this conversation, for it set up a chain reaction in the mind of one campus minister, which is still "running," in regard to the relation of the church's ministry to the academic community. The conversation with Robert Kent raises persistent and perturbing questions for which the campus ministry staffs of all denominations are urgently seeking answers, and the directions in which those answers are being sought will be briefly described and critically evaluated, with comments concerning their adequacy for the future, in the pages that follow.

First, then, we will suggest five facets of the life of the church and the university and their interrelationships which make creative experimentation on the part of the campus ministry necessary. Second, we will survey the kinds of creative and experimental forms and structures of ministry currently being tested and projected. Third, we will subject these forms and structures to critical evaluation, both positive and negative. And, finally, we will stick out our necks with some predictions and hopes for creative experimentation in the future.

THE NECESSITY FOR EXPERIMENTATION

Campus ministry — a frontier FOR the church

The FOR in the title of this subsection is deliberately emphasized, since, to anyone who has served both in a local parish and in the more specialized campus ministry, it has often seemed that the latter is regarded by many parish pastors, church officials, and especially church college administrators as a frontier *against* the church rather than a part of its legitimate and urgent mission posture. Howard Moody's perceptive remarks concerning his own denomination might well be descriptive of the infighting that goes on *within* many denominations as various vested interests vie for larger shares of budgets and personnel and for the prestige which an increase in either seems to afford: "As a denomination we seem bent on selling ourselves in the open market of competitive Christendom; we feverishly search for the fresh format, the novel gimmick, the new approach which if packaged properly will lead to a new inpouring, perhaps of the Spirit, but, more important, of people into the churches." [1] And in the same article, Moody defines "frontier" in the sense it is intended in the title to this section: "I would like to use the word 'frontier' to designate the locus at which the church genuinely encounters the world — and it is for certain a world we have never lived in before. How will our Baptist churches face up to that world? How will we throw off the irrelevant aspects of our past?" [2]

Moody's remarks are but symptomatic of a host of voices being raised within the church today, all of them directed toward alerting us as to how little genuine encounter there is between the church and the structures of the world — a world strange and fearful to us because it is so radically different from that in which the church has been able to make its impact in prior generations. Books like Martin E. Marty's *The New Shape of American Religion* (Harper & Row, 1959), Gibson Winter's *The Suburban Captivity of the Churches* (Doubleday, 1961), and Peter L. Berger's *The Noise of Solemn Assemblies* (Doubleday, 1961) have sensitized many churchmen to the need for radical changes in the forms and structures of congregational life and denominational organization if the church is to regain contact with the world at its intersections of greatest power and vitality.

Similarly, in regard to the academic world, other perceptive voices have indicated the growing estrangement of the church and its ministry from the life of learning in such books as Arnold S.

[1] Howard Moody, "American Baptists: To Break the Bonds of Captivity," *The Christian Century*, April 10, 1963, p. 456. Copyright 1963, Christian Century Foundation. Reprinted by permission of *The Christian Century*.

[2] *Ibid.*, p. 457.

Nash's *The University and the Modern World* (Macmillan, 1943), Sir Walter H. Moberly's *The Crisis in the University* (SCM Press, 1949), and two more recent ones, Alexander Miller's *Faith and Learning* (Association Press, 1960), and Denis Baly's *Academic Illusion* (Seabury Press, 1961).

Charles S. McCoy, professor of religion in higher education at Pacific School of Religion, sums up the present situation:[3]

> Whatever the background, it is clearly the case today that a wide gulf of estrangement has developed between the church and the university. The academic community has deep suspicions of the church, held not only by non-Christians but also by many church members on college faculties. The church often regards the university with hostility. Educators often regard religion as a threat to free inquiry. Church leaders are often sure that college teaching deliberately undermines the faith of the students. On the one hand, scholars have little respect for most Christian learning; church colleges are generally regarded as inferior. On the other hand, churchmen regard vast expanses of American higher education as totally secularized and faithless. . . . Churchmen tend either to exalt the university and its personnel as filled with a mysterious, unapproachable wisdom, or to degrade the academic community as a society of irrelevant absent-minded eggheads.

Surely here is a locus where the church needs desperately to learn new ways of encounter with a world of which it is too much ignorant, inexcusably fearful (was not the Reformation spawned in just such communities?), and from which it has much to learn if it desires to minister to a world-coming-to-be, rather than a world-that-once-was. And the scouting thrust of the church's vital encounter with this rich frontier of the world's life is already available and at work in its campus ministry staff; the main body of troops are the students, faculty, and administrators on those campuses, who must be disciplined, equipped, briefed, supported, and encouraged by the whole church of which they are a part.

Present inadequacy of earlier forms, structures, and patterns

It might be expected that the forms of the church's ministry in academic communities — where change, growth, new insight are

[3] Charles S. McCoy, "The University and Its Culture," in Richard N. Bender (ed.), *On the Work of the Ministry in University Communities* (Nashville: Board of Education, The Methodist Church, 1962), pp. 44, 46. Used by permission.

sought and encouraged — would have been kept flexible, plastic, and constantly subject to critical evaluation. To some extent such has been the case. But too frequently also, as in more stable circumstances such as local churches and denominational offices, there remain forms and patterns anachronistic to the function needed and the task to be performed, forms which have long outlived their usefulness.

Beginning with voluntary student Christian associations in the late 19th and early 20th centuries (cf. chapter 4), the church's ministry was carried on in the 20's, 30's and 40's through various non-denominational groups, principally YM and YWCA's; also through denominational student fellowships, which began to be organized on an intercollegiate and national level as early as 1922 (Lutheran Student Association of America). Between 1935 and 1955 a number of denominational national student work offices were initiated to take the lead in appointing personnel and in securing the financing necessary for both the continuation of the student movements and the parallel development of organized ministries and student centers.

This work received more and more impetus as it became increasingly apparent that larger numbers of Christian students were finding their way to private and public colleges rather than to church colleges. The concern was rather parochial, with each denomination seeking to maintain contact with its own students, and the pattern has come to be known as the "church follows its students" phase. Conservation of the faith of the faithful was the hope, and the means was the provision of student centers to serve as centers of a Christian social life and a spiritual, ethical, and moral "haven" from the "godless campus." [4] On campuses where little provision was made for students' social life, and in the years before the present proliferation of student unions had begun, such centers provided a "home away from home," especially for students denied access to membership in the somewhat exclusive fraternity and sorority communities.

[4] I am indebted for some of the material in this section to a paper by Herluf M. Jensen, former executive secretary of the National Student Christian Federation, "Some Thoughts about the NSCF as Community and as Organization," prepared for the III General Assembly, NSCF, Lake Geneva, Wisconsin, Sept. 3-10, 1961.

During and after World War II, both the student movements and the student work agencies of the churches became aware that theirs was a mission task and not merely a job of preserving faith in the faithful, and the claims of the ecumenical movement began to break open parochial attitudes, especially in the student movements. Theological literature concerning the church's task in the university began to appear, such as the books of Nash and Moberly mentioned above. Social and recreational concerns began to be replaced, or at least supplemented and enriched, by study retreats and conferences. The Christian community on campuses began to see its task not simply as holding the faithful or recovering the fallen, but as participation and witness in the whole gamut of academic life. The change was expressed symbolically when departments of student work or student service began changing their names to departments of campus Christian life or divisions of college and university work. This change was not merely one of designation, but reflected a new conception of the scope and range of the task facing the church as it sought genuine engagement and encounter with the university while each did its own valid and authentic work.

Rapidly-changing academic scene calls for experimentation

As the church turns its attention away from a narrow, parochial, self-conserving kind of campus ministry, it finds itself confronting a complex, anxious-yet-confident, mushrooming, sprawling, giddy-with-growth community which is today's college and university — whether community college, junior college, state-college-become-university, or major state university with graduate schools increasingly calling the tune.

The most visible change evident to the church as it surveys the campus scene is the meteoric rise in numbers of students — a change from 200,000 seeking higher education in 1900 to approximately 4,000,000 in 1963 and a fantastic estimate of 10,000,000 by 1970. Whereas one in twenty-five high school graduates sought a college degree in 1900, today almost one in three intends to do so. And, to make the picture more vivid, experts predict that the *shortage of college teachers* in 1970 will be the same figure (200,000) as the *total number of students* in 1900! The resultant building boom on college campuses, especially in federally-financed dormitories, but also in classrooms, student unions, and even such special facilities as fine arts buildings and theaters, meets the eye on almost any campus one visits. And, in addition, whole new campuses are springing up in every part of the country, from a new downtown campus for a great state university, to community or city colleges, to a host of new two-year extension centers which will feed students into the more complete facilities of the mother institution.

While the various denominational campus work agencies have expanded rapidly as to the number of staff on campuses and the number of campuses staffed with professional workers, it is increasingly being asked whether the church can find either personnel or money to keep up with such fantastic growth. Possible creative solutions move in the direction of greater ecumenical joint-staffing and a much expanded role for lay ministry — but this line of thinking anticipates later pages of this chapter.

A second revolutionary change is perhaps less visible, but even more significant and pervasive in its implications for the university and the church's role in it. This is the vast explosion of knowledge, particularly in the scientific disciplines, with the university involved in vast research (and the consequent communication of its fruits in teaching) which reaches in spatial terms from the bottom of the ocean to the farthest reaches of the latest radio-telescope; in scope from the discovery of DNA to the desalination of ocean waters; and in pragmatic terms to the outdating of textbooks within five years from the date of their publication. It has led to whole new departments in the university, to narrower and narrower specialization on the one hand and insight into new unities between disciplines on the other, and to new approaches to curriculum, ways of teaching, and more honest appraisal of what *must* be taught and what will only clutter up students' notebooks and heads.

A corollary of the expansion of knowledge is the fact that increased demands are being made on the university for research by both government and industry, and an inordinate amount of research money is being poured into certain segments of the university by various government agencies.

The pressure on faculty and students alike (to say nothing of administrators, personnel services, and housing officials) which the combination of expanding numbers, exploding knowledge, and drastically stepped-up research brings, also gives the church pause as it seeks to provide for this whole vibrant, pulsating, intensely alive community: (1) maturity of faith through study, (2) wholeness and integrity through worship, and (3) meaningfulness and purpose in vocational responsibility and service to neighbor.

Campus trends, developing and receding

With a background of earlier forms and patterns of campus ministry now before us, and with a quick glimpse at the rapidly-changing scene as we look with new seriousness at the university communities in which our ministry is set, what can we now discern concerning patterns of life and action which will suggest and affect the direction of creative experimentation in campus ministry?

In a paper cited earlier (*cf.* footnote 4), Herluf Jensen, former executive secretary of the National Student Christian Federation, has listed with sensitive awareness some of the rather clearly discernible trends which need to be considered in future strategy.

He says that there is a *receding* interest in religious emphasis weeks, in social life (recreation) within our student fellowships, and in the strictly sectarian programming, — in general, a receding interest in all that goes on in student Christian centers and foundation houses. On the other hand, he says that there are *developing trends* in serious efforts of study, in small groups (especially those gathered around social and political concerns) , in various forms of voluntary service projects, in corporate team ministries, in concern for international students, in awareness of social and political issues, in ecumenical contacts and relations, in international travel by students, in the disciplined involvement in Christian intentional communities (*cf.* later pages for specific description of these) , and in a growing willingness on the part of campus ministry staff to accept ecumenical responsibility (*cf.* later illustration of this) .[5]

As we look specifically in the next major section of this chapter at the imaginative experimentation with new forms and patterns of campus ministry, we shall see how greatly the direction and intent of experiment has been influenced by the discernment in almost all denominations of the above-listed trends.

[5] For a complete listing of Jensen's trends, see chapter 15, "The Church Alive in the University."

The need to take seriously the university's own authentic task

Alongside the various revolutionary changes taking place in the academic community itself, there have also been radical changes taking place in the church's intellectual life, *i.e.,* in its theology. Some of these have been described in chapters 2 and 3, but a brief synopsis is in order here. These include the recovery of a vital biblical and evangelical theology, especially since World War I, and really only available to us in America in the last two decades – a theology in reaction to the optimistic and rationalistic theology which held sway in the late 19th and early 20th centuries. With this has come a rediscovery of the nature of the church as God's people, clergy and lay, active in serving love in the world. With it also has developed the realization that other structures and organisms of society have their own valid tasks, and that the world as a whole can and must be the theater for the Christian's enactment of his life of witness and service. Thus has come reemphasis on that yet-to-be-fulfilled insight of the Reformation: that the central role of the laity in their function as both gathered and scattered (dispersed) church requires penetration of every segment and dimension of society in which their daily lives are lived out.

As Howard Moody has reminded us, in the previously-cited article, however, this theological revolution "will be complete when it opens new ways for church and world to meet – and when the church becomes willing to live in and for the world, hearing its abuse, being reviled by it, and bearing its burdens." And he asks of his own denomination what might well be asked of Christians of every persuasion: Will we "be able to move beyond church-world dialogue to a church-world involvement in which [we] love the world – even as God does – enough to be thoroughly immersed in it and concerned enough to defy it, not because it is immoral or evil but so that it might become faithful to its true nature?" [6]

Churchmen writing in regard to higher education have constantly reminded us that the vocation of the university community is *primarily* intellectual; Professor Roger Hazelton has spoken of the task of being both a Christian and a student as one in which you are "basically a student and centrally a Christian"; College president

[6] Moody, *op. cit.,* pp. 457, 458.

Howard F. Lowry has indicated that the most difficult task of the college is to get a student to sit down fifteen consecutive minutes in front of a book (in *The Mind's Adventure,* Westminster Press, 1950).

The call for those of Christian persuasion to be "involved" in the university world, to love it and be "thoroughly immersed" in it so as to help it become faithful to its true nature, has been brilliantly and passionately articulated by Charles McCoy as he states his "strong convictions" about church and university.

> I believe the church, in its ministry within the academic community, must take the university with much more seriousness than has been the case in the recent past. We must work harder to understand the university—its nature, its purposes, and its problems. A minister is prepared to work effectively in the university community only if he has respect for the great heritage of Western higher education and has genuine love for the university and the persons who make it up. We must recognize the estrangement existing between church and university. We must keep pace in our understanding with the changing face of the American campus. And we must participate in the struggles which harass and perplex the denizens of the academic jungle, whether administrator, professor, or student. Only in these ways can we learn to speak relevantly to the uncertainties and hopes of higher education. Only then can we provide leadership in the church and glimpse the challenge of Christ's ministry in the university.[7]

Whether we in the church can move toward completing the theological revolution of the last twenty years in America — whether in our ministry in these vibrant, pulsating, intensely alive communities we can become the agents of God's redemptive love and purpose for them — it is too early to predict with accuracy. But that a beginning is being made will become evident as we now survey some examples.

KINDS OF CREATIVE AND EXPERIMENTAL FORMS AND PATTERNS OF CAMPUS MINISTRY BEING CURRENTLY TESTED AND PROJECTED

If we turn our thoughts back for a few moments to the conversation between Robert Kent, law school senior, and a campus minister, with which this chapter opened, we might now be able to sense some of the insights as well as some of the perturbing questions which resulted for the campus minister.

[7] McCoy, *op. cit.,* p. 47.

It seemed abundantly clear to him on later reflection that, if the Christian gospel were to address Robert Kent, several factors, largely ignored or inadequately appreciated by the church in its ministry on campuses, had now to be seriously grappled with:

(1) The locus of excitement and intensity of interest, the place where Robert Kent was evidently most alive and stirred, was in his study and his summer experience preparing him for the profession of law.

(2) When the campus minister expressed interest in what excited and made a great deal of sense to Robert Kent — though he (the minister) was unable to experience, except vicariously, that excitement and sense — he did recognize that he had really encountered Robert at the height of his powers, at the heart of his experiencing and feeling, at the place where his nerves tingled and his emotions were most stirred.

(3) At the same time, it was apparent that to intrude foreign and technical theological understandings that had no recognizable connection to Robert's own excitement about law and his study and experience with it, was to move toward disengagement from him, to put distance between them.

(4) Coincidentally, it occurred to him that what he was experiencing with Robert Kent was not unrelated to his own sense of distance, the inability to share deeply the life of his own lawyer-brother over the past half dozen years.

(5) When Robert Kent raised the question concerning the role one's own experience plays in shaping one's religious convictions, the campus minister came to a dawning awareness of how valuable *listening* to this student had been in expanding the range of his (the minister's) own experience and of the need to stretch the theological categories *he* was familiar with to include that wider range.

(6) The question similarly began to emerge as to whether some way did not have to be found to stretch the range of Robert Kent's experiencing excitement, and interest beyond the narrow scope of legal matters to the broader and deeper and wider-ranging host of questions of meaning and purpose, nature and destiny, with which the Christian faith claims to have to do.

The fact that similar experience and insight has produced parallel

questions and suggested initial experimentation toward more satis-
fying answers than conventional campus religious ministries and
programs were providing is evidenced in certain specific, identifi-
able forms and patterns being tested and improved.

The Christian Faith-and-Life Community at Austin, Texas

Following World War II and under the stirrings of both the
theological revival and the appearance of the World Student Christian Federation's materials on the "university question" (the
theological examination and critique of the university itself; cf.
reference to Nash, Moberly, Miller, and Baly books above), the
(Presbyterian) Westminster Foundation Director at the University
of Texas, the Rev. W. Jack Lewis began to conceive of an experiment in lay training in a state university community.[8]

Taking his cue from what he observed in the lay evangelical
academies developed in Germany after World War II, and from
similar lay training centers in Holland and the Iona Community
in Scotland, the community which emerged at Austin under Lewis'
guidance included in its development the following features:

(1) Provision for a limited number of students to live together
for an academic year under a discipline of worship, shared meals,
free-time seminars, and lectures.

(2) The development of a curriculum of study which, in close relationship to the intense community experience with its worship,
continuing conversation, and opportunity for pastoral guidance by
theologically-trained staff, would:

(a) Help the student overcome his religious illiteracy, not
only for his own integrity as a student, but that he might then
be an adequately equipped layman to participate knowingly in
the church's mission.

(b) Raise questions concerning his own self-understanding
as a person living in a fast-changing world and provide adequate
theological and cultural symbols for the articulation of his experiences of himself and his world.

[8] For a fuller picture of the Austin Community, the reader is referred to the
article by Dr. Parker Rossman, of Yale Divinity School, "The Austin Community: Challenge and Controversy," in the Spring, 1962, issue of *The Christian
Scholar,* pp. 44-51, to which we express our indebtedness.

(c) Be brief enough to be covered in two semesters of an academic year, yet meaty enough to raise the central question of the meaning of human existence; to suggest answers from the history of Christian ideas including selections from Old and New Testament, the Church Fathers, the writers of the Reformation, and contemporary theologians; and to raise and seek answers to the question of what it means to be a responsible man of faith in the various orders of life.

(3) The provision of opportunities for dialogue with the culture of the current day through the use of art forms (art, movies, slides, tapes, music, drama) in after-dinner conversations, and in worship.

(4) The inclusion of students from a variety of university disciplines, several cultures and national backgrounds, and a cross-section of denominational and religious backgrounds to provide an interdisciplinary, ecumenical, and international and interracial possibility for mutual enrichment and serious interchange.

This is an all-too-brief attempt to encompass in schematic form the rather complex and very imaginative development of the Austin Community, and two brief paragraphs from Dr. Rossman's more thorough treatment of it must suffice to lift up what this writer conceives to be its greatest strength:

> From the first there was visible power within this community of students and staff because of the discipline, the worship, the common life, and the seriousness of study which characterized its common life. The Christian Faith and Life Community rests upon the conviction that the vocation of the student is thorough-going study. The student's regular academic work is stressed as primary; it is his present vocation and his preparation for future service in society. Nothing in the Community is allowed to detract from this primary responsibility. On the other hand, there is also a dimension of supplementary theological and Biblical study which is planned to clarify that vocation, to provide intellectual stimulation, and to give him understanding of the human situation today and of the need and problems of the Church.

> Yet, the *aim* of Christian work is not merely to study the Christian faith, but to focus upon mission! Theological categories are important so that the laity may be able to articulate for themselves and others that which they feel to be important. Thus [such a] campus Community sees its study of religion as integrally related to liberal education, i.e., "to help the student develop a self-understanding to which he

can meaningfully relate all the factual knowledge he possesses. It provides the chance for the kind of serious conversation through which he can learn to think critically." In other words, the Community *helps the student to think through the meaning of his academic work, of study, itself; of liberal education, itself; and of the university, itself; as well as of his own intellectual vocation within the perspective of the Christian's vocation in the world.*[9]

Although begun in the framework of campus work at the University of Texas, the Austin Community has now become a lay training center with many other facets beyond the communal disciplined study and worship effort. Some of these are parish laymen's seminars, vocational conference seminars, parish ministers' colloquies, theological studies for married student couples, and a number of others. True to its original experimental nature, the Austin staff is now turning its attention to various new avenues of approach, partially necessitated, one suspects, because of a division among its ten-member staff just over a year ago when seven staff members left the Texas community to serve the Ecumenical Institute at Evanston, Illinois. The Rev. W. Jack Lewis, who continues as Executive Director of the Community, writes in a letter of June 5, 1963:

> There are now four full-time theologically trained men who make up our Collegium: they are Episcopalian, Methodist, American Baptist and Presbyterian, U.S. Beginning in September, we will be consolidating our college work and adult work in the same area, utilizing our Laos House . . . for intensive 44-hour seminars. For a few years we will not have our regular residential program for students but will be experimenting with existing groups within secular groups on campus to see if the break-open type seminar will provide penetration within these secular groups.
>
> Next fall we will be working with 750 persons, ranging from teenage through middle age, both men and women. Some of these seminars will be "inter-age" to see and explore the possibilities of breaking barriers of communication between the age groups which today are so separated by rigid images which each holds of the other. During the fall we will be working on three weekends with 25 members each time of various campus religious foundations and in the spring with an equal number from fraternities, sororities and other campus groups. . . .
>
> We will be developing several vocational type seminars in the future but these will be predicated upon an initial seminar . . . dealing with

[9] *Ibid.*, pp. 46, 48.

the meaning of human existence and the possibility of full humanness. Once the theological foundation has been established, we feel that a person can move anywhere in advanced courses which we might be offering. We feel that one weakness of the European academics, despite their tremendous contributions to all of us, is that they fail to do the theological groundwork before moving into vocational and social issues. We have discovered that the methodology of teaching in a weekend seminar which includes a mealtime conversation, intercession at meals, reading from the Scriptures and the Church fathers at the opening of the meals, art-form discussions and corporate worship, when providing the context for lectures, essays and seminars, offers the possibility of a "Gestalt" for the participants as few things could do. The possibility for a person to receive his past and be open to the future is one of our prime concerns.[10]

Other "intentional" communities — residential

There is little doubt that the Austin Community was the stimulus for the establishment of similar "intentional" communities throughout the country — so much so that Herluf Jensen identified as a major trend in campus work the development of Koinonia Houses and Faith and Life Communities, and the disciplined involvement in Christian intentional community.

Almost all of these have made minor or major modifications of the Austin Experiment to adapt it to their own campus environment. Residential communities have been established at Brown University, M. I. T., Yale, Wisconsin (American Baptist), and most recently at the State University of Iowa at Iowa City (National Lutheran Council). A recent article in *The Lutheran,* biweekly periodical of the Lutheran Church in America, indicates how and why such a community gets started and the kind of adaptation made from the Austin Experiment:

> Having discarded all notions of a campus pastor being able to minister to thousands [of students] through traditional means and having

[10] In his June 5 letter, Lewis also writes: "Your letter points up the necessity for our Staff to write a general history and description of the nature and scope of our work. . . . I feel that the historical development was described fairly accurately by Professor Parker Rossman of Yale Divinity School . . . under the title 'Protestantism in the University: and the challenge of a new idea.' Mr. Rossman wrote six chapters which were mimeographed and last year were condensed in *The Christian Scholar.* . . . Chapter One of his paper is entirely on the history and development of the Christian Faith-and-Life Community on the college campus."

shelved plans to establish a student congregation (there are several Lutheran congregations in town), [the Lutheran Student Foundation] dispatched [Campus Pastor] Arne Kvaalen to Texas to take a look at the "Austin Experiment." . . .

Kvaalen was impressed by what he saw. Christus House, an Iowa adaptation of the Austin experiment, came into being with three small dormitories (for undergraduate men, women, and graduate men) built into former residential homes, and a newly erected fellowship hall. It got off to a shaky start last spring. Initial response on the part of students was slow.

But a few interested young people brought friends along and, when the fall semester opened, Christus House was filled to capacity (34 about equally divided between men and women) with Lutherans accounting for about three-fourths of the total. Art, science, and pre-med students led the list: . . . In the fall Jim Anderson joined the community as resident chaplain. . . .

He lives in a closet-like room behind the office of the men's dormitory and carries out an intensely personal ministry to the students, at daily matins and vesper services, during and between meals, and in the after-hours period that lasts at Christus House until deep into the night.

"They come to me to talk about anything that may bother them, but mainly about the problem of being a student and of finding a direction in life," he says. "We may start out in the kitchen, move to the fireplace, then to the lounge or the library in the girls' dorm, finally wind up at the Student Union or walking the streets of Iowa City at 2 in the morning."

The discipline at Christus House is simple. Students applying for room and board (at $65 a month) are pledged to attend daily matins or vesper services, to be present at supper with its "directed conversation" (discussion of topics presented by residents or guests), and to take part in, and prepare for, weekly seminars conducted by the pastors.

Keeping of the discipline is reviewed at biweekly after-dinner gatherings at which students tell the groups where they have failed to keep their promise. This is not a "confession of sins" but a device to keep the commitment of the community alive. . . .[11]

Pastor Arne Kvaalen, who initiated the experiment, came from a campus pastorate in North Dakota to the University of Iowa to get a master's degree in fine arts (a circumstance which may indicate why many students in the community are from the art discipline) and later returned to his original pursuit. In a letter to an alumnus of the Iowa Foundation, shared with this writer, he indicates other dimensions of the experiment:

[11] Robert E. Huldschiner, "Students Are People—An Experiment in Ministry on a State University Campus," *The Lutheran*, April 24, 1963, pp. 6-10.

We have a residential community as a primary structure which makes possible a worship-centered ministry of preaching-teaching with an intensity and depth heretofore unknown to us in this work. . . . 33 students are involved in a disciplined life together of daily worship, hour-and-a-half seminars each week in Biblical studies and Lutheran theology, and in a suppertime discussion period each night with all kinds of vital subjects from Dietrich Bonhoeffer's book *Life Together,* worship and liturgy, to the Cuban crisis and the Christian's posture in the face of thermonuclear war.

In addition another 15 students join in the weekly seminars so that a total of about 48 students are involved in the theological study. To the ten week-day worship services we have added Sunday evening vespers at the request of the non-residential students who join those in residence at the Sunday evening supper-discussion.

We have started a Bible study group in one of the women's dorms and a supper-time study-discussion group in one of the men's dorms with more to follow. . . . Some exciting things are happening among the students involved.

One of the modifications from the Austin experience in this Iowa community is the emphasis on the use of the liturgical worship of the sponsoring denomination and the emphasis (at least thus far) on attracting most of the community members from that denomination's constituency and giving conscious attention to the study of its own theological tradition. This change may indicate a weakness similar to that for which the Austin Community has been criticized, namely the lack of theological variety among the staff. But it may also indicate a strength for which the Austin Community was also credited — "being rooted in specific theological convictions which give character and incisiveness to its work." [12]

Having known personally and somewhat intimately the fine Community of Life and Faith initiated on the University of Wisconsin campus under the direction of American Baptist university pastor, the Rev. Richard Broholm, the present writer would indicate his own high esteem for the work of that community and for the very manifest enrichment in self-understanding; in the heightened capacity for theological sensitivity to the vocation of the Christian student and lay witness in secular structures; and perhaps especially in the deepened grasp of what it means to live in community, which occurs among participants.

[12] Rossman, *op. cit.,* p. 51.

Yet, like the Christus House Community at Iowa, the lack of an ecumenical basis of support has meant here also a lack of theological variety among the staff, and therefore the lack of the kind of creative tension which evidently gave the Austin experiment a great deal of its power of creativity and depth. On the other hand, both the Iowa and Wisconsin communities have consciously sought to work within the framework of the institutional church and to be a source of renewal which would benefit the more regularized forms of denominational and congregational life — an identification apparently less real and less sought after in the Austin situation.

An occasional paper, prepared by the staff of the Wisconsin Community, and entitled "Some Reflections on a Residential Community of Life and Faith after Five Years," indicates both some of the unresolved problems and some of the as-yet-unexplored possibilities for the Community of Faith and Life. Among these are financial and recruitment problems. Only thirteen of seventy-seven American Baptist churches in the state give any financial support, and most of these are small donations. (The writer would share the staff's view that this lack of support stems from an outmoded and anachronistic view of the church's relation to higher education and of a suspicion of ecumenically-tinged efforts in campus ministry.) Here again, as Howard Moody has suggested, there is an urgent need in this and other denominations to "break the bonds of captivity" to ways of thinking that just will no longer do if new ways are to be opened for church and world to meet.

Similarly, ways of achieving ecumenical support for a denominationally-directed program, both in financing and recruiting students, are being sought, but much discussion and goodwill between campus workers have not yet led to viable solutions.

Two major questions, having to do with the kind of experience which the Community provided, were asked of students who completed their year of residence. Their replies give us specific insight concerning the meaning of the experience to them.

To the question, "Is the program too intensive, too disturbing for most students? Does it tend to accentuate emotional instability beyond the point of healthy self-criticism?" two students replied:

> The Community dispelled for most of us any fond hopes about the ease or simplicity of any kind of corporate life. We shall never again

take lightly Paul's words about walls being broken down. Marriage, employment, voluntary associations, all have taken on new, less romantic, more human significance. The Community in its purge of the community-myth has forced us to take seriously the theological implications of "aloneness."

I found that I was questioning all of my motives, that I was too preoccupied with being sensitive and responsible. In many ways the Community made life a hell for me by forcing me to be even more introspective than I already was.

And to the question, "Does the Community tend to undercut loyalty to the institutional church?" two students replied with the following comments:

If I were to make some personal statement about the Community of Life and Faith I would venture a guess that without it I should proba, bly have remained loyal to the church but have denied the world. A worse judgment I could not pronounce on any Christian.

As to moving away from the institutional church and the Community's possible tendency to encourage this, the Community has had an opposite tendency in my own personal experience. I had moved away from the institutional church more than a year ago and had no serious thought of drawing closer. At the same time the Community seemed to offer a "responsible" and "honest" way of looking over the church again. The entire Community experience has left me with more understanding of the Church's struggle and warmth for its efforts.

Perhaps we have given undue attention to these "intentional" communities as experimental new ways of reaching the college mind, but if their establishment continues to be a major trend (as Herluf Jensen has suggested), or if they are an experiment today but "may become the pattern of campus ministry in the future," as Huldshiner reports (cf. footnote 11), it is necessary that wider segments of church membership be informed about them and contribute to their critical development and support.

Non-residential communities

Non-residential, but covenantal communities (*i.e.,* whose members "covenant together" to share in certain disciplines of worship, study, meal fellowship) have been developed on a number of campuses such as Emory University at Decatur, Georgia, the St. Paul campus of the University of Minnesota, and (under the sponsorship of the Wesley Foundation) the University of Wisconsin. The commitment in these communities is much less intensive, the demands on time much less strenuous, and the curriculum of study rather less extensive than in the residential community. Members usually commit themselves to at least one regular worship service together, the sharing of one meal a week together with preparation for and attendance at one seminar, and the reading of certain common theological fare. Personal interviews are often required to enable staff to ascertain the members' seriousness of motivation and faithfulness of commitment.

A more recent experiment which is being watched with considerable interest is that initiated by the Rev. Robert L. James, Jr. and later led by Tom Wiesser [13] at Temple University in Philadelphia, a large commuter school, to develop a Faith-and-Life Institute geared to the commuting student. Since it is estimated that by 1970 almost half of all the students in the United States will be attending this kind of huge metropolitan commuter school, and since much of the traditional pattern of campus ministry is impossible and irrelevant in commuter schools, the necessity for such an attempt is clear.

W. Jack Lewis describes this new modification of the Austin Community very briefly in his letter of June 5: "The commuter brings his overnight bag to the campus on a given day and at the end of his classes goes to a residence set aside for the purpose, where he then participates in worship, dinner, lecture, seminar, spends the night, has worship and breakfast the next morning, goes to school and returns to his own home that day."

A tentative outline of plans for the Institute, in mimeographed form under date of March 22, 1961, first describes the nature of Temple University, then the peculiar features of the life of commuter students and continues:

> The heart of the Church's ministry in this situation is in the life and work of the Christian members of the university community (rather than in the work of the campus ministry staff as such) . . . .
> One part of our responsibility is to help new students—freshmen and sophomores—discover the dimensions of the Christian way of life in the university for themselves. The Faith and Life Institute is proposed as the center of our common effort with these students.
> About sixty freshmen and sophomores will be "enrolled" each se-

[13] According to information in letter of June 5, 1963, from W. Jack Lewis.

mester, and each student will be urged to attend for three semesters. These sixty students will meet in seminar groups of about fifteen, each group coming to the institute one evening a week regularly. The seminar cirriculum will deal with the Bible and biblical theology, church history and the development of the different traditions, Christian ethics and the church's relation to the world. It will be specifically designed to provide knowledge and understanding of Faith and Life for these young laymen.

The paper then indicates that since other lay academy experience has made it clear that "common life" is an essential factor in the fruitfulness of such a seminar, it is proposed to provide such life in a house located near Temple University to be purchased by the Protestant Advisory Board for this purpose. The residence would then be used in the manner indicated by Lewis in his brief description of this experiment in the June 5 letter. Additionally:

> It is proposed that the Institute be staffed by a full time director of studies who, in addition to the Seminar program, will develop week-end conferences for students and others on Faith and Life as it relates to various fields of work. This will serve both as "Seed-Bed" for new insights for the Seminar, and as follow-up for upperclassmen who have been in the Seminar previous years. It will provide a much-needed opportunity for students, faculty, and practitioners to seek together for new patterns of Christian life. A seminary intern and his wife will live in the center, providing chaperonage and supervision of the property.

The Temple University experiment unquestionably projects a community experience with significant new features which will be of peculiar interest to the church's ministry on both the growing number of community college campuses (such as the two-year University Extension Centers in Wisconsin and the junior colleges in California and elsewhere), and also on those larger campuses with longer histories which have always attracted a large proportion of commuter students (*e.g.*, the University of Minnesota, the University of Wisconsin in Milwaukee, and the new downtown Chicago campus of the University of Illinois.)

We turn then, to other experimental forms, with this last insightful comment by Professor McCoy lifting up one among many reasons for the attraction which these "intentional communities" have had on compuses: "College students seek personality in a new world of impersonality at college, and, therefore, join fraternities, sororities, cooperatives, and other groups in which they can share and be recognized as persons." [14]

The Christian Faith and Higher Education Institute

It is apparent from the above description of the Austin Experiment and its modifications that the churchmen (primarily campus ministers) who have initiated and developed them have of necessity experimented with forms of group life, content of curriculum, teaching methodology, patterns of conversation, use of art forms in many media, and liturgical order and expression.

As we have seen, what was learned in the Austin Experiment has been widely shared and used, largely in campus ministry situations, but certainly not exclusively there. One of the continuing criticisms of the Experiment, however, is that adequate means of communicating to the whole church what has been learned, particularly as it is relevant to renewal at the congregational and parish level, have as yet not emerged.

Similarly, if we center our attention more narrowly on the church's responsibility in the arena of higher education, it is evident that the communication of new, promising, and creative ways of ministering in this context has not been going on in a way that leads to an informed and involved constituency among the general church membership (which is a *major* motivation for the writing of this book!).

It is also becoming increasingly clear that the development of new and helpful resources for the church's task in higher education will not occur in the measure, depth, scope, and richness which is potentially possible, unless present haphazard efforts are supplemented and perhaps disciplined by structures created specifically for that purpose.

The Christian Faith and Higher Education Institute, under the leadership of the Director of Studies, Jack Harrison, is a structure intended to meet just such a need. Supported financially by the United Church of Christ and the United Presbyterian Church, U.S.A., and headquartered at 1405 S. Harrison Road in East Lansing, Michigan (contiguous to the campus of Michigan State University), the Institute has a study and strategy committee made up

[14] McCoy, *op. cit.*, p. 42.

of persons chosen for their competence without regard for denominational affiliation, both churchmen and educators. Originally conceived of as a regional structure, the Institute now conceives of itself as a school without geographical locus, and does not carry on all its work in one location, but instead goes wherever the work may demand.

As indicated in a descriptive brochure it has published, the Institute is commissioned "to discover and develop resources for both the church and higher education." Continuing, the brochure breaks down this task into four areas of responsibility and describes them as follows:

1. EXPLORATION AND EXPERIMENTATION

In this area, the Institute conducts conferences with groups of campus ministers, college chaplains, college town pastors and university scholars and laymen in order to find out the kinds of issues that need to be explored further or intensively studied. Individual laymen and clergymen serve as part-time consultants to help discover issues either in the church or in higher education for further exploration or intensive study. For example, in the academic year of 1963-64, a professor from a theological seminary has served as an Institute Theologian to explore as thoroughly as possible the issues involved in Theology and Natural Science. His work will result in a report of his experiences and his reflection upon the issues involved in both church and higher education.

In the area of Exploration and Experimentation the Institute attempts to discover issues and to evaluate them for further exploration or intensive study.

2. INTENSIVE STUDY AND DEVELOPMENT OF RESOURCES

In the area of intensive study the Institute has commissioned two seminars to conduct three-year studies in the fields of Medicine and Economics.

The Seminar in Medicine is to study the issues common to Theology and Medicine concerning man as a human being rather than a machine in the scientific research aspects of Medicine in medical education and in the practice of Medicine. Directed from the West Side Medical Center in Chicago by a Presbyterian University Pastor, the work is being done by laymen in Medical Science along with theologians.

In order to understand fully the issues involved in the vocation of an economist, the Seminar of Economists will study the ways by which economists can come to understand their work and compare this to the ways by which people in other fields of learning understand their work. By including ethical and theological considerations as well as economic considerations in the study of this important university subject, the study will lead into the issues confronting man again as a human being versus a machine. The seminar is being conducted by a university professor of Economics at South Dakota State College.

Both of these seminars have already published some of their results through articles in professional journals and as bibliography for economics and ethics.

Another area of intensive study is under development which will involve laymen scholars from universities who will study and reflect upon the work and ministry of the church in the world. They will produce a set of essays about the life of the church in the world where the problems of freedom and obedience will be fully set forth.

3. CONSULTATIONS IN PROGRAMS FOR OTHER GROUPS AND INSTITUTIONS

When called upon, the Institute serves as a consultant to other groups and institutions making resources available to strengthen their program.

In its first year, the Institute has served such groups as The Committee on Campus Christian Life of the Michigan Council of Churches and the Campus Ministry Boards of several denominations in Michigan by securing the services of Michigan State University to set before responsible agencies for campus ministry in Michigan the changing patterns of higher education in Michigan.

The Institute has also helped the faculty of the Presbyterian Theological Seminary of the University of Dubuque, with the Steering Committee of Michigan State University, to carry out a school for the seminary faculty on the subject of Pedagogy in Higher Education. The proceedings of this school have been published by the Institute and distributed to seminaries and theological schools thoughout the United States and Canada.

The Institute provides leadership and staff to help in Michigan State University's Town and Country Pastors Leadership School in the summer.

The Institute has also provided leadership for a consultation on Campus Ministry at Delta College in Bay City-Saginaw, Michigan, for the benefit of the pastors of churches serving the tri-county area and consequently serving Delta College. These pastors included Protestant, Roman Catholic and Jewish pastors consulting together on their common ministry in higher education.

The United Campus Christian Fellowship National Council has asked the Institute to consult in a program in the summer of 1964 which would set before the National Council the work of the university in the United States. The Institute is able to bring resources from higher education as instructors in such a program for the benefit of the National Council of the United Campus Christian Fellowship. The proceedings of this conference will be published for the use of students, faculty and campus ministers of many churches.

4. PUBLICATION AND DISSEMINATION OF RESOURCES

The Institute will seek to have material published in existing organs of publication and it will itself publish such items as are of special interest to special groups and assist in the dissemination of resources already developed.

The Institute has published the proceedings of the Dubuque Faculty School on Pedagogy in Higher Education and has distributed these to theological seminaries and schools.

To provide for the exciting possibilities of a conversation between theology and university disciplines, the Institute has begun the publication of a series of papers by laymen. The following have been published: The Resources of the Christian Faith for the Scientist by a physicist; Faith, Learning and Commitment, and The University as a Model for a Campus Ministry by a research professor in Floriculture Marketing. These papers have been widely distributed to campus ministers in the United Campus Christian Fellowship, the Protestant Episcopal Church, the American Baptist Convention and the National Lutheran Council. The intent of the papers is the development of a conversation among university scholars that can be of the highest order as a resource to both church and higher education.[15]

It seems clear that care, patience, and disciplined planning are to be the keynote of the Christian Faith and Higher Education Institute and that resource materials of real worth and merit will continue to flow from its efforts.

Other experiments in relating Christianity to university disciplines

There is a clearly recognizable movement in campus ministries toward taking more seriously the primary task of the university as manifested in the various disciplines of the academic community and in the related teaching, research, books, and articles. Though many small groups, organized along lines of intellectual interest and usually related to one or more parallel university disciplines, have come into being on various campuses, very little has been written about them, and little has thus far been done to share insights gained from them or resources found helpful in them. Because of their extreme importance and consequent probable continuing usefulness (especially with the potential "resource development" for just such groups being initiated by the Christian Faith and Higher Education Institute), the writer will describe several

[15] Jack Harrison, *Christian Faith and Higher Education Institute* (Lansing, Mich., 1964).

such groups with which he is acquainted from first-hand experience so as to begin the process and stimulate the wider dissemination of information about them.

The conversation with Robert Kent (a pseudonym) with which we began was one of a host of conversations with law students, lawyers, and one professor, Wilbur Katz, at the University of Chicago in which the writer sought to ascertain the possibility of a continuing discussion on that campus of issues in the legal profession as they might be helpfully illuminated by theological insight and vice versa. Professor Katz, an Episcopal layman and an active supporter of such dialogue, gave encouragement and provided contact with lawyers in the Chicago area who might be interested, since it was hoped that such discussion would be mutually enriching if engaged in both by neophyte students, still academically concerned with the law, and experienced lawyers who would relish continuing contact with what was being taught in the law school.

Fortunately there were several people in the Chicago area who had participated in such dialogue on the East coast, primarily under the stimulus of William Stringfellow (a theologically articulate young lawyer then with the East Harlem Protestant Parish), and in conferences at Packard Manse, an ecumenical retreat center, led by Bishop James Pike.

Primarily as the fruit of their experiences, it was decided not to use theological materials as the central focus, but rather to use a modification of the "case study" procedure with which law students and lawyers were more familiar. Through personal calling, both on law students, lawyers, and some Divinity School students and professors, and with additional help in finding interested people on the part of campus ministry colleagues, a group was gathered and met on a continuing basis. Several of the lawyers shared in the development of case study materials in which questions were raised of import for both the legal and theological people in the group.

Members of the group later shared in the planning of a National Conference on Christian Faith and Law, sponsored by the National Student Christian Federation and the Society for College Work of the Protestant Episcopal Church, held in the fall of 1957. Shortly before the conference an issue of *The Christian Scholar* had appeared on the theme "Christian Faith and Law," and other resource materials were available from the Packard Manse conferences, from European vocationally-oriented seminars, and from special lectures at Columbia University Law School and New York University Law School. The theme of the conference was "Love for Justice," and lawyers, judges, law students, and law professors from across the country participated. Papers were presented by Professor Katz, by Professor Harold Berman, of Harvard Law School, by Paul Lehman, Professor of Christian Ethics at Princeton, and by Professor Markus Barth, of the Divinity School of the University of Chicago, and were later printed in *The Oklahoma Law Review* in a special issue. Professor Jacques Ellul of Bordeaux, France, originally scheduled to give a presentation, was unable to do so, but prepared a written statement also included in the issue. His book, *The Theological Foundation of the Law* has since been translated and is now available in English.

Some months after the writer left Chicago, a joint seminar was conducted by Professor Katz of the Law School of the University of Chicago and Professor Barth of the Divinity School on the concept of righteousness in law and theology.

Since moving to the University of Wisconsin, the writer has worked on a more occasional basis with four or five professors and a number of lawyers and law students in similar kinds of conversations and discussion. He has taken courses in legal process, jurisprudence, and church-state relations. In the latter two, he had opportunity to lead the class in one session on the place of "natural law" in modern Protestant ethics, and in another he led a discussion on a provocative paper by William Stringfellow in the *Ecumenical Review* on "The Coming Conflict Between Law and Theology," dealing with the question of proper relations between church and state.

It became apparent rather quickly that if one was to be in touch with the most vital forces in a university in which the natural and physical sciences play such a predominant role, both in terms of the University's reputation and traditions and in terms of rapid and vast growth in both teaching and research in these disciplines, one had better find ways of being in conversation with both faculty and students working in those fields.

Fortunately, a number of professors in the science fields were involved as members of the State Foundation Board and on the Local Directing Committee of the Center. With the aid of several of these men, together with a small number of graduate students who had expressed interest, a weekly discussion group on Science and Christianity was established which has continued for several years, and has a mailing list of over fifty graduate students and faculty. Many kinds of resource materials have been found fruitful in this group and the practice of a weekly mailing which tries to pick up the main trend of the previous week's discussion and provide provocative excerpts from both theological and scientific literature has given continuity and depth to the group's life.

A special issue of *The Student World* under the theme "Christians in a Technological Era," was used nearly one whole semester, and a good part of another semester was given to discussion of a paper by a Dutch Professor, van der Velde, published by the English SCM entitled "Science, Secularism and the Gospel." Members of the group now frequently share articles from scientific or other journals which have stimulated their thinking, such as one by Yale Professor Henry Margenau in the Yale Alumni publication on "The New Style of the Sciences," or an article in the journal of a Chicago fine arts radio station called *Perspective,* which is the record of an interview with British mathematician Jacob Bronowski entitled "Asking the Impertinent Question." Bronowski's M.I.T. lectures, published in paperback under the title *Science and Human Values,* have also been used in the group.

Physicists, biologists, mathematicians, chemists, medical students, a neurologist, a cancer researcher, and faculty and graduate students from a number of other disciplines have been part of the fluctuating, changing, but always exciting group that share in these conversations.

Related to these ongoing conversations was the invitation to Bishop Hans Lilje of Hannover, Germany, jointly made by the Lutheran Student Foundation and the University Knapp Lectureship, to give three public lectures at the University on "Science and Christianity." In conjunction with Bishop Lilje's visit, a weekend conference, particularly directed to high school and college and university science teachers and parish pastors, was held on the theme "ONE MAN: Man of Science/Man of Faith — A Conversation Between the Insights of Modern Science and Modern Biblical Faith." Sponsorship was shared with the Board of College Education of one of the Lutheran bodies supporting the Foundation and with faculty from Luther College as well as faculty and graduate students from the University of Wisconsin who aided in the planning. The intent was to share more widely with parish pastors and the scientifically-trained members of their parishes some of the resources and insights gained in the Wisconsin discussion experience, as well as that which could be brought together for such an occasion.

More than seventy people shared in the weekend conference. Fifty of them were high school and college science faculty, doctors, and scientists in industry; the remainder were churchmen with varied responsibilities for adult parish education, youth work, lay theological training. Presentations were made by Bishop Lilje and various church-college and university scientists; in addition, an Old Testament scholar spoke on topics like "Quests and Questions of the Scientist," "The Nature of Ultimate Reality," "Man and Creation in Biblical Perspective," "Scientific Methodology and Theological Thinking," and "The Vocation of the Christian in Teaching Science." Preparatory materials including a copy of the book *The Simplicity of Science,* by Entomology Professor Stanley D. Beck of the University of Wisconsin, who was one of the lecturers, were sent out. Later, mimeographed copies of the presentations plus an extensive bibliography prepared by the writer were shared with participants and with many interested individuals and groups who requested them. Stimulated by the fruitfulness of this conference, similar conferences were projected for other locations.

The necessity for the campus ministry, on behalf of the whole church, to continue this kind of attempt to relate the Christian faith to the vitality of the scientific disciplines on our campuses, is suggested by Harry Morton,[16] scholarship secretary for an agency of the World Council of Churches. He indicates that the underlying factor in our age of swift and baffling change is the scientific and technological revolution which is forcing man to see and understand himself in a new relationship to the cosmos. Morton has asked whether God might not be using science to bring to an end

[15] Cited by Herluf Jensen in his paper on the NSCF (see footnote 4).

a world characterized by liberal arts culture ("not because that culture is bad but because it is anachronistic").

A similar viewpoint was expressed some years ago by Prof. Denis Baly in a study book prepared for the United Student Christian Council (predecessor to NSCF) in 1956:

> It is very revealing that there seems to be more joy in Christian circles over one atomic physicist who is outspokenly religious than over ninety and nine ordinary Christians who have no pretensions to scientific learning. Likewise, in the academic world there is often profound surprise over a clergyman who reveals himself as possessing serious scientific knowledge. . . .
>
> The whole scientific revolution which has been proceeding and developing during the modern period is certainly not of the Devil, as the devout fundamentalist believed, nor is it, as most people would probably argue today, merely neutral. Anyone with a sound Biblical foundation must believe it to be of God. . . .
>
> Perhaps the biggest thing the university has to say to the Church is just that the scientific revolution has now taken place and that, therefore, what could have been forgiven in the past cannot be forgiven now.[17]

A similar warning has been made in the book by the British scientist and literary figure, C. P. Snow, *Two Cultures and the Scientific Revolution,* in which he chastises those identified with a literary and humanistic culture to become literate about what has been happening in the burgeoning scientific revolution of our day.

Another perceptive critic who speaks from within the church has argued poignantly both that the scientific revolution is of God and that the church may not now be forgiven if it refuses to take this fact seriously. Dr. Harold K. Schilling, Dean of the Graduate School and Professor of Physics at Pennsylvania State University — and author of the very excellent book, *Science and Religion: An Interpretation of Two Communities* (New York: Charles Scribner's Sons, 1962) — has addressed an eloquent plea to churchmen:

> I am a scientist. Science is my Macedonia. For this occasion I take the role of the Macedonian and assign to you that of Paul and his companion. Your land across the waters is for the most part that of the non-sciences. You have been doing mighty deeds over there, interpreting the Gospel to men of public affairs, of the professions, and of the

[17] Denis Baly, *Chosen Peoples* (Philadelphia: The Christian Education Press, 1956), pp. 48, 59. Used by permission of the United Church Press.

arts. You have addressed yourselves to the problems and anxieties of the common man. You have made distinguished contributions to the knowledge and practices that characterize that land. But, alas, only a few of you have entered our country. Hence my plea that you come over and help us. . .

My plea . . . is first that all of *you* come over and become acquainted with our ways. They are not understood very well, though no doubt this is partly our fault. Second, I plead that many of you become as expert about our land and devote yourselves as assiduously to its problems as others of you have in the realm of politics and statecraft, labor and business, and still others have in the arts.

Some of us belong to both the community of science and the community of Christian faith and have been trying to do what we could to hold science and religion together, to show the relevance of each to the other. It seems sad to us that in general contemporary theologians appear quite uninterested in this. Could it be that this follows from their having divorced history so completely from nature that God seems to act only in history, and that therefore the study of nature seems irrelevant theologically? At any rate we are puzzled by this state of affairs. Moreover many theologians talk as though only that area of human existence is real or significant that is portrayed by the novelists, dramatists and artists, who by and large have not yet discovered science—except in its materialistic aspects. Quite unnoticed seems to be the fact that, for better or for worse, a large and influential sector of mankind finds science to be at the very core of its spiritual life. Can a theology of the nature of man be completely adequate if it disregards that fact, and fails to take into account those attributes of man that are revealed by the existence and remarkable, even though only partial, success of science?[18]

Here again, as in reflection on the conversation with Robert Kent, it appears that if we want to confront seriously those immersed in the natural and physical science disciplines on our campuses, we shall have to touch them at the heart of the excitement which is "at the core of [their] spiritual life." We must expand the range of our own experience to include some measure of what is so urgently their experience, stretching our theological categories to include that wider range.

Other creative forms and patterns, briefly listed

Lack of space forbids any thorough description of other imaginative ways being explored for campus ministry, but we will briefly

[18] Harold K. Schilling, "A Contemporary Macedonia Plea," *Union Seminary Quarterly Review*, January, 1963, pp. 113, 121.

list a few additional ones with which we are personally familiar, a list which could be greatly lengthened by even a cursory visit to any of the large number of college and university campuses across the country.

(1) Joint study conferences at which two or more separate denominational groups seek to learn each other's ways of worship, doctrinal stance, temper, and flavor — as in the Episcopalian-Lutheran Study Conference at Stephens College, Columbia, Mo., in the summer of 1962, or the Hillel/LSAA Retreat on "Law, Love's Discipline," 1963.

(2) Jointly sponsored lecture series — such as that sponsored by the Protestant Centers, YMCA, Hillel Foundation, and St. Paul's Catholic Chapel at the University of Wisconsin, summer, 1963: Dr. Erwin Hiebert, Professor of History of Science, University of Wisconsin, speaking on "Moral Implications of the Use of Nuclear Energy"; The Very Rev. John Egan, Director, Office of Urban Affairs, Catholic Archdiocese of Chicago, speaking on "Race's Challenge to Religious Institutions"; Dr. Paul Holmer, Professor of Theology, Yale University, speaking on "Science, Knowledge, and Faith"; and Dr. Germaine Bree, Professor of French and Humanities, University of Wisconsin, speaking on "Implications of the Artist as Revolutionary for the Roles of Teacher and Student."

(3) Drama or theater groups, sponsored by religious centers, to bring less-well-known but significant plays to the campus — such as the Mime and Man Theatre sponsored by the various religious centers at Madison, producing plays by playwrights like Ionescu, Camus, Strindberg, O'Neill, Ibsen, and Jean Genet, and providing for discussion with the audience afterward, led by campus ministers together with speech, literature, or theater and drama people on the campus.

(4) Sharing the sponsorship of outstanding lectures with the university or one of its departments — such as the bringing of Finnish Christian psychoanalyst Martti Siirala to the University of Wisconsin with help from the Psychiatry Department to lecture in the Medical School, meet with psychiatric interns and Psychiatric Research Institute people, and give a public lecture, as well as meet with a Faith/Psychology discipline study group jointly sponsored by several centers.

Since our primary task in this chapter has been to survey and describe recent trends in denominational campus ministries with an eye toward those creative and experimental ways of ministering to the college mind which are deserving of wider awareness among the general church membership, we will make only brief additional comments of an evaluative and critical nature.

It may be that some readers will be disappointed or chagrined that little evidence has been given in these pages for the continuity of patterns of ministry on the campus with which they were familiar in their own student days and about which they have some nostalgic memories. Some reasons for the necessity of experimentation were given in the opening section. But another dimension of the church's relation to many of the structures of society ought at least to be alluded to, namely that we no longer live in a society in which the church "calls the tune" in very many, if any, of the societal structures with which it indeed must often now struggle to restore vital confrontation and communication. If some of the above ways of ministering in the university seem to involve risks, if they seem to be directed toward moving the ministry of the church, clergy and laity alike, out into less familiar territory and by less churchly-oriented forms and patterns, then perhaps a reminder of the exposed position from which the church ministers in our day is in order. Speaking more particularly of the situation in England, but in tones increasingly relevant for the church's mission in the American academic scene, Sir Walter Moberly writes:

> "Real Christianity," it has been truly said, "has gone almost dead on the modern mind." We Christians in the universities are ourselves profoundly affected by the secularist climate. To demand a consciously Christian university as part of any short-term programme, is vastly to underestimate the magnitude of the change required, not least in ourselves. . . . The national mind is not now Christian in the sense that it once was; and, at best, it cannot again become Christian by any speedy process.[19]

If some of the new patterns and forms of ministry described above seem to bear fruit slowly, and involve much smaller num-

[19] Sir Walter Moberly, *The Crisis in the University* (New York: The Macmillan Company, 1949), p. 102.

bers (though more intense work with these), it may indicate a more faithful and acute understanding on the part of the church of the immensity of the task before it, and of the necessity of a more disciplined and carefully trained and equipped force needed to carry it out — and we might well look to the intense relationship of our Lord to just twelve disciples as our justification for experimentation along these lines.

Secondly, and almost in contrast if not contradiction to what was just said, the creative ways being experimented with are based also on new insights concerning the presence in the university community of resources and attitudes on which the church has too little counted as supportive of its ministry there. Charles McCoy has put his sensitive finger on some of them:

> Let us not assume too easily that professors and students are atheistic because they are skeptical. Christian faith has more to fear from Christianity reduced to a dull habit than from the probing mind of a concerned skeptic. As a perceptive editorial in a recent *Christian Advocate* suggests, we may have more "waiting agnostics" than militant unbelievers. There is a waiting and an emptiness and a hoping in the campus atmosphere today. It is an emptiness in the quest for meaning which plagues faculty and administrators no less than students. In higher education today, with its changes and with its promise, Christians are called to proclaim God's redeeming Word in Jesus Christ. . . . This is the university faculty. . . . Don't charge them off as atheists because they raise questions. If we are sensitive today, we can perceive real issues of theology and faith emerging in every field of study.[20]

Experienced campus ministers on many campuses will testify that as they have learned to listen with more patience, have involved themselves in the lives and vital interests of those who make up the academic community, they have been enabled to become increasingly aware of the sometimes inarticulate anguish among campus inhabitants for that Word which frees and liberates them from self-justifying and status-preserving thinking and acting, and opens to them possibilities for a joy too often missing in their academic vocation. It is only as the result of such loving listening, as suggested to us in the conversation with Robert Kent, that the church's ministry, clerical and lay alike, will be enabled to carry on such a relationship with the academic community that:

[20] McCoy, *op. cit.*, pp. 33, 40.

When the service of the pastor or of the layman reaches out to meet the need of a student or colleague in loneliness, anxiety, or despair, they ally themselves with what is behind and beneath everything and which outlasts all else. To nurture the community which, in the name of Christ, sees human need—the shelving of ultimate questions about life and death, the settling into cynicism of the scientist, the satisfaction with formality of the artist, the degeneration of philosophy into the definition of definition, the forcing of proximate answers into ultimate ones—the congregation, seeing such needs, lives in their midst and can bring the healing of the Gospel to meet them. In such encounter, the Christian community is born and set into motion, living its life and giving its service out of the depths of corporate worship, led in its life by a pastor whose integrity of thought and character and seriousness of purpose are expressions of the Church's concern for higher education."[21]

THE FUTURE

Some things may be said with certainty, even in as rapidly changing a scene as that of the church's ministry in higher education. As indicated above, experiments with various modifications of intentional communities, with their possible rich contribution toward a disciplined and intelligent laity so desparately needed for renewal of the church on every level, will undoubtedly continue. It may be that they will more and more be ecumenically based after initially being denominationally originated, so that they may be more adequately staffed for more theological variety and to make possible the depth of help for needs they so often uncover in the intense experience of selfhood and community they provide.

Small group work directed toward engaging the thought of the church with the thought and life of the various disciplines of the university will also continue and demand both more staff and more adequately trained personnel. Dr. Franklin Littell has suggested the pattern which in all likelihood will emerge here:

> What sense can be made of a seminar of Methodist doctors or Baptist lawyers or Presbyterian engineers? . . . As on the mission field, dividing engineers, school teachers, doctors, government officers, lawyers, chemists according to denomination is to expose the naked sectarianism

[21] "The Mission of the Church in Higher Education," paper prepared by Professor J. Edward Dirks for the meeting of the Synod of New England, United Presbyterian Church, U.S.A., at Northfield, Mass., in June, 1961 and reprinted by UCCF Publications Office. Used by permission of J. Edward Dirks.

of much denominational promotion. It embarrasses the faithful and hardens the heart of the scornful. The problem of relating the Christian message to real problems and real decisions of a specialized nature is new and strange and complex enough without splintering the leadership groupings along denominational lines. . . .

The pattern of religion in higher education on the future American university campus will not be set by a modestly attended chapel service or little marginal clubs of students on the rim of the campus, split up on denominational lines. Rather will the faculties and departments be divided by comity agreements like those in the mission fields, with, for example, the Baptist student pastor ministering to the business school, the Methodist to the school of medicine, the Presbyterian to the department of the humanities, and so on. Each campus religious worker will be part of a team to bring the whole Word to the whole educational community.[22]

It is probably true, especially in the rapidly-expanding state universities with their huge graduate complexes, but perhaps also in the smaller schools where several denominations will cooperate in providing a ministry, that increased attention will be given to the more permanent members of the academic community, *i.e.*, faculty and staff and the long-term graduate student. A suggestion that the campus ministry move in that direction was recently made by Dr. Ernest C. Colwell, President of Southern California School of Theology at Claremont. This ministry, he said, "should be aimed directly at the permanent members of the campus community, the faculty and the staff, and only secondarily at the transients, that is, the students. If the ministry to the university is to be effective, it must win adherence from faculty and staff through whom the major, and the most extensive influences reach the lives of the students." As a specific way of approaching the faculty, Dr. Colwell suggests modification of the "Danforth Associates" program of the Danforth Foundation: "I suggest that the church might pick out *church people* who are also faculty or staff in the university, appoint them officially as ambassadors to students, recognize them financially if possible and certainly in every other significant way." [23]

[22] Franklin H. Littell, *The German Phoenix* (New York, Doubleday & Co., Inc., 1960), pp. 163, 165-166. Copyright © 1960 by Franklin Hamlin Littell. Reprinted by permission of Doubleday & Co., Inc.

[23] "Blazing New Trails in Campus Religious Life," a talk given to the Convocation on Christian Higher Education, Cincinnati, Ohio, Jan. 6, 1962, sponsored by various Methodist educational agencies.

The result of an imaginative denomination selecting twenty thousand such associates, "selected from the faculties and administrative staffs of the colleges and universities of this country would hold up the hands of . . . Foundation directors, of college chaplains, of pastors of the college church, or the church in the nearby community to the achievement of a more effective ministry."

Two final comments, one a warning and one a prophecy, complete our look at the future. The first, by a student who has described several experiments of renewal in the church, including the ecumenical Church of the Savior in Washington, D.C., an experiment in a disciplined, decentralized, and lay-run congregation, warns:

> It is a strong temptation on the part of many to try to transplant the Church of the Saviour, the Christian Faith and Life Community [the Austin Experiment], or some other new form into a situation which is completely foreign to the soil in which the original concept grew. This is always unwise and usually impossible. This does not mean that each situation demands a radically different form of ministry from another, but that the ministry of the church must be tailored to the indigenous factors in the local situation.[24]

That the experiments described above have, in fact, almost always been "tailored to the indigenous factors in the local situation," seems abundantly evident, though it can be said from experience that too often the easy way of unimaginative and dangerous copying of what has proved fruitful elsewhere is taken by inexperienced or insensitive workers.

Finally, that the mood of experimentation and exploration of new forms and the risks accompanying such a mood will be with us for a long time is lucidly indicated by Dr. J. C. Hoekendijk, Professor of Modern Church History at the University of Utrecht, Holland, in an exciting article entitled "On the Way to the World of Tomorrow":[25]

> As we look discerningly around, we can somehow already form an idea of what is to come. About two things we shall quickly come to agree: we shall have to cross cataracts of time, turn another page and live in dis-

[24] "The Student Looks at the Local Church," by Wayne Proudfoot, in Richard N. Bender (ed.), *op. cit.*, p. 64. Used by permission.

[25] In *Laity*, Bulletin No. 11, August, 1961, p. 8. Published by Department of the Laity, World Council of Churches, Geneva, Switzerland.

continuity with the life of yesterday. The great slogans of modern man
—continuity and progress—have been changed by post-modern man into
change ("change will be the only unchangeable") and *renewal*. And
this again implies facing a period of fundamental *uncertainty*. Already
the secure ones are suspected and ruled out as an anachronism, and soon
what we do will become more obviously a risky adventure: simply because we do not have time to get the necessary information in order to
act wisely. What information we finally get will repeatedly prove to be
too little, too late. Therefore the many who give us information about
the world of tomorrow urge us to play down our longing for certainty
and to endure the uncertainty without panic and fear; to accept what
is risky, to live by improvisation, and to experiment.

Hardly a better text could be provided to close this survey of the
ways in which the church is presently carrying on its task in the
academic communities of our land.

WILLIAM B. ROGERS

7: The Role
of a
Christian Faculty Movement

SEVERAL YEARS AGO a student group on a state university campus asked some key faculty people to make up a panel in order to discuss their particular academic tasks in a context of Christian vocation. This program turned out to be something less than a success, theological training, either in the classroom or in the church's campus program, while the panel members — good churchmen all — had to put it mildly. Many of the students had been exposed to some not. While the students had a nodding acquaintance with and concern for the Protestant doctrine of vocation (in fact this is why they planned this program), the faculty members had to fall back on platitudes of advice which amounted to "be good" and "go to church." Some of the students were quick to see their advantage — with bloody results before the evening was over. The effect of this little episode on the senior participants varied. One faculty member came by the Student Center the next day to pick up three books on Christian vocation. With others, the only discernible result was a slight strain in the relationship with the campus minister.

William B. Rogers is the executive secretary of the Faculty Christian Fellowship. His previous experience includes campus ministries at Hampden-Sydney College in Virginia and North Texas State College, and an executive position in the university Christian mission of the National Council of Churches.

139

This incident illustrates a present-day fact of life for Christians in their concern for higher education. *The church is on the outside looking in.* Although there was a time in American history when the Protestant church largely dominated the educational process, especially at the college level, this day has long since passed and will not come again. There is today a pervading, even aggressive, secular outlook, and the fact of contemporary religious pluralism multiplies the problem for persons with a religious concern. The church college, itself tending in the direction of secularization, continues to diminish in its influence on higher education, and simultaneously the state university increases its ascendency, with its access to the tax dollars so necessary for large-scale expansion. At least, this trend poses a series of questions the church must face anew as those strategies which were geared to other generations become increasingly archaic. At most, it implies that the disestablishment is an accomplished fact in higher education and that Christian faith must learn to deal seriously with the secular in a society which will no longer give any special place to elements of its Christian heritage.

The ambiguities of this new situation are apparent in the quite different treatment which different expressions of religion are characteristically given in higher education. On the one hand, the Judeo-Christian tradition, one of the roots of western civilization, is usually ignored in academic studies while its twin, the Graeco-Roman, is given prominence. Here is one obvious result of the secularization of higher education. The university may well have good reasons for keeping religious studies out, divided and contentious as the different traditions seem to be. Curiously, however, the university often makes a token acknowledgment of the *practice* of religion, sometimes providing chapels, allowing "religion weeks" and otherwise identifying in fringe matters with the religious outlook of its constituency. A good example of this is a prestige university, in part state supported, which makes elaborate provision for a three-faith chapel and a religious activities building housing the various denominational and student movement programs, but which has neither curricular provision for religious studies nor an interdisciplinary program indicating the importance of this area to the vocation of the university. What is not generally realized by university administrators is that worship is the most divisive element of Christian practice, while there is a common area of agreement among different religious traditions concerning biblical, historical, and critical studies which could provide the basis for a western religious curriculum, even in a public institution.

The point of departure, then, is what goes on in the classroom — or that which is at the core of the university's vocation. The criterion of permissiveness with regard to religion seems to be its distance from the curriculum. Incidentally, it is precisely at this point that recent Supreme Court decisions have challenged the practice of religion in public education. These decisions have carefully distinguished between the *practice of worship* and *teaching about religion,* the latter apparently creating no particular problems for the church-state issue. At least the judicial process has ferreted this out as a critical issue concerning what is to be permitted in public education. This obvious point has all too often been overlooked by the university: A fundamental root of western civilization has been largely ignored, to the detriment of a liberal curriculum, in reaction to the church-state question and out of fear of religious controversy.

The university, however, is not alone in the attempt to keep religious matters on the periphery. The church itself in recent history has consistently relegated its concerns to the fringe and thus has helped remove itself from the center of the university's life. It has given over the business of education to the state, and it has virtually abdicated from the real vocation of education. For example, the denominational centers ringing the campus have sometimes plucked their students out from their normal student involvements and their natural witnessing arena on the campus to a separate existence unrelated to the university's vocation. On the other hand, however, the transition in student work from the local church to the denominational center within the past generation has at least brought some increase in its relevance to campus life, since the parish structure with its necessary orientation toward the community rather than the university is seldom adequate to face the peculiar challenges of the campus.

Since the university's vocation is study, a vocation which incidentally is being taken more and more seriously on the campus, it would seem that it is at this level that the church should form its primary strategy. But the church has conspicuously neglected the university's vocation in the recent past and in so doing has made itself irrelevant to its primary task. This trend, fortunately, is being reversed in the concentration of energies upon programs which are more integral to the university's existence. Hopefully this will end the recent historical innovation of preoccupation with the fringe of education rather than its heart. However, the task is more difficult now.

The Role of Faculty Christian Fellowship

It is within this context that Faculty Christian Fellowship has found its place and purpose over the last ten years. The professor is obviously a key figure in any consideration of the university's vocation. There is no lack of professors and college administrators who are good churchmen. However, the problem is that a doctoral-level understanding of an academic discipline is often paired with a quite different level of understanding of faith. The resulting ambivalence in the lives of many of these splendid men and women is demonstrated by the practice of sharply segregating their church lives from their academic lives. Too many, unable to relate faith to their specialized fields, become schizoid in the sharp segregation of these elements of conflict. Faith is inevitably the loser. Not only is the professor an ineffectual witness to his professional involvements if his life of faith has not been subjected to the same kind of intellectual discipline as his academic field, but his professional competence fails to inform the church. When his services are used by the church, this use is characteristically in areas far removed from his vocational competence.

A continuing problem in this country is an intellectual obscurantism among many within the church who somehow assume that faith is not compatible with the best disciplines of study and learning. This is irony carried to an extreme since it has been the church which has kept learning alive and has sponsored its increase through the centuries — for instance in medieval Europe and in the first hundred years of our life as a nation. The obscurantist attitude today is exemplified most pointedly by the successful mass media evangelists, the great city crusaders, and radio and television preachers whose names are bywords in society at large as well as within the church. These, unhappily, capture most of the publicity given to

Protestant Christianity in this country and consequently dominate the image of the church in the popular consciousness. But within the university this kind of anti-intellectualism constitutes a real impediment to evangelism. It proclaims a nineteenth-century theology (I would insist that it is not first century) which is still jousting with the windmills of a nineteenth-century version of science and a nineteenth-century intellectual world view. Need I add that today's intellectual community is repelled, has no way of coming to terms with such a version of Christianity, and too often repudiates anything related to it?

Christian faith itself is universal. Undoubtedly there are some who require the formula version which is the hallmark of this enterprising obscurantist group — but not many are to be found in the university. The universality of Christian faith (good news which shall be to all people) requires that the church go all out in proclaiming the gospel in all its fullness, intellectually and esthetically, with its implications for every facet of every life. This approach is particularly critical within the culturally affluent milieu of the university. Christian faith must be related to the intellectual disciplines, confront head-on the pluralism of the university (or the multiversity?), make its claims of discipleship among those of the intellectual life, and reassert itself as being relevant to the vocation of the university. To this end the church would do well to devote a considerable portion of its best resources (especially human) to this task.

This emphasis is subject to its own set of abuses. It becomes easy to intellectualize faith at the expense of living it — for instance, to substitute highly rationalized disputations about its nature for the involvement and commitment which constitutes its real life. One does run into esthetic and intellectual dilettantism in the church's efforts within the university. The Faculty Christian Fellowship has undoubtedly perpetuated its share of this kind of thing. But such abuses are an inevitable reaction to the obscurantist force which threatens Christian faith from within, and they are an inevitable risk of a strong intellectual emphasis.

The blight of ignorance afflicts the church at all levels — reflecting not only the failure of the American general educational system to deal adequately with our religious heritage, but, more important, reflecting also the church's neglect in preparing its own for life within the university. The failure of the church's educational program is most obvious from the campus perspective. Student and professor alike come to their university tasks largely innocent of disciplined training in faith which is relevant to the university vocation. Consequently the ultimate confrontation must take place in higher education. When this does happen, it should be in the main arena of university life, not in some peripheral side show, if the good news is to speak to people and to issues — if it is to sound through the din of the academic marketplace. Consequently the church in the university becomes not only a training group for faith but simultaneously the front line of involvement with the world.

All this adds up to the conclusion that a Christian faculty movement must frankly be directed to a high level of intellectual integrity and scholarship. It cannot in good conscience ignore either the vocation of the university, the church's own intellectual tradition, or such a strategically important segment of the life of the world. This does not mean that the typical faculty member can be approached only through his grey matter. He is not a disembodied intellectual. He is a person, with all the human relationships and involvements of family and community of anyone else. Perhaps the average faculty member may not even be said to be an intellectual, however this slippery term might be defined. Nonetheless, this neglected area of Christian involvement can be ignored only at continued frightful cost to the church and its effectual witness.

The Faculty Christian Fellowship has for ten years attempted to project itself into this breach. The child of concerned faculty Christians and of the Protestant churches related to the National Council of Churches, it has taken on for itself the tremendous task of affirming Christian purposes in ways indigenous to the campus and the university's vocation. Its letterhead describes it as "a community of teachers and scholars seeking to determine the Christian's responsibility in the academic life." This definition would seem to limit its task to inquiry rather than implementation, but a listing of objectives found in its publicity shows the more inclusive aim:

1. To help college and university faculty members increase their understanding of and commitment to the Christian faith
2. To relate the insights of the Christian faith to the vocation of the

teacher and to the subject of his teaching and writing
3. To promote fellowship among Christian faculty members
4. To help discover the teacher's responsibility in the academic community in cooperation with students, administrators, church leaders, and others
5. To explore within a Christian context the responsibility of the academic community for human culture and contemporary society
6. To encourage contact and conversation between all members of the academic community who take the university and their work seriously
7. To act as a liaison and service agency for denominations, foundations, and other agencies working with faculty on behalf of the concerns of religion in higher education

Some time ago at an Executive Committee meeting of FCF, the late Alexander Miller said: "The task of FCF is communication, not organization." This statement at least describes an important function of the national office in providing a clearing house of information and activities of the movement. In the earlier years, as the veterans have often pointed out, it was assumed that there was a core Christian community among faculty — that our primary task was to identify it and call it into visible existence. We are no longer so sanguine, at least as far as identification can be made under some rubric such as Faculty Christian Fellowship. Although many faculty study groups were developed, conferences organized on a local or regional basis, a concerned and informed group of faculty called out (with some becoming identified with the national FCF or a denominational group such as the Episcopal Guild of Scholars) the original expectations for community were never realized. When membership in FCF as a national movement was abolished in 1962, this step was a tacit acknowledgment that we can serve our concerns in other ways than by concentrating upon a visible faculty community with whom we have direct contact and by whom we have a specific identity. This is also a tacit acknowledgment that the name represents a facility rather than a community as such, and consequently may be subject to change. The FCF's responsibility is to function as the only broadly representative ecumenical agency serving in this strategic area.

The fact of the matter is that FCF cannot at present pinpoint a comprehensive philosophy and policy. This is evolving only as it attempts to come to grips with its present task. FCF has always deemphasized structure and organizational involvements (perhaps wisely, when we realize how circumscribed by organization most college staff are). However, simple realism dictates that — with FCF's broad denominational kaleidoscope, extensive geographical coverage, and multiplicity of involvements — it shall not avoid a consistent and comprehensive pattern of relationships requiring organization.

At one recent general committee meeting it was pointed out, almost in despair, that we have no adequate theology for our work, no developed rationale which can give coherent direction to a faculty movement at this time. To this condition John Coleman, a Canadian mathematician, replied in memorable fashion: "Theology follows the life of faith. An ecumenical theology follows the ecumenical community. We cannot wait for it." This is the premise on which Faculty Christian Fellowship is at present operating. Many theoretical and structural questions remain unsolved. But we fully intend to use the resources we presently possess to get on with the life of faith and to function responsibly within the ecumenical community.

THE PROGRAM

This attempt to function responsibly is represented by a number of program elements. The following list is by no means exhaustive, but it represents typical faculty activity which is related to an ecumenical Faculty Christian Fellowship. Present concentration is upon three parallel projects, all bearing upon the relation of faith to the various academic disciplines.

Discipline-research groups

Perhaps the most basic problem still requiring searching examination in the whole "faith — higher education" milieu is that of the relationship of faith to the various academic disciplines. Difficult as it is even to approach the issues raised in such a dialogue, it has been deemed essential to delve seriously into a program of discipline inquiry by FCF. Groups of outstanding scholars have been assembled in various fields to explore this relationship in depth. The difficulties in the group process are reflected in the slow development of this program, but progress is being made in the fields of psychology, sociology, philosophy of education, political science, history, and philosophy, and there is ground for hope that other groups will be added to this list. The outlines of the plan were set forth in 1956. At that time the consensus was reached that the "process of continuous discussion among Christian scholars should determine and make explicit critical and interpretive concepts and methods derived from the Christian faith, which can function creatively in the intellectual disciplines and the reciprocal contributions of the work of the scholar to Christian theology." The process was divided into three parts:

1. The relation of Christianity to the intellectual disciplines
2. The relation of Christianity to the whole body of knowledge
3. The relation of Christianity to the whole life and structure of the university, placing the intellectual aspect of the university's life in its proper relation to this wholeness of life. This involves a recognition of the fact that, while the intellectual enterprise must come first in this process, the conclusion might well be a subordination of the intellectual to some other aspect of the life of learning or a redefinition of the intellect to include more than is presently accepted

Some have challenged this procedure as being unable to do justice to the essential quality of Christianity and that of the discipline. Others have felt that the group process presents too many difficulties and that the FCF purpose can best be served by individual work. Whether done individually or in groups, however, a growing body of literature investigating the disciplines from a Christian perspective has been one result of this ferment. As the discipline groups themselves have developed, participants have testified to the cogency of dialogue and encounter with others centered upon such fundamental issues.

Faith-learning studies

More recently the need has been seen to make the results of discipline efforts more generally known and available for individuals and for campus study groups. The result is a series of short discipline studies prepared in a broad range of areas, which are available from the FCF offices, 475 Riverside Drive, New York, N.Y., 10027.

These study guides contain the following elements, though some variation is to be expected among the different guides:

1. The raising of the critical questions in the relationship of the faith to the particular discipline
2. The suggestion of a point of view in the direction of resolving difficult questions, but with the clear recording of disagreements to the recommended perspective and the noting of other alternative approaches
3. An exposition of some currently available books and articles which either deal directly with the issues or provide some needed background. This is more than a book listing with annotations; it provides a description of material available. Of course, in many cases, there is at present very little available on the specified subject

The national conference

Discipline inquiry was also a major area of the national faculty conference at the University of Chicago Center for Continuing Education, August 23-28, 1964. Its purpose was:

1. To advance the exploration of the relation of faith commitments to the academic disciplines and the vocation of the teacher
2. To contribute to the formation and identification of the Christian community of scholarship and to seek means of improving communication among the members of this community

The conference, planned for about 300 scholars, assumed both theological understanding and competence in some academic field. It was not designed for those whose primary need is for an elementary course in theology. Although there was an open invitation, it was accompanied by a "tough" invitational.

Other activities

While these three items constitute the special preoccupation of the national office at this time, there are many activities which continue to be carried on under the FCF aegis. Of critical importance are these publications:

1. *The Christian Scholar* is a quarterly journal which has as its announced purpose "the exploration of the meaning of Christian faith and thought . . . in relation to the whole range of the intellectual life and to the whole task of higher education." A journal of the Commission on Higher Education of the National Council, it has a history closely parallel to FCF and is perhaps the most vital instrument over the ten-year period in the development of a Christian faculty movement.

2. Also a quarterly, but smaller and addressed to a mass readership of faculty, is *Faculty Forum*. It is prepared by the Methodist Church to serve the whole faculty movement. It is the news-and-features organ of Faculty Christian Fellowship, each issue usually containing an article of some substance, at least one book review, and various items of news and coming events of general interest. About 35,000 copies are distributed each quarter and the influence of this publication is being increasingly felt with is ecumenical use.

There are other periodicals which FCF heartily indorses, such as denominational publications which also have a wide circulation. For several years the FCF office published an *FCF Bulletin,* many issues of which were valuable in setting forth a philosophy of the parent structure. The format is now used for the series of study guides, since such a specific house organ is no longer critically needed in an inclusive movement.

Another important area of effort is the series of state and regional conferences which now cover much of the country. This program, kept going by the devotion of the concerned professors and the support of denominations and other institutions, provides considerable stimulation for a continuing movement.

In a sense all these varied efforts are directed toward the concerned campus group and the individual teachers who make it up. We have no way of knowing the number of these campus groups which meet more or less regularly in sustained study, inquiry, and conversation out of concern for faith in academic context. The present efforts at publication and communication have such groups as their ultimate focus. Usually the groups develop a plan of study or inquiry, though in other cases there are larger gatherings for a meal and an address on a subject of more general interest. In either case all the participants, whether churchmen or not, are representative of Faculty Christian Fellowship.

There is one point of universal agreement in the experience of these campus groups: A Christian faculty movement cannot function denominationally. Neither the temper of the university nor the inclination of participants allows for separatist activity in matters which are of equal concern to Christians of all stripes. Frequently, specific denominations or their representatives will take the lead in sponsoring certain activities, whether locally or on a regional or national scale, but the character of all such activity is of necessity ecumenical. This factor makes particularly significant the relation of Faculty Christian Fellowship to the National Council of Churches, as well as its constant conversation with university teachers in other countries and with elements of the World Council of Churches and the World Student Christian Federation. Its status within the National Council is that of a "related movement" (in contrast to being an actual unit of this ecumenical agency), in order to maintain its integrity as a movement whose initiative comes primarily from within its ranks. However, it cannot eschew its essential nature and identity as an arm of the body of Christ.

In parallel to this ecumenical scope as related to the church, Faculty Christian Fellowship also represents the whole academic spectrum and the whole gamut of human temperament. Hopefully this broad range represents Christian universality at its best, but there is no compromise in the affirmation of its Christian core and purpose. There is always a temptation to identify with a particularist or parochial perspective, both theologically and academically, but the strong tendency has been to shy away from any such closure which would exclude some on the basis of an academic, rational, or temperamental standard. A faculty movement must maintain its inclusive character, representing the church as it does, but always in conversation with an enlightened climate of liberal studies, including the humanities and the sciences.

THE FUTURE

No one is fully satisfied that Faculty Christian Fellowship is adequately fulfilling its unique role — or even that it has found its final task, but one thing is sure. With the continuous changes taking place in higher education and in society generally, it can never be content merely to sustain its policies and programs of the years without searching reexaminations of its purpose. It would be rash at this point to try to indicate where the future will take us. But one obvious question will have to be faced soon if we are to be realistic in our continued involvement within American higher education.

The secularization of all forms of public education in this country (and most forms of private) — for better or for worse — is becoming increasingly obvious. Christian faith, especially in its Protestant form, is becoming more and more "disestablished." One can no longer assume that education will reflect the prevailing attitudes of the formerly dominant political and cultural group. The WASP (White Anglo-Saxon Protestant) culture no longer prevails without challenge. The process of secularization is developing rapidly in this country (a fact already in most areas of European life, of course more obviously in Eastern Europe). In other parts of the world, where one could never assume anything but a very superficial "Christian" establishment, even if indeed that existed, nothing can be assumed today, especially where there is a blanket condemnation of "colonialism" and everything associated with it. In America the process of secularization seems furthest advanced in higher education, perhaps resulting in part from the university's militancy in freeing itself from the former control of the Protestant church. This trend has already led to the condition described earlier of an important segment of Western culture being excised from the curriculum, whether by design or default.

The recent strategy of the church, by now painfully aware of its dislocation from its former position of ascendency, has been to try to arrest this almost overwhelming current. For a number of years some have been preoccupied with "the university question" as a proprietary right resulting from their understanding of the unity of knowledge and their reading of the history of the university. While it has been acknowledged that Christians have neither the resources nor the will to control higher education today except in fragmentary or token ways, a theologically ordered unity of knowledge is pursued as a current pioneering venture. Some, while having no interest in grounds, buildings, and endowments, have worked toward creating a new establishment, an intellectual "city of God," wherein a comprehensive Christian world view could again assert itself in the academic marketplace. This effort is well represented within the discipline groups of Faculty Christian Fellowship. This is an example of the effort to combat and overturn the secular in the name of Christ.

A radical new approach to the phenomenon of the secular, building upon some of the insights of Bonhoeffer, is gaining currency within the church today, particularly in Europe. It would seriously challenge the effort to reestablish the old sacral order in any form, but particularly in terms of principalities and powers, and it would affirm the secular as being within the province of God. Questions which this perspective might raise in American higher education must be among the concerns of a Christian faculty movement. Should we, for instance, continue to try to break through with our message and world view in opposition to typical secular attitudes characteristic of higher education in general and some disciplines in particular? Is it our primary purpose to make the university over in a Christian image? Should we eschew our special privilege and position in the past establishment and accept realistically the secular order in which we more and more will live? Is it our task to concentrate upon a style of Christian life and existence in a society which allows a Christian no special place and recognizes no exalted Christian rationale and wisdom? In the affirmation of Christian faith are we willing even to acknowledge that we may be something less than intellectually respectable according to the pervading secular attitudes?

Here is a developing issue within a Christian university movement among students and faculty. Is a rational Christian world view alone tenable for ordering the universe, or is the secular an order of God's creation with its own tenets, to which we must relate in "a world without religion?" It is easy to predict that this issue will become more and more insistent as we become increasingly aware of the secular currents of the day and live closer to the Christians in those societies where the establishment is only a memory of the past (and not necessarily a good one). The raising of these questions at least has the merit of rocking us back on our own personal establishments as we search out our own motivations for this task.

Whether our particular Christian aim is to remake scholarship from within, or to come to grips with an unalterably secular world of the university which is also a creation of God, a Christian faculty movement finds its identity and purpose as an arm of the body of Christ. There are times when it has asserted its autonomy in identifying with the campus and its vocation, seemingly at the expense of its essential identity with the church, but it can not long be separated from its fundamental nourishment. It would soon wither and die like any other rootless plant. Our relation to the church gives us our particular purpose in affirming a strategic lay role for faculty and in projecting the inclusive character of a faculty movement.

The church needs this arm, particularly if it has a concern for its own renewal. Here are the intellectual capacity and the academic perspective, both to provide the critique and to help restructure the church in the new secular society. But, for the present at least, a vital Christian faculty movement has its primary responsibility within the complexities of higher education, to be the church in all its integrity within this most strategic segment of American society.

A. STANLEY MacNAIR

8: Preaching
to the Academic Community

THROUGH THE FREQUENT AND SOBER ANALYSIS to which the life of the
church today is subjected runs a recurrent theme: that the church
has "lost provinces" in which Christian influence once was strong
but now is negligible. Christian teaching and witness, critics declare,
have little effect upon such important aspects of the common life
as the plastic and performing arts, politics, labor and management
organizations, psychiatry, or literature. To put the matter in another way, the church appears not to have much to say to many
prevailing centers of influence which formulate the policies under
which we live, establish the trends of modern history, and provide
the raw material out of which we fashion and criticize the patterns
of our lives.

Upon the campus, concentrated as in no other type of community, representatives of and apologists for such power centers
constellate. There may be found the theorists, the analysts, the
critics, and the devotees of the way of life we designate "American"
— of the culture we call mid-twentieth century, of the religious scene
described as post-Christian, of the space-age technology, the abundance economy, and the welfare sociology.

For 13 years A. Stanley MacNair was pastor of the University Baptist Church
in Seattle. He is currently the professor of guided field work at Central
Baptist Theological Seminary.

155

The church does not speak compellingly to the academic community. That much is certain. The prevailing temper of the campus takes little account of the persistent strength of the Christian faith. A tendency rather exists to discount and to deprecate religion in terms of its least meaningful and authentic expressions, a tendency best described in George Hedley's word, as "superstitious."[1] He lists nine notions currently held by many of the "intelligentsia and the enlightened": (1) that the content and emphasis of religious thought and teaching undergo no change; (2) that we can understand our cultural heritage without knowledge of our religious traditions; (3) that religion is necessarily at odds with fact and reason; (4) that religion is not a valid field of scholarship; (5) that people who use symbols have to take them literally; (6) that religion is an escape mechanism; (7) that religious people are socially unconscious; (8) that ideals are impractical; and (9) that values can be achieved and maintained in isolation.

Hedley asserts these notions to be superstitious because they are unexamined premises. Modern intellectual unbelievers, he says, "have chosen to fear and to avoid without ever having used their abundant opportunity to learn and to know. . . ."[2] Such a mood may be superstitious to the core, but it is prevalent. Can the church speak to the campus? If it can, since these are the charges commonly laid against the church by the campus, they must be taken into account. The witness must be designed to speak directly to the condition, the needs, and the biases of "Academia." That is, the church leadership must know the world in which it lives, must know the gospel through and through, and *must make linkage between the two.* "Church leadership" means the pastor, and "linkage" may best and most consistently be achieved through the ministry of preaching.

How shall he preach to Academia? How may he shape and point the message? First the congregation must be defined.

The preacher to the academic community occupies one of two basic positions. Either his entire constituency and spiritual responsibility resides within and partakes of the life of an institution of higher learning, or his parish embraces both the learned community

[1] George Hedley, *The Superstitions of the Irreligious* (New York: The Macmillan Co., 1952).

[2] *Ibid.*, p. 137.

and a nonacademic or "town" constituency. Pastors of collegiate churches, chaplains, and preachers to the college or university do not face some of the perplexing and provoking dichotomies faced by the parish minister. They can apply the principles and practices set forth below, without dilution.

Most ministers, however, serve an academic community as one segment of a wider responsibility. If the church is located in a town, the town is also the site of a college, whose members are part of the total town life, including its religious manifestations. If the church is located in a city, it lies in the neighborhood of a college or university campus. Members of the academic community in this instance relate to the entire urban or metropolitan complex, while maintaining a substantial number of primary relationships within the college district — which is probably the locale of the church.

In either instance the presence of the institution of learning constitutes a significant part of the responsibility of the church and provides a segment of the congregation having an importance far out of proportion to its numbers.

That the minister serves a community wider than, but including, the "gown" creates some conditions and poses some problems peculiar to his ministry. He may feel torn between competing interests, antithetical viewpoints, irreconcilable philosophies. Even more, he may see himself as a man who talks alternately to two groups, neither one of which hears, or wants to hear, what he says to the other.

He who would address a congregation composed partly of professors, administrators, and students of a college may drive four pegs of principle into the wall, and upon them "hang" his preaching ministry. They are absurdly easy to say: (1) His call was to preach and not to lecture. (2) To preach is to proclaim the gospel. (3) He preaches to a specific congregation. (4) Preaching addresses the whole of that congregation. Those who come to worship expect to hear the Word of God interpreted in terms each one can hear, assimilate, and heed. Let us inspect these propositions.

1. The minister's call is to preach and not to lecture. He is a herald of the gospel, a proclaimer of the Word, and not a professor of religion. The pulpit is not the classroom. The temptation to win the approval of the academic portion of the congregation by adopt-

ing the tone and method of the classroom is dangerous. Even should the victory be won, it would be a Pyrrhic victory.

This is not to say that preaching is lacking in educative elements nor that its practice precludes learning, for both are part of the fabric of homiletical work. It *is* to say that, when pulpit discourse partakes of the nature and method of the lecture platform, it loses effectiveness. By lecturing, the minister ceases to be a herald. More than an advocate he begins to sound like an analyst, cool and objective. While the analysis of a problem or of a segment of life experience may be an essential element of preaching, to make it the substance of a sermon is to emasculate the proclamatory role of the preacher. The gospel is more than a set of propositions to be presented systematically and explained or defended. The gospel expresses a relationship between a man and his God. It declares an indispensable social relation between man and man because of God's prior relationship to each of them. Since God is a partner to both relationships, analysis breaks down, for the Eternal is not subject to our analytical categories. The element of mystery and the note of faith are present in preaching as they are not in lecturing.

While the lecture seeks to present some aspect or facet of human knowledge in organized and assimilable form, the sermon attempts the presentation of truth in such guise as to bring men through an act of will to the point where decision must be made.

The professor lectures to a slender segment of the community, the young, with academic background, who have been screened by entrance requirements and prerequisite courses, and who are committed to study or to flunk.

The preacher, on the other hand, meets the community in cross section, more or less. For the most part they come voluntarily (although some young people and an occasional adult may have suffered duress). Attendance at worship has not been subject to an admissions committee or an academic counselor, nor have they enrolled for a specific course. No member of a congregation expects to be given a compulsory assignment. Freely have they come, freely must he give. The expectation to hear the gospel preached moves a congregation to assemble.

The academic elements within a congregation share in this general expectation. It is not to hear a lecture but to worship God and to be illuminated by his word that they, too, have come.

2. The preacher's job is to proclaim the gospel, a task which presents him with several responsibilities. First, the biblical illiteracy of our time is great and growing. In one test after another students and others answer the simplest questions of fact and identification wrongly, and interpretative questions wake no flicker of knowledge from them. That many of the students have been exposed to the teaching of Sunday church schools and the worship of the church makes no decisive difference. To the vast majority of people the Bible is a closed book, an unheard witness, not ill described as "the best seller which nobody reads."

When he employs the Bible in preaching, therefore, it is the obligation of the preacher to give sufficient explanation so that what the biblical word is will be understood, and its connection with the lives of his people will be grasped.

Besides biblical ignorance the preacher must reckon with theological ignorance. A firm grasp of the principal ways in which the faith is verbally expressed ought to be the heritage of every disciple, but is, in fact, a rarity. What content is poured into such terms as God, Christ, Man, Sin, Redemption, Hope, so commonly spoken? How is the present usage of these terms related to the content given to them by past generations? The man in the pew most likely doesn't know. He couldn't care less, it may appear. Yet proclamation of the gospel is related to the theological forms and interpretations in which it has been, and is now being, cast.

In some way the preacher must attempt to liquidate this illiteracy, to inform the ignorance of Bible and of doctrine. In a sense this phase of preaching is preliminary to proclamation, but, unless it be done constantly, proclamation will fall upon dulled ears.

The gospel may be a stumbling block "to Jews and folly to Gentiles." To modern ears accustomed to hearing about adjustment and conformity, God's truth may sound like an affront to common sense, an offense against man. To be called sinner, to be reminded of deep-lurking evil, to be confronted with one's self as he is — these things please us moderns no more than they have pleased men of other times. Jesus was put to death for the offense of confronting men with themselves in the light of God's nature and demands.

That we "needs must love the highest when we see it" proves to be a poetic fancy without a corresponding prosaic fact. The preacher is called to proclaim prophetically and winsomely at the same time. The gospel — spoken boldly forth against the crusted custom, the familiar evils, and the close-held sin — forces the hearer to consider anew the work of God. Prophetic preaching roots in description, the description of things as they are, but seen *sub specie aeternitatis*.

Thus he who would preach must concern himself with content, and with prophetic proclamation, but these do not exhaust his task. Preaching has comfort as one of its aims.

In preaching comfortably, the minister acts as priest and pastor, bringing to bear resources of strength and reassurance, of understanding and acceptance, upon the needs and struggles and resignations and tragedies of those to whom he speaks. Those who occupy the pews bring with them a freight of the world's dark side. Worry, illness, grief, pain, guilt, resentment are upon their backs. To put both the burden and the burdened upon the shoulder of God is one dimension of the preacher's work.

3. The minister preaches to a specific congregation. His words are not addressed to people in general nor do they fall in a vacuum. There before him sits a peculiar people, the congregation to which God has mysteriously related him. Even beyond peculiarity, this people is unique.

What he does say must be addressed to the sheep of his own field, not to those over the fence or over the mountain or over the sea. These who sit before him, it is their sins which must be exposed, their heartbreaks assuaged, their flagging hopes revived, their crusted eyes opened, their anxieties probed and made bearable, their lives made new through God's powerful Son and Spirit.

To address himself to matters which do not touch *this* congregation is, for the preacher, an act of irresponsibility. A congregation is as stubbornly unique in nature as are the individuals who comprise it. Sermons delivered "in general" may convey a theoretical meaning, but do not touch down where men live. To the particular quality which makes a congregation itself and not some other, a man must set himself to speak.

4. The minister preaches to the whole congregation. No more

exacting demand can be imagined than to speak to the diverse spiritual states of some scores or hundreds of persons. Here are to be found children and their grandparents. The wise and the foolish have come. Those easily moved sit alongside others of tougher fiber. The insightful one and the obtuse share the same pew. Success consorts with failure, and gullible and skeptical men share the same hymnal. "Town" and "gown" mix and mingle, while student, professor, and dean are counted in the midst.

Must he preach to them all? He must try! Thereby arises many a man's nagging sense of insufficiency. Ever comes the tempter: Against so wide a cross section of community life even the widest pattern of "shotgun" preaching will leave whole sections untouched. Hence, says the tempter, it is wisdom's part to focus upon a particular group, perhaps the largest one, or the most responsive, or that which wields the greatest influence, and let the rest get what they can. A minister may gain a reputation as a scholarly preacher, or a nature lover, or a teller of tales, while hungry sheep look up and are not fed. Thus, when the congregation contains an academic segment, the preaching may serve more to meet the needs of that segment than others, or, quite as likely, may overlook the needs of the campus in addressing the probably more numerous non-academic elements. Either way the principle of preaching to the whole congregation is breached.

The foregoing paragraphs have stated an obvious truth, that preaching is directed to the whole of a particular, unique congregation, and that it means to proclaim the gospel in its content, challenge, and comfort. Another line of argument has been that, only rarely, does a congregation represent the academic community wholly or in major part.

What may be said of the preacher's approach to that section of the congregation that may fairly be described as academic? Or, to put the matter in another way, is there a difference in the way he preaches to such a congregation rather than to another; and, if there be, what is the difference?

Within the academic community the life of the mind is more marked and more characteristic than in society as a whole. The theories and interpretations of knowledge, critical analysis, and attempted syntheses are "in the air." Professors and students use a scholarly "jargon" as a *lingua franca*. The intellectual issues of the time are presented, criticized, and compared. The main currents of modern thought run strongly through the community.

That these qualities are present has implications for preaching. No one dare stand in the pulpit without an awareness and some understanding of the questions that are being asked on campus and the answers that are being suggested. These constitute the real issues of life for a significant fraction of the church, and responsible preaching must deal with them — deal with them in the context in which they are raised.

It is plainly no duty of the preacher to give the answers which scholarship gives. Nor is it allowable to him to decry the questions. His responsibility is to see what the questions ask about man in his relationships and to declare what answers the gospel has to give to them at this juncture in human history. Further, the declaration needs to be couched in the terms set for it by the terms in which the questions are posed. When the Christian answer is verbalized, it must make contact in communicative fashion with those who put the questions.

"There is one Lord, one faith, one baptism," not many. We do not proclaim one gospel for the learned and another for the unlearned, one way to Christ for the Ph.D. and another for the day laborer, one Christian life for the professor and another for the plumber, one ethic for the student and another for the salesman. There is one faith which people of many backgrounds and stations and skills can express, each in the way most appropriate to himself and in terms which are meaningful to him.

First, therefore, preaching to an academic community calls for breadth of understanding and awareness of the principal thought-forms of the age and the characteristic ways in which these are expressed. Prevailing systems of thought can be met and mastered only upon their own grounds. Purely defensive campaigns are not worthy of the Christ whose word to his disciples is "I have overcome the world." Offensive action, the carrying of the fight to the opponent upon his own field, beating him at his own game, has been the way of the church at its most responsible. The church's charter demands that it be in the world but not of the world. The preacher to the academic community needs to know the categories and modes in which men of intellect think, as a necessary precondition to a proclamation of the gospel of salvation which such men will understand and respect.

Our age, like all others, has its distinguishing thought patterns, its main streams of inquiry, its reservoirs of presuppositions. The preeminence of science has led in this century to the triumph of empiricism. The scientific habit of observation, description, collation, hypothecation and verification in repetitive cycles has become a norm for thought, often indeed the only norm and the sole test of validity.

Two world wars and a wasting depression between them have sorely shaken man's belief in the good, the true, and the beautiful. Our time in history has been dubbed the age of anxiety. Fear, guilt, despair — all experienced in immediacy and depth — have produced a pessimism expressed in a wide series of forms ranging from nobility to nastiness. The angry young men of Britain; the unkempt beatniks of our metropolises, the dramas of Becket and Tennessee Williams; the symbolic fiction of Kafka, the atonal music of Schoenberg; the broken and distorted art forms of Picasso; the somber and uncompromising hopelessness of the philosophies of Sartre and Camus all exemplify the trend.

In American society anti-intellectualism has a long history and a not insignificant strength. In modern dress, supported by an expedient alliance of hyper-fundamentalist religion and hyper-reactionary political and economic forces, anti-intellectualism has emerged to march under the self-styled banner of "militant anti-communism," tainting with Red all who disagree with its formulations of American life, American history, and American policy.

Each of these patterns confronts the preacher with an urgency: What does your faith say to *this?* How can you meet the challenge that only empirically verifiable truth can claim to be truth, the challenge that the world, experienced existentially and faced realistically, calls for a brave, unhopeful despair, the challenge that the tempered and balanced tradition of scholarship makes one "soft on communism."

Each of the patterns also issues in practical dilemmas which the preacher ought to seek to resolve. What relevancy has the Bible or the "spirit of Jesus" which can be tested empirically? How can the

Christian hope break through the crust of despair? What can be the basis of a powerful confrontation of communism by Christians and the church?

Accuracy is a second demand upon the preacher to an academic community. To be sure, homiletical craftsmanship calls for accuracy in every sermon, but the issue is more closely drawn when in the congregation are specialists in a dozen fields of thought and students in as many more. Nothing so closes the mind of a hearer as to hear ignorant, half-informed or misinterpreted content delivered portentously as the word of the Lord. "Before you describe grape-growing and draw spiritual comparisons again, come out to the vineyard and see how it is done," commented a sage deacon to the writer. The parallel is appropriate.

Third, deal with the real issues. The various philosophies of the day are materialistic, nihilistic, pessimistic to the core. The atheist existentialist and his brother the "beat" poet speak a profound and disturbing challenge not to be met by demolishing a straw man constructed especially for the occasion; nor will Camus be refuted by lambasting Thomas Hardy.

To learn what the real issues are is simple compared to the intellectual effort required to understand them and to elucidate them in terms of the Christian gospel. Knowledge is said to proliferate at a gallop nowadays, approximately doubling within each decade. Perhaps the rate of growth is even more rapid within some scientific disciplines.

Obviously the preacher cannot become an expert even upon a small scale, let alone upon a grand scale. He can, however, acquaint himself with the main lines of inquiry upon which decisive work is proceeding. This indeed he must do, lest a major new discovery radically reshape a whole field of learning and thrust upon the church the urgent task of assimilation and reinterpretation of new knowledge within ancient truth.

A good *vade mecum* for such a journey of acquaintance is *An Outline of Man's Knowledge of the Modern World*. According to Lyman Bryson, its editor, this volume written by thirty-three contributing specialists has as its purpose "to guide the reader toward a useful understanding of the scope of a particular subject, the kind of thinking that is current among the leaders in the field, and the significance which the subject has in the world in which we live." [3]

Fortunately for the preacher the mass of fact in any area or subject is considerably less significant than the basic concepts about which they are arranged. The grasp of concepts lends ordered understanding of the real issues facing our generation, and the preacher to the academic community may come to his pulpit more assured.

Learning conceptually about our mid-twentieth-century world enables the minister to bridge the gap between the academic and nonacademic sections of the congregation. The layman easily is bewildered by the jargon of the school. Intradiscipline verbal shorthand, so valuable for precise discourse among peers, leaves the outsider thoroughly outside. Even within the academic community itself, physicists, psychologists and paleontologists find the technical vocabulary of the others opaque. If this be so, the plight of the "ordinary" layman may be imagined; yet to be effective in Christian witness he must be in touch with the principal currents of thought about our world. The minister may become guide and interpreter if he himself keeps in touch.

Regard for the whole thorny, many-sided truth is a fourth principle of prime concern when preaching to an academic congregation. Beware the too-easy generalization. Avoid an interpretation based on too narrow a segment of the evidence. Admit the areas of ignorance and plainly label opinion by its name. Preacher or no, no man is infallible, and we hold the word of God in earthen vessels. Student and scholar alike will listen with gratitude to one who reserves his dogmatism to the areas where certainty prevails and who sets forth his own views modestly.

Fifth, a seeking attitude commends itself to the academic community. "Not that I have already obtained" falls on more receptive ears than "I am Sir Oracle, and when I ope my lips let no dog bark!" At the college, men and women spend their lives opening doors into new understandings of the world. Often the contribution of a life of scholarship seems insignificant. Of Ernest DeWitt Burton

[3] Lyman Bryson, ed., *An Outline of Man's Knowledge of the Modern World* (New York, Toronto, London: McGraw Hill, 1960), p. 3.

it is reported that his study of the Epistle to the Galatians resulted after twenty years in conclusions which he stated on a single page. The work, however, has never had to be redone. That the preacher shows evidence of growing-ness and search is an aid to his effectiveness.

A sixth principle needs to be added: Sound a declarative, positive note. The preacher can speak with competence and authority about the Christian faith in God who has made us, has redeemed us through his son Jesus Christ our Lord through whom we belong to his body the church, and in whom we have entrance into his kingdom of eternal love. So let him speak. Open-mindedness, sympathetic understanding of other positions, and modesty cannot be excuses for approaching Christian realities tentatively. Preaching is proclamation, and proclamation demands boldness. Of a book published a generation ago a reviewer scathingly said "It is a clarion call to nothing in particular." The preacher has particulars to describe, Christian particulars which enshrine the ultimates of God's love and purpose *vis a vis* humankind. To speak boldly of these, with winsome clarity and spiritual authority, is the minister's foremost responsibility in preaching to an academic community as to any other.

Perhaps a word of warning ought to be set down here. Preaching which takes the above principles seriously emerges only from preparation of the most painstaking and careful sort. A flying visit to the study to scan a few pages, to search a concordance, and to scrawl a few notes between meetings will produce no word from the Lord to a congregation tinged with Academia — or to any other. To read, to ponder, to compare, to pray, to wait, to write, to revise, to master, these are the avenues which converge upon a theme with power. Preaching wrought thus carries its own dynamic to delimit, to illuminate, to explain what a Christian fact means in the complexities of life where a modern college or university sits. Preaching thus proclaimed declares Christ to be as central, normative and decisive to the men who inhabit that institution as to men of any other condition or community.

"Complete education must provide at least three sorts of equipment for life," says Robert L. Calhoun, "specialized skills, specialized knowledge of many sorts, and a perspective or unifying frame through which the details become a systematic whole." [4]

This third major factor must present two sides: an inclusive theoretic outlook or point of view from which the world and oneself can be understood after a fashion, and a no less inclusive practical dynamic or loyalty by which all that one is, thinks, and does may be vitalized and directed.

A principal task of the preacher to an academic community is to address himself to perspective-making. Upon the one hand he is challenged thus to preach because all too often the provision of this third sort of equipment for life is neglected by the learned community itself. It was Walter Moberly whose use of the term "multiversity" shocked the academic world into the pained admission that it had largely failed to provide integration and synthesis of knowledge. "A university," remarked a whimsical dean, "consists of many departments connected by plumbing." A quarter century has passed since Moberly's challenge, and the many programs and experiments in integration demonstrate the seriousness with which academicians viewed it. Yet, for great numbers of students, college work consists of discrete courses and disciplines through which runs no thread of continuity.

Perspective-making would remain a task of the preacher even were the college fully able to provide synthesis of knowledge. Christian faith makes the staggering claim that truth is one and that the fully apprehended truth of God in Christ enables one to make sense of the complicated world. "In him all things hold together" is the way St. Paul puts it (Colossians 1:17).

The failure is partly to be explained by the enormous proliferation of knowledge, partly by the attendant (and necessary) specialization, partly by other factors like the rapid growth of student bodies and the now-waning "cult of objectivity" with its professed abhorrence of presupposition and commitment.

A rigorous demand is laid upon the man who would preach to Academia. Its members who sit under his ministry require a wholeness of world view unlikely to be sufficiently emphasized upon the

[4] Robert L. Calhoun, *The Place of Religion in Higher Education.* The Hazen Pamphlets, Number Two (Haddam, Conn.: The Edward W. Hazen Foundation, Inc.), p. 5. Also published in *Religion and the Modern World* (Philadelphia: University of Pennsylvania Press).

campus. They need a principle of integration to hold together their bits and pieces of learning. To energize their being and thinking and doing, the dynamic of commitment is wanted. Through the presentation of the gospel a wholeness of view is proclaimed which imparts to life a cohesive principle and demands a consonant response of committed action.

9: Foreign Students
and the American Campus

THE MOVEMENT OF STUDENTS from one part of the world to another had its origin in earlier centuries. The Greeks had foreign students in the famous schools of philosophy, and in the Middle Ages wandering scholars came from all parts of Europe to study at the great universities.

Writing on the theme of cross-cultural education, Dr. Yasumasa Kureda writes:

> What distinguishes today's scholars abroad from those of the past is that they are living in a time symbolized by de-colonization, independence, nuclear weapons, and global integration. We are in a world in which we must live with people of divergent cultures. The Nepalese student who has never seen traffic lights is in classes with students who are dreaming of becoming astronauts.[1]

According to a historical sketch by Dr. Benjamin Schmoker, the general secretary of the Committee on Friendly Relations Among

[1] National Association of Foreign Student Advisers, *Newsletter,* April 15, 1963.

Margaret Flory is the secretary for student world relations of the commission on ecumenical mission and relations of the United Presbyterian Church in the U.S.A. As such, she is responsible for stimulating student work abroad, the ministry to overseas students in the U.S., and such ventures as ecumenical work camps, overseas study seminars, and the junior year abroad and frontier internship programs.

Foreign Students, the first foreign student in the United States was Francisco de Miranda, who in 1784 came from Latin America to enroll at Yale.[2] He arrived fifteen years before the University of Göttingen in Germany conferred the first degree on an American student. In 1859 Dr. Yung Wing received his degree from Yale and returned to China. An American sailing ship brought Joseph Hardy Neesima from Japan to the Phillips at Andover Academy in 1865; after continuing his education at Amherst and Andover Theological Seminary, he returned to Japan in 1874 and became the founder of the famed Doshisha University. In 1904 there were 2,693 students from 74 lands in American colleges, universities, and technical schools, and by 1911 the number had grown to 4,856.

Dr. John R. Mott by this time had become aware through his world travels of the immigration of students for academic purposes. Inspired by the challenge of influencing right international and interracial relations through student exchange, he took the leadership in bringing into being the Committee on Friendly Relations Among Foreign Students which was "to serve all students irrespective of race, nationality or religions." This committee, which had its 50th anniversary celebration in 1961, has provided port-of-entry services, fostered development of community programs, sponsored VISIT and the International Camp Counselor Program, and carried on services in counseling, provision of information, and publications.

At the time of its inception the committee was the sole professional organization serving foreign students, but the passage of the years brought hosts of other efforts. In 1919 the Institute of International Education was founded. The first International House was constructed in New York City in 1921, followed by similar ventures in other cities. The Experiment in International Living, dedicated to the provision of homestays, came into being in 1932. In 1938 a Division of Cultural Relations was established in the U.S. Department of State. In 1941, inspired by Dr. John A. Mackay, the Board of Foreign Missions of the Presbyterian Church launched a program of grants to overseas churchmen. The Smith-Mundt Act was passed by Congress in 1948, providing for a cooperative

[2] *Manual for Student Christian Workers on the Christian Ministry Among International Students*, 1957. Published by United States Christian Council.

exchange program between the United States and other countries. Another important development in 1948 came with the formation of the National Association of Foreign Student Advisors. There are now more than 1,700 foreign student advisors officially named by educational institutions, and each year NAFSA sponsors an annual conference, a series of regional workshops, and a publication program. We have mentioned only a few of the many organizations and programs serving foreign students; the situation cries out for coordination and for a new dimension of depth.

When the Fulbright Act was passed in 1946, there were 15,000 foreign students in the United States. In 1955, when the Institute of International Education published its first issue of *Open Doors,* there were 40,000 foreign students, faculty members, and physicians in American colleges, universities, and hospitals. The 1964 issue of *Open Doors* reports that the 75,000 foreign students counted in the Institute's census represent a 16 per cent increase over the previous year. Both figures, the number of foreign students and the rate of increase, are the highest on record. Every September these statistics are transformed into the living reality of people, as practically every university town in the U.S.A. welcomes its share of Iranians and Indians, Brazilians and Nigerians to its campus and its homes.

In the early days of the foreign student migration toward the United States, the majority of students came from Canada and Europe. Now less than one quarter come from these areas. The rest come from the developing areas of Asia, Africa, and Latin America, where opportunities in higher education are limited and where a whole generation needs to be trained in lightning speed to provide leadership in all walks of life for the new nations. In 1963, students were sent by 152 countries to the U.S.A., where they were enrolled in 1,805 educational institutions. The largest number came from the Far East. Seventeen countries had one thousand or more students in the U.S.A., with Canada (7,004) leading the list and India (6,512) following as a close second. Fifty-one per cent of all the foreign students reported in the census were enrolled as undergraduates. Among far eastern students, there were considerably more at the undergraduate level. As in previous years, engineering continued to be the most popular field of study (22%) followed

by the humanities (19%) and the natural and physical sciences
(17%). Also as in previous years, one fourth of all foreign students were located in California and New York. Forty per cent of
the students were concentrated in no more than thirty-two institutions.

But it is impossible to think of foreign students in terms of statistics, for each one is a person with a past, a present, and a future —
a person whose experience in the United States will be affected by
many factors, such as age, academic ability, marital condition, skin
color, nationality, religious conviction, political status, relationship
of his country to the U.S.A., facility in English, financial backing,
and whether or not he is a sponsored student on scholarship. As
Ulrich Mauser states: "The foreign student does not exist as a
category; his presence on the campus defies all generalizing tags." [3]

"What's in a name?"— a question as old as Shakespeare — is pertinent as we think of the student who travels to another part of the
world for a part of his education. "Foreign student" has been the
title used officially by governments and educational institutions.
In Christian circles there has been a good bit of disquiet with this
term. "Overseas student," "student from abroad," and "international student" are all attempts to find a more adequate expression,
and yet the term "foreign student" persists in spite of dissatisfaction
with it. This writer uses all of these terms freely, and any of them
may be encountered by the reader in continuing to read the content
of this chapter.

Students coming to the United States from practically every country and political area of the world have faced the usual problems
of cross-cultural adjustment. Delia and Ferdinand Kuhn vividly
describe some of these in an article which appeared in the August
21, 1960, issue of the *New York Times Magazine*.

> A large chunk of the troubles that beset foreign students in their per-
> sonal and academic lives can be traced to their ignorance of English.
> . . . the English taught in Tokyo, Manila or Calcutta may sound like
> Greek in New York or Ann Arbor. . . .

[3] Ulrich Mauser, "A Theological Perspective on the Ministry of the Church to
Foreign Students." The Committee on Christian Work Among International
Students, National Student Christian Federation, New York, May, 1961.

A second set of troubles grows out of the mystery of the American system of higher education. It differs from other systems, and most foreigners are ill-prepared for it. Bit by bit they discover what is expected of them: classroom recitation, regular homework, surprise quizzes and mid-term examinations.

The informal American pupil-professor relationship startles them. . . .

The stranger on the American campus stumbles into a whole thicket of troubles for a third reason: He is . . . often too young to be on his own. The normal frustrations of youth loom larger when one is alone and far from home. . . .

But at any age the newcomer faces problems of food, clothing, shelter and communication with those around him. A student from the tropics, for example, feels the shock of cold for the first time. Many are overcome by the first effect of American food. All have to learn the value of dollars. . . .

Finding a place to live can be embarrassing . . . too many landladies have a way of saying 'full up' when an Asian or African presents himself at their doors. . . . On the campus, everyone says 'Hi!' to the foreigner with a warmth such as he rarely meets in his own country. Yet, when it comes to real friendship, the American student seems preoccupied with his own affairs.[4]

Longing for contact on a deep level, foreign students are disappointed when fellow-students share only the "epidermic" part of their lives. The easy cordiality which at first seems so appealing does not often lead to deep interest.

An Indian student, Sam Gupta by name, has expressed this feeling of loneliness and isolation in a poem entitled "An Overseas Student":

> I am lonely.
> I am lonely in this kindly crowd.
> There is no warmth in this bazaar
> Of official courtesies.
>
> There are no demands, there are no reproaches,
> There are no belongings, there are no loyalties —
> Like a piece in a museum
> Or in an antique shop.

[4] Delia and Ferdinand Kuhn, "Why Foreign Students Become Cases," *New York Times Magazine*, August 21, 1960, pp. 114-115, © 1960 by the New York Times Company.

      (— Junk with a price tag on —)
      The gay tourists move around
      To cover "this too": in time
      Those hackneyed curiosities,
      "Where do you come from —?"
      "What do you do —?"
      To add another name to their list of international
          "friends." [5]

As suggested in these lines, both bewilderment and resentment frequently grow out of the difficulties found in the sphere of social etiquette or relationships with the opposite sex. Almost all foreign students have expressed the humiliation of serving as program showpieces or being given (in the phraseology of African students) the "zoo treatment." The lack of knowledge of the history, geography, and culture patterns of their countries is shocking and disconcerting to them. One Egyptian girl, when she arrived, said that the other students had expected her to be riding on a camel and wearing a veil.

Financial problems are also a major source of worry and strain. Money doesn't go very far in the U.S.A. If he has to work, the foreign student may find manual labor distasteful, since he isn't used to it. Living in an affluent society often takes its toll, resulting in the temptation to live beyond one's means by incurring debt or expecting expensive gifts from generous Americans. The tendency to be tempted by continuing educational opportunities and to want to stay on for one more degree and yet another is very widespread. This often leads to the extension of the study period when there are no financial resources, thus precipitating a crisis for the students and their American associates.

There is overwhelming evidence that the racial situation in the United States has been a stumbling block in international understanding. Many students with dark skin have been exposed to severe prejudice in attempting to secure food and lodging; others constantly fear that they may face embarrassment. In an article in the December 1, 1961, issue of *Presbyterian Life,* the Reverend James Bryden, a university pastor at Howard University, cites the experiences of a West African woman student.

[5] Used by permission of Sam Gupta.

She had been invited by white friends from Pennsylvania to drive to colonial Williamsburg. She went. There they wandered along charming colonial streets and into quaint shops. They witnessed "The Common Glory," a pageant which brought to life the heartbreaking struggle of the American Revolution. They heard stirring music and memorable words about freedom. Then, driving back to Washington, the girl from Africa "was mistaken for an American"—the party was refused service in one restaurant, and in another where the management did serve them, the girl was terrified and made physically ill by the demonstration of white customers against her.[6]

One has only to travel abroad with listening ears to learn how widespread this kind of incident has been. It can only be hoped that, in this period of the continuation of the American Revolution through the present struggle for racial justice, overseas students will help us by understanding, prayer, and participation as they have helped us through their judgment in the past to see more clearly this great sin on our national horizon.

Perhaps this is a good point at which to point up the special difficulties of African students. Although they represent only seven per cent of the foreign student population in the United States, with a total of 5,000, they are rapidly increasing — more rapidly, in fact, than other groups. They also account for a larger number of problems confronting foreign student advisors and counselors than perhaps their numbers would warrant. There are many contributing factors, of which one is skin color. They have found themselves on campuses where they were accepted in the school itself but not in the surrounding community. Many have come on such a financial shoestring that they were constantly in financial trouble, especially during holiday and summer vacation periods when they were without support and could not find jobs. Coming out of the security of the extended family system, they have not always found an "uncle" to help provide for their needs at the proper time! Because of their desire for education on the graduate level, far too many have had to remain outside their own continent of seething change for far too long a time.

Because the foreign student often has so many problems to bring to his counselors, problems as varied as the human race, he him-

[6] James D. Bryden, "Howard: Crossroads University," *Presbyterian Life,* December 1, 1961. Used by permission.

self is sometimes thought of as a problem. However, in a paper entitled *Developing Patterns in the Ministry Among International Students,* Raymond DeHainaut states:

> Many people who are close to this work among the increasing numbers of international students realize that we have received by their presence an opportunity for the enrichment of American life as well as a problem. It is not surprising that many of the campus ministers to foreign students that I have visited were talking about the foreign students' ministry to us and to the Church. I feel that in my own contacts with students from many lands I have gained much more than I have given.

This reaction would be echoed by anyone who has sincerely given himself in friendship and service to people of another nation, church, and culture. The need to understand each foreign student as a person and to learn something of his needs and aspirations is obvious. There are certain characteristics which one can anticipate. The student who comes has usually one primary educational objective — to prepare himself for his chosen vocation. He wants adequate training for his life and work in his homeland in the years ahead. If he is a mature student, he will allot his time and attention to those experiences that will help him fulfill his educational objective. He is an individual in a strange new culture, understandably cautious in responding to the habits and customs of that culture. If he is here under the sponsorship of his own government, the United States government, a church, or a private educational agency, he will be more or less subject to the requirements of the sponsoring agency. If he is unsponsored, he will probably need financial help unless by chance he comes from a wealthy family. As an individual far from home and from family he has spiritual needs whether he is a Christian or a non-Christian. In the words of Benjamin Schmoker, "There is a fundamental need for security and for a sense of belonging. He needs abundant faith in himself which is dependent upon the demonstration of faith that others can give." [7]

It may be helpful at this point to include some paragraphs from Dr. Hector Valencia, of Colombia, who has studied in the United States at three periods — in 1945, 1948, and 1953. He asks the ques-

[7] *Manual for Student Christian Workers on the Christian Ministry Among International Students, op. cit.*

tion: "What attitudes and experiences make the difference?" and in reply mentions six expectations of the foreign student.

1. *Fair treatment:* In a world full of injustice, hate, and suspicion, the growing indivdual is very conscious of his rights. He wants to be treated as an equal and resents any slight discrimination. . . . The injustice becomes not only a personal matter but also an insult to the country and race the student represents.

2. *Understanding of his cultural background:* It is assumed that a student going to a foreign country has done some research about that country. In many cases, extensive reading and preparation have taken place for months before actually traveling. . . . He, therefore, expects to find people in the community who are able to talk intelligently about his own country and its characteristics. Nothing is more discouraging for a student than to realize that the people in the country he has chosen to pursue advanced studies, and which he thinks more enlightened, know little beyond their own culture and local geography. . . .

3. *Opportunity for self-expression:* Provisions should be made by different agencies interested in the welfare of the student for him to frequent, and join if he wishes, interest groups such as foundations, art, science, and literature societies where he can express himself and interpret his culture in a creative manner. There seems to be a need to tell about one's own country and its multiple manifestations.

4. *Orientation on current problems:* Modern man, whatever his profession, cannot ignore world problems. He is involved in them and has to share the burden of seeking solutions for them. It is important to present to the foreign student a clear picture of these issues and the solutions which Christianity offers within the framework of western civilization. This should be done without apology. On the other hand, one has to be aware of the mistakes committed in the name of this civilization and of the changes taking place in the world today and consider them as a challenge for the invigoration of Christianity and the Church. . . . The foreign student should have the opportunity of clarifying his thinking and of renewing his faith in the Christian Church and in democracy. . . .

5. *Financial help if needed:* Although the student planning to study in a foreign country should be sure of his financial ability to support himself while studying, there are emergencies for which he might need help. Miscalculation of costs, sudden sickness, economic difficulties in the family, etc. may present themselves and the student should have a place where he can borrow for these emergencies.

6. *Spiritual guidance:* This is one of the most neglected areas among foreign students. . . . Opportune guidance in this realm will avoid separation from the church and softening of Christian principles and morals.[8]

While it is admitted that the authentic locale of the foreign student is in the academic milieu, it is also true that the actions and attitudes of the surrounding community are an important factor. Some studies have highlighted the importance to him of adult friends apart from those persons to whom he is officially related in the university. These friendships are most naturally formed in the home — around the fireplace in the living room, at the common meal in the dining room, or over the dishes in the kitchen.

More recently the somewhat superficial emphasis on hospitality has given way to the "host family" idea, with emphasis on relationships of depth which will last throughout the time the foreign student is in the U.S.A. All across the states, host family programs are sponsored by many different types of groups, both secular and religious. One of the most significant of these has been under the leadership of the Episcopal Council for Foreign Students.

Their main concern in developing local and diocesan committees has been with the "quality of the hospitality rather than with quantity." They have placed a great deal of stress on interpretation of hospitality as a two-way street and on the importance of training host families in cross-cultural understanding. The Rev. Philip T. Zabriskie, president of the council, has explained the council's policies in these terms:

The theology of the Episcopal Council for Foreign Students is rooted in a respect for human freedom. The love of Christ is something we dare not use as a bludgeon. It is a long hard journey from a Church reception for foreign students to an intimate discussion of faith between close friends. Most of the students you meet will never advance far on this journey, but one may. . . . It is a long hard journey, but friendship, when it is true, is never easy. The type of friendship of which we speak is the very essence of our faith. It is a gift from God.[9]

[8] *Perspectives on Studying Abroad.* Preparatory material for Consultation on "A New Ministry in a New World."

[9] From an address by Mr. Zabriskie, paraphrased in part in the Council's Manual, *Sojourners Among Us.*

Many columns have been printed in "dos and don'ts" brochures to help American families in hosting foreign students. Some of the recurrent emphases are (1) that genuine interest and desire for friendship is the only authentic reason to invite overseas student guests, (2) that a humble, teachable spirit is more important than a passion for service, (3) that knowledge of the student guest's homeland, politics, economics, and culture is essential for mutual encounter, and (4) that being on the defensive for the short-comings of one's homeland may close the door to fuller under-standing and deeper communication.

In comments addressed to hostesses in the February, 1962, issue of the NAFSA *Newsletter*, Mr. James Bentley states:

> "Understanding" means "standing under" another person's culture, his value system, his personality, and his habits. . . . When you truly subject yourself to the presence of your guest, you run the risk of being changed by him, but without this risk there are no grounds for estab-lishing trust.

The story will never be fully known or told of the new insights which have come to children from foreign student guests. An initial interest kindled in this way is often fulfilled in later years, as hands clasped around the table in a Kansas town become hands clasped around the world in Chiengmai, Nairobi, or Taegu through mis-sionary or diplomatic service.

The seventeenth Quadrennial Conference on the Christian World Mission held at Ohio University, Athens, Ohio, marked a turning point in the reflection of the churches and the student Christian movements in their thinking about the Christian ministry among international students. This was a new kind of conference which brought together some 3,500 students, about 1,350 of whom (or roughly half) came from some ninety-eight countries outside the U.S.A. The type of encounter which took place at a very deep level was startling to both the American and the foreign students. The conference left in its wake some wistful thinking about how wonderful it would be if this kind of confrontation on political, social, economic, and religious issues could take place on the local campus where a miniature world community exists but never mani-fests itself.

In due time the Student Volunteer Movement and the United

Student Christian Council combined to bring into being the Committee on Christian Work Among International Students — a Committee which continued under the National Student Christian Federation when the new organization came into being in 1959. Although the Committee (made up of representatives of the various churches and member movements of NSCF who are assigned special responsibility in this area, selected international students, and American students who have studied abroad) worked without staff in its early years, it managed to carry on a publication program for campus Christian workers and to sponsor eastern and western regional workshops and a National Training Seminar. In the spring of 1961 an emergency program to assist African students was launched.

One of the major efforts of the Committee has been to sponsor ecumenical ministries in areas of large concentrations of international students. These are patterned after the Protestant Foundation at the University of Michigan, a pioneering effort which was initiated in January, 1947, when a Baptist missionary volunteered to spend her furlough working with foreign students. The Michigan work proved so valuable that it was continued under new leadership, and in 1953 the Protestant Foundation for International Students was formally incorporated. It has been an ecumenical effort with a wide base of support including the United Church Women, the University Office of Religious Affairs, the local cooperating denominations, and their national counterparts. In its staff and its board the Protestant Foundation has been blessed with dynamic leadership which has resulted in waves of influence and insight to other campuses where there are large concentrations of students from abroad. The changing philosophy of work reflected in a significant study completed in 1961 reflects the changing situation as both the world and the university scene in the U.S.A. become more thoroughly internationalized. The following paragraphs on goals is from the report of the Committee on Evaluation and Review:

1. To serve in the name of Christ in a ministry among students of all faiths and cultures, seeking to understand each person's total needs and bring him into responsible and effective relationships with persons representing community resources relevant to his needs.

2. To nurture the spiritual growth of Christian foreign students and to encourage them to continue their participation in the corporate life of the Church through affiliation with a local parish or congregation.

3. To be a ministry of reconciliation by providing opportunities for vital encounter between international students of differing religious, political and ideological positions who are often removed from channels of conversation.

4. To help the church through providing its members, lay and clergy,
   A. with training and opportunity to participate in this specialized ministry;
   B. with opportunity to know students from abroad, the richness of their cultural and religious traditions, the needs and contributions of their countries with opportunity to understand the churches from which they come and the world mission of the Church particularly as it relates to the problems and issues of the day.

5. To realize in our midst the World Christian community and make it known; to deepen the understanding of the Christian faith through the sharing of international and inter-denominational insights; and to undergird the witness to this faith within the University community.

6. In all of these endeavors, to seek the guidance of the Holy Spirit.

Since 1956 a number of ecumenical ministries, similar in purpose and pattern to that at the University of Michigan, have been established in accordance with the recommendations of a paper entitled "Criteria and Procedures for Developing an Ecumenical Ministry Among International Students on a Local Campus." These developments have taken place in the following centers of large concentration of foreign students: University of Chicago, Massachusetts Institute of Technology, Harvard University, University of California (both the Los Angeles and Berkeley campuses) , Ohio State University, and Washington, D. C. (where a number of institutions are served) . At this writing, negotiations are in progress with local committees at Michigan State University and Purdue University. The first of these ministries was in Chicago, where the work was started with the part-time assistance of a graduate student. By 1961 the

Interchurch Committee had secured highly qualified personnel on a full-time basis and had prepared through the struggle of discussion a statement of purpose beginning with the following theological premises:

> The ministry of the Interchurch Committee is premised on the conviction that God has confronted us in Jesus Christ as Creator, Judge, and Redeemer and continues to confront us concretely in the needs of our fellow man and the events of history. Thus, this ministry comes into being in response to the Living Lord who calls all Christians to minister to those in need and to respond to the unfolding creative possibilities of every time and place. As such, this ministry is an ecumenical ministry, motivated by concerns which cut across all denominational lines.
>
> Because the Christian church is called to radical openness to events, its life and work should be characterized by sensitive alertness to the peculiar situation in which it finds itself. The creative opportunity of the international student situation at this university calls for a "ministry of encounter," enabling international and American students to meet one another at significant levels. In such encounter, judgment is discovered, alienations do exist, conflicts arise and are perhaps even heightened, but reconciliation and movement toward creativity is made possible as well. If the church is true to its heritage, it does not just pick up pieces; it also helps create opportunities for raising ultimate questions and sharing ultimate concerns.

The following paragraph of a section entitled "The Shape of the Ministry" also seems worth quoting:

> In light of its theological premises and in response to this situation, the Interchurch Committee seeks to encourage dialogue and involvement in common issues across lines of nationality, culture, and religion, in as many ways as it finds possible. In general, the efforts of the Committee, under the guidance of the Minister to International Students, are directed toward:
>
> —enabling the fullest possible realization of international encounter within denominational structures existing on the campus and in the university community;
> —establishing such new structures as the situation seems to demand;
> —the exercise of a vigorous personal ministry by the Minister to International Students and the denominational chaplains;
> —cooperation with other agencies serving international students.

God has used the charisma of fellow-Christians from other lands and churches to help us understand his action in the development of international communities of students. In 1954 Jacques Beaumont, of France (now director of CIMADE), wrote a widely-circulated paper entitled "The Christian Witness to Foreign Students," in which he outlined the missionary task of student Christian movements in the U.S.A. in relation to foreign students as including these elements:

> To show them a Christian community, a living church
> To show them an intelligible Gospel related to a culture in movement and change, a culture of this modern age
> To show them a Christian faith related to a political world with some sensibility to the changes which have occurred since 1900.

He also highlighted the urgency of foreign students' contributions in awakening American students to what they are as "Christians, as citizens of this world, as citizens of the American democracy" as well as to what they are not and what they could be. Mr. Beaumont wrote feelingly about the "healthy shock" which foreign students will present if we will "trust them and hear them."

In 1955 André Appel, then the university pastor at Cité Universitaire in Paris, conferred with many persons involved with the ministry to foreign students in the United States, sharing his own insights on the biblical basis for ministry in a paper that was later to find its way into a workbook, *Resource and Reflection,* published by the National Student Christian Federation. In 1948 Walter Leibrecht addressed a Washington workshop on the subject "Christian Encounter and Witness to Non-Christian Students." There followed the contribution of Christoph Hahn, also of Germany, who presented a paper to CCWAIS entitled "The Christian Ministry to Foreign Students." A third German contribution came in a paper presented by Ulrich Mauser at the Consultation in Mill Valley in December, 1960.[10] The papers by Leibrecht, Hahn, and Mauser are also included in *Resource and Reflection.* Dr. Mauser highlighted the double aspect of the ministry which both the church in this country and the foreign student have to fulfill to each other.

> Whenever a Christian student from abroad lives together with fellow Christians in this country, a Christian brother meets his Christian brethren. Certainly, in this brotherhood of believers, men and women have

[10] Ulrich Mauser, "A Theological Perspective . . . ," *op. cit.*

a mission to fulfill to each other. The mission is mutual love, mutual help, mutual criticism, mutual encouragement.

The entire paper is worthy of reading and rereading, study and restudy, but for our purpose we can extract only some brief sections to give an idea of mood and content.

> The foreign student is, like every other member of the congregation, primarily a gift of God given to the Church . . . a gift which, by virtue of his being a foreigner, is at the same time markedly distinct from other members of the congregation. He brings his own background and experience into the church, and the very diversity of his heritage makes him a particularly valuable gift to the life of the Church here.

Dr. Mauser feels that the presence of the Christian foreign student opens Christian eyes to see "the nation-transcending quality of the Church," stimulates a concern for Christians all over the world and identification with their burdens and their joys, brings a realization that the Christian faith is not confined to any political camp or any economic point of view, and reveals that the cultural forms which shape the church's life all over the world vary greatly. Indeed the foreign student will have made a great contribution if he is able to convey that to live as a Christian is not to be confused with "the American way of life." If these things are to happen, then the foreigner must speak frankly in Christian love, and the people in the churches must be willing to listen and to learn from those whom God has given them as neighbors and as friends.

As the foreign student population has increased, bringing a miniature world community to almost every campus large or small, it began to dawn on church leaders and on some congregations that God had placed a missionary opportunity on their doorstep. They saw that they could not deny that God might have something to say to them through the presence of Christian students — the gifts of churches in other lands. It thus became clear that Christian fellowship with this kind of ecumenical understanding was rare but they worked patiently toward bringing it about. This involved interpreting the international dimension of mission to make manifest that, as W. A. Visser 't Hooft points out, every church in the world is in need of that great enrichment which would come to it if it should open its mind and heart and life for those gifts of grace which it can receive through the ministry of other churches. This fellowship of giving and receiving has been expressed in many ways — through participation, for example, in youth conferences, church retreats, church school teaching, and singing in the choir — thus providing a sustaining relationship with a given Christian community.

Perhaps it would not be amiss at this point to draw upon personal experience. As the "foreign student advisor" of the United Presbyterian Church for over a decade, I have learned that Christians from all over the world need to know and to speak to one another frankly in Christian love just for the sheer purpose of manifesting the truth of the gospel. Several years ago an African student from Cameroun came in to say "Goodbye." Weighing his words carefully and speaking with the slow, measured speech of one who is still getting used to the language he said, "Before I came to the United States I knew only my brothers in Christ in the Cameroun. Now I know and love brothers in Christ from all over the world."

Through the years this and other experiences have brought home to me the truth of J. B. Phillips' statement:

The Englishman, the African and the Indian, for example, may exhibit a certain limited wholeness in themselves and in their own church, but it is only when they learn to work together that they begin to realize a greater wholeness than they had previously imagined—the wholeness of the "one new man" in Christ.[11]

This is what a young Philippine psychologist meant when she wrote of an experience of several students from different parts of the world sharing as a team what God had done for their people through Jesus Christ. "With the kind of discussion we had that night, I always feel a deep elation, for somehow the symbolization is clear; the circle of Christian love is completed when people from different parts of the world speak with one voice."[12] Thus I learned how important it is to plan occasions when Christian students from many lands, including the United States, come together for worship, study, discussions, and fellowship.

One way of fostering this world-family feeling has been through monthly "Family Circle" letters of encouragement sent each month to several hundred students who come from related churches abroad.

[11] J. B. Phillips, *Making Men Whole* (New York: The Macmillan Company 1952) , p. 66.

[12] From a letter to Margaret Flory.

This is a method of communication which has been useful in the Christian church since the days of the Apostle Paul. A host of reactions like the following have helped the writer to know the meaningfulness of this method of communication. "With every Family Circle letter comes a feeling of kinship and oneness with other members of the Circle. . . . It drives away whatever loneliness is ours, whatever misgivings we may experience as we fit ourselves into a society, which, while friendly and generous, is strange and untried in some ways."

Providing Christian literature to aid in the strengthening of devotional life and to keep students informed on developments in the life of the church both in the United States and at home is an important means of Christian nurture. When the right material is in the hand, and the mind is open, the power of the Holy Spirit can work miracles with the printed page. One cannot overemphasize the importance of maintaining a link with the church back home in India or Indonesia, not as mere sentiment but rather to understand that God is calling the community of Christians to be and to do, both at home and in their newly-adopted country.

Exposure to church life in the United States in a variety of situations is important. This means contact with churches both large and small for extended periods rather than one-night speaking stands; it means the opportunity to see Christian community centers in the remote areas and in the inner city; it means observing the ministry among American Indians and migrant workers; it means experience in conferences and retreats — all this to supplement the regular participation in the life of a single local church near the campus. When one sees an international student ushering on Sunday morning, singing in the choir, teaching a class of small children, or making a poster for the bulletin board, then one realizes how important it is for faith to move from the mind into the working hand. Thus, changing the preposition *for* to *with* has been one secret for involving international students in a meaningful local church or student group experience.

It is quite evident that the presence of overseas students can provide an important thrust for the unity of the church in the United States. Coming from the United Churches in Asia, for example, they may be utterly confused by the denominationalism in our country.

A word of judgment upon the denominational approach so widespread in this country is stated by P. T. Thomas, a graduate student from India at the University of Chicago:

> Each denomination has its own employee to serve its students. No one group is responsible for the whole campus. Again the conception of the ministry as the denomination doing something for its students is dominant. The church's (*i.e.*, the denomination's) responsibility is to provide a man to "do the job." The Christians do not seem to recognize that they are a community for the sake of the larger campus community.[18]

Seeing one's patterns of work through the eyes of overseas people is often very salutary in bringing fresh understanding of the present situation and determination for change. Many university pastors in recent years have come to the conclusion that the ecumenical approach to the foreign student is the only one which is valid. Likewise, working together in this ministry has raised questions about the compartmentalized denominational approach to the rest of the campus in which they have been trapped for many years. On a number of campuses now there is concern for the development of the Christian community in the university, each group contributing resources as it can for the sake of a total impact in the name of all. In some cases this has meant the assignment of one person to be a coordinator of the foreign student ministry.

Along with the increase of foreign students in the United States has come an increase of Americans studying abroad. Between 1954-55, the academic year for which *Open Doors* first furnished information about United States students abroad, and 1961-62, the most recent year for which data is available at this writing, the number of U.S.A. students abroad has increased by 70%, from around 9,000 to over 16,000. This movement of students out from the United States and back again has provided a more internationalized setting on the campuses. Furthermore, it has increased the foreign student's circle of friends who know what it means to make an adjustment to another culture and who therefore have a new affinity for the overseas person in their midst. Over and over again, former Junior Year Abroad students are heard to say: "Now that I know what it is like

[18] *Student World*, Vol. LV, Fourth Quarter, 1962, Number 4, Serial Number 218, p. 481. Used by permission of the World Student Christian Federation, Geneva, Switzerland.

to be a foreign student, I am going to be a better friend to the
foreign students on my home campus."

Another notable factor is the increase in the number of families
in any community who have lived and worked abroad and whose
home is evermore open, especially to the students from the country
they have learned to call a second home. Thus we may be well on
our way to an internationalized lay expression in many of our
campus communities. It seems very clear from the vantage point at
which we now look at the ministry among foreign students that this
work cannot be something apart from the whole task in the academic community. At the same time very special attention must be
given to it, recognizing the kind of needs which are generated in
crossing from one culture to another. It is the mood of the day to
talk and write about the role of the laity. Among foreign students a
true lay ministry should be the goal even though there may be some
place for professionally-trained persons. The direction before us,
however ideal it may seem, is the whole Christian community carrying on the ministry, exercising concern and love for one another,
and assuming the responsibility for pastoral care. The role of the
worker with special responsibility is to equip others for their
ministry.

A confirming note in this regard comes from the pen of Reginald
Smart of the International Ministry at Harvard, who writes as
follows:

> Only when all available persons are prepared to accept responsibility
> for one student or student-family will the pastoral responsibilities of the
> Church be in any way adequately discharged. In practice this involves
> real friendship, visitation, counseling, expression of concern where it is
> needed. Any worthwhile ministry should multiply itself and perhaps in
> time a special person will not be needed, because the Church will be
> effectively ministering to the whole community of which foreign persons
> are an integral part rather than a field for specialists.[14]

Those who are associated in these days with foreign students,
either professionally or informally, have the advantage of a good bit
of research which has been carried on in recent years in regard to
cross-cultural adjustments in general and to certain exchange pro-

[14] From an unpublished manuscript, reprinted with permission of Reginald
Smart.

grams in specific. The most recent of these is the report of the U. S. Advisory Commission on International and Cultural Affairs, published in April, 1963, which is addressed to the Congress and the American people. This was a broadly based survey of 2,696 former grantees from 20 countries who came to the United States between 1949 and 1960 under the educational and cultural exchange program carried on by the Department of State. A distinguished committee under the chairmanship of Dr. John W. Gardner, president of the Carnegie Corporation has quoted and summarized the findings in the following way:

1. "Testimony is overwhelming from all sources that the program as a whole is effective." The Commission found that the number of grantees with hostile or negative attitudes who were unable to benefit from their educational opportunity were a "fractional minority."

2. "There is impressive testimony that the exchange program increases mutual understanding." Increased understanding of America and Americans was cited as one of the most outstanding results of the program.

3. The evidence is abundant that the exchange program has succeeded in helping dispel among foreign visitors many misconceptions and ugly stereotypes about the American people. The report continues to state that "particularly singled out for comment were the vitality of American thought, the American sense of drive and organization, and a group of warm personal qualities differing notably from the stereotyped qualities which grantees apparently had expected to find."

4. The exchange program does not bring out a uniformly favorable point of view on all aspects of the American scene; the reaction of former grantees varied considerably with the country from which they have come, and with the particular aspect inquired about. It was found that in general the grantees from Europe were most critical, and from Latin America the most laudatory. As to aspects of American life, scientific development received the highest commendation; race relations, the lowest.

5. "The program has been outstandingly successful in providing a valuable educational experience to foreign grantees." Only 2% of 53,000 found the influence on their professional field other than favorable.

6. The evidence is significant, though somewhat less conclusive, that the grantee's visit has also benefited his home country. "This has been through the transmission of valuable skills, knowledge, and attitudes."

7. "The program has effectively established channels of communication between the people in other countries and the United States." In this regard broader perspectives and a wider international outlook were repeatedly cited. Surprisingly enough a great majority keep up significant contact with friends and professional colleagues discovered during their stay in the United States.

Although the Commission found the program as a whole to be effective, it has made some helpful suggestions for improvement. These include (1) a concerted effort to seek out and select more persons with particular promise and talent from underdeveloped areas, (2) a relaxing of English-language proficiency requirement, provided that intensive language training is given in the United States prior to the beginning of studies, (3) attempting to concentrate on the seeking out and selection of candidates who are "sufficiently vigorous and restless to help promote desirable social and economic change," (4) the setting-up of field selection centers to assist U.S. universities and private agencies in choosing properly qualified students, and (5) adapting all programs for foreign students and visitors to provide more time and opportunity for meeting a wide cross-section of American families.

A summary sentence which gives the report its title "A Beacon of Hope" is the following:

"In a time when most international activities seem almost unbearably complex, hazardous and obscure in outcome, the success of educational exchange is a beacon of hope." [15]

It has seemed advisable to cite this report at length because it is one of the most recent and extensive pieces of research and because it throws light on the whole international educational effort.

The specialists who deal with international exchange programs are worried about the immediate years ahead. In a ten-year period from the mid-fifties to the mid-sixties there has been a 92% increase

[15] U. S. Advisory Commission on International Educational and Cultural Affairs, *A Beacon of Hope—The Exchange-of-Persons Program* (Washington: Government Printing Office, 1963) , p. 61.

in the number of foreign students in the United States, and it has been predicted that by 1970 there will be one hundred thousand persons on educational assignments in the United States. By that time the pressure on the part of American students to enroll will almost have doubled, with close to six million students trying to get into college. In view of this congestion, certain questions have been raised about the feelings of alumni and parents and even legislative bodies toward the continuing increase of overseas students in our midst. And yet the January, 1963, issue of *Think* magazine carries statistics indicating that in the United States only 1.5% of the total student population is from abroad in contrast to 30% in Austria, 7% in France, and 10% in the United Kingdom.

Recent studies indicate that the United States should be receiving more students from abroad in the years ahead in order to fulfill its responsibilities to the developing nations. In 1960 the Ford Foundation printed the report of its distinguished committee on the university and world affairs which stressed the redesigning of the curriculum to meet the needs of foreign students and at the same time to prepare to receive more students.

> With mounting domestic enrollments there are pressures to reduce or hold at the present level the numbers of foreign students received at particular institutions. Any such policy is not responsive to the needs and opportunities, particularly in those countries of Asia and Africa that are just beginning to develop their own educational systems or are adapting and expanding older systems for the needs of modern nationhood. For a number of years to come, the universities and colleges of the United States and other countries with highly developed educational systems will have to fill the critical gap between the educational needs of these countries and the limited capacities of their own educational institutions.[16]

But Melvin Fox, of the Ford Foundation staff, also makes the point that the United States needs the influence of foreigners as much as the foreigners need American assistance. One of the principal tasks we have in the West, he says, is to learn to live in a non-Christian, non-Caucasian, perhaps non-democratic world. Therefore, he believes, it is critically important that our colleges and universities begin to develop a broader base for the traditional disciplines than the wholly western orientation on which they now rest. Foreign stu-

[16] *The University and World Affairs* (New York: The Ford Foundation), p. 32.

dents and scholars represent a major resource in the efforts American universities will make to do this.

As the process of internationalization becomes more evidently a manifestation of God's plan for his world, it is clear that the challenge has many foci. For the university itself it means far-reaching changes in curriculum.

> A first-class liberal education in the second half of the twentieth century should unquestionably include an effective international component. Few universities or colleges have yet organized themselves to meet this standard. A searching examination of existing curricula would lead in many cases to the conclusion that some existing courses should be reorganized and combined or should even give way altogether to make a more adequate place for world affairs.[17]

Serving the underdeveloped nations will mean our provision of personnel abroad for many types of programs, as well as our receiving students and faculty in our own country. Internationalization is indeed a two-way process, as Joe W. Neal asserts in the April, 1962, issue of the *NAFSA Newsletter*.

> As universities move to streamline overseas programs, they will grow more conscious of the fact that they cannot become internationally minded when their interests cross the national boundary, while still remaining isolationist on the campus, and they must move toward being internationalized.

In line with this thinking there are already a number of campuses where an international office has been set up in which the following kinds of responsibilities are coordinated: foreign student advising, educational opportunities overseas for faculty and students, the receiving of international visitors, and cooperation in special programs with educational institutions abroad.

Through these pages there has been reference to both secular and Christian efforts on behalf of the international student. This seems an appropriate example of D. T. Niles' assertion in the last chapter of his book *Upon the Earth* that there are two sides to ecumenical vision and strategy:

> There is, on the one hand, the side represented by the organs of the churches and, on the other hand, the side represented by secular movements. Both must be taken equally seriously. The missionary enterprise and the ecumenical movement must provide the means of interlocking

[17] *Ibid.*, p. 17.

man's eternal destiny and his present life, interweaving the life of the people of God which is the Church with the lives of men as men which is the World.[18]

Confirmation is given to the importance of interlocking the Christion and the secular by André Appel, of France:

It is my conviction that all Christian organizations involved in foreign student work would find it to great advantage to carry on a real dialogue with secular organizations similarly engaged. With their knowledge of what the Bible says about "strangers" they could contribute greatly to a clear definition of student exchanges . . . they would have to warn not only of the danger of false universalism and false brotherhood, but also of nationalism and attitudes of cultural and technical superiority. On the other hand, Christian student workers can receive much from the methods worked out by secular organizations.[19]

In 1960 a Commission on Work Among Foreign Students was created under the auspices of the World Student Christian Federation. A major effort of this group was the holding of a consultation on the theme "A New Ministry in a New World" at the Ecumenical Institute at Bossey in April, 1963. Nine delegates from the United States were in attendance, and the ecumenical discussions which took place there confirmed several convictions which had been growing in the midst of those who have been serving in the ecumenical ministries.

The emerging world civilization places today's students in a radically new kind of world. Jean Paul Meyer, of France, stated: "We are exposed by God to the four winds of history, to the changing air of history, to the birth of the new international world that God is making right now, under our eyes." The thousands of students who are studying outside their own countries symbolize the new day — its complexities, its frustrations, and its opportunities. These students are moving in many directions across the world and not just from the West to an area of rapid social change. They are a modern diaspora, in the words of Dr. Hoekendijk, and their scatteredness offers a great ecumenical opportunity to the local Chris-

[18] D. T. Niles, *Upon the Earth* (New York: McGraw-Hill Book Company, 1962) , p. 268.

[19] Andre Appel, "The Biblical Basis for a Ministry to International Students," *Resource and Reflection* No. 3. (New York: National Student Christian Foundation.)

tian community which receives them. The ministry involved is a mutual one. The receiving group needs to serve and to listen, to offer pastoral care and at the same time to learn from the gifts of other churches whom God has sent. As one of the leaders of the Bossey Consultation has stated: "The Christian foreign student or teacher is as much a member of the ministering community as are those who are native to the country. By his presence and participation he enables the local Church to enter more fully into the world-wide mission of the Church."

The Bossey report describes the foreign students as a sign in our midst:

> They enter our universities from different parts of the world, far from home, and remind us that the world is one and that the Church is world-wide. They remind us that together we share in the world mission of the Church which is hampered by, among other things, the disunity of the Church. They help us to understand what mission means and involves, in a world of rapid technological advance, in a world of violent nationalism, in a world watching the re-emergence of Islam, Buddhism, and the spread of various types of scientific humanism and nihilism.

It may well be that the Bossey Consultation will prove to have been the kind of catalyst on a world basis which the Athens Conference of 1955 was on the American scene.

A major message on Theological Reflections on the New Ministry in the New Age was given at Bossey by Dr. Paul Löffler of the staff of the Division of World Mission and Evangelism of the World Council of Churches. In a section on theological reflections he summarized the renewed theological understanding of the Christian ministry by drawing on the New Testament insights reflected in a series of meetings on Christ's Ministry and Ours, and one on New Forms of Christian Service and Participation which had been sponsored by the East Asia Christian Conference. In brief capsule form, there are five major points:

> 1. Our ministry is not a matter of reaching out into unknown territory but of following Christ in step-by-step obedience into every new sphere of the world which he has conquered already. Every Christian ministry, inasmuch as it means sharing in Christ's ministry, must be the expression of a liberated life in Christ as a factual reality.

2. The goal of Christ's ministry, in which we share, is the reconciliation of the total world to God. But then fresh thinking is called for with reference to our traditional understanding of reconciliation. In the first place, the New Testament is not concerned with the reconciliation of individual persons as an end in itself. Agreed that Christ stresses persons in his ministry, but his goal is the reconciliation of all humanity. The ministry of reconciliation is essentially missionary in character. The very word "reconciliation" itself implies a new relationship between the Christian and his non-Christian brother as a result of their encounter. This is to say that the Christian does not convert the non-Christian but is with him reconciled into a new context of greater wholeness. Reconciliation is not to bring people into our camp but to move out ourselves and to challenge others to move out of their camp so that God can give us together a fuller life.

3. The one ministry of Christ is given to all God's people together. The basic unit is on the one hand the local congregation of all those who believe and who are together responsible, and on the other hand the church universal, the new Israel which shares in the joint task of service and witness to the ends of the earth.

4. The one ministry of all God's people is carried out through a variety of different vocations—the corporate ministry of the church does not consist of a number of activities or programs but of a living relationship between persons who with their gifts enrich and complement each other, leading to a joint witness in the world.

5. In conclusion, Christ the Servant, the incarnate slave who dies on the cross and rises to eternal dominion, is the only valid image for our ministry.

With the preceding five points as a basis, Dr. Löffler then proceeded to formulate "a few first affirmative conclusions which point like signposts into the direction we should march":

1. The existence of an authentic corporate life in Christ in the university world is the first condition of a Christian ministry among international students. According to Dr. Loffler, this implies three things: firstly, a life together of Christian students representing various cultures, countries, and communities; secondly, this Christian community and its ministry have to be concerned with the wholeness of reconciliation. This is the Christian extra, the very essence of the life of reconciliation, that it offers the international student community not a set of interesting programs and study groups, but a point of wholeness where people are liberated for

each other. Thirdly, wholeness can be restored only through the total salvation of Christ. Neither silent Christian presence nor service by itself, nor verbal evangelism is the full ministry of Christ.

2. If Christ's ministry is to the whole world, our ministry is not for students but with students in the university world. Dr. Loffler emphasizes that we must accept the new international university world as the God-given one, and we must come into a real encounter with it.

3. The new ministry in the university world has to be ecumenical. The demand today, according to Dr. Loffler is something much more radical than we have known, namely "a new ministry which is not just an extension of the old national one, but a new gift of the Holy Spirit. . . . The essential point that has not yet been brought home to student communities in an international situation is that you can no longer even understand your own national situation without mutual exchange with foreigners."

4. The new ministry must express the total variety of gifts and serve the totality of needs. Dr. Loffler refers to the various gifts (*charismata*) given by the Holy Spirit—the liturgical riches of Eastern Orthodox Christians, the insights gained in the encounter with a technological and secular world which western Christians can contribute, the spiritual depth of Asian Christianity, the joy of African worship and Christian life. Secondly, he speaks of a variety of needs: "Obviously, the foreign student will have problems of his own which demand special pastoral care. . . . The life in Christ liberates us from any ideological principle of equality. We can be free to serve each person as a unique historic being, and each national group according to its needs." Thirdly, he makes clear that "in the pluralistic and highly specialized university society with a Christian community out of many nations and denominations, the only adequate form of the ministry is that of a team representing the different cultural and racial backgrounds, a team of full-time members and lay workers. The challenge is to develop a pluriform pattern of service which will adequately express Christ's ministry in the university world."

5. The ministry of "servanthood" requires a radical approach to the present organizational structures. Here Dr. Loffler points out that "our structure is designed to draw people into either an open or a closed membership circle," in contrast to a growing conviction that "the only workable and reasonable structure and

strategy in a modern secular age is that of dispersed cells of mobile units functioning within, not at the fringe of the unit of society—in our case, the university." Secondly, he affirms that "servanthood" demands a functional organization which serves people in their changing relationships rather than provides program. "We must examine much more thoroughly the pitfalls of our organizational structures which force us sometimes to do things which we cannot accept theologically, and, more often, to leave things undone which we ought to have done," he adds. In the end Dr. Loffler highlights the need of study of "the role and function of the international university both as a community of learning and living and in relation to its task in society at large."

Dr. Löffler's message to the consultation has been quoted at length because of the author's belief that these affirmative conclusions do indeed point like signposts into the future — a future that will be marked by continued student and staff mobility, by increased emphasis on the international character of many disciplines, by the international circulation of books and periodicals, by curriculum changes, by growth in prestige of international academic organizations, in short, by the internationalization of the academic world of higher education to a degree undreamed of even ten years ago.

At this point the writer would urge a careful reading of the report of the Consultation entitled *Foreign Students: A New Ministry in a New World,* which describes the new world of higher education, quotes Dr. Löffler's address in full, outlines a thesis for action, includes a most helpful section on Christian students among students of other faiths, another on guidelines for the selection, orientation, and support of foreign students, and a study outline raising strategic questions in regard to the following: International community in higher education, the Christian ministry in the academic community, and the implications of the life and mission of the church. The questions raised will press in upon us for a good many years to come.

Perhaps we can now see a foretaste of what is to come in the United States in the days ahead. Former President Cornelius de Kiewiet of the University of Rochester looked forward as he wrote:

America's consciousness of its world must undergo the same transformation that occurred in Western Europe in the sixteenth and seventeenth centuries as a result of the great voyages of discovery. . . . To a degree we do not yet recognize, with an unparalleled speed, we are discovering a new world . . . Our educational habits and practices have of necessity been deeply influenced by Western Europe . . . Yet there simply must be room in general education . . . for the opportunity to bring into focus the new world.[20]

As the international world becomes more and more a living reality on our campuses, let us pray that, through the guidance of the Holy Spirit, forms of life and work among Christians in the academic community will emerge in recognition that all Christians in any locality are the church in that place and they share responsibility for participating in Christ's ministry. Let us pray that the resources needed for the fullest expression of an ecumenical strategy in the new internationalized world of higher education will be forthcoming from the churches; let us pray for a universal realization that the ministry cannot be for foreign students but must be *with* and *among* them in exactly the same way as with other members of the academic community; let us pray for an understanding of the lordship of Jesus Christ in the university world and what this means for the Christian community in the university; let us pray that student Christian movements and campus Christian life ministries will express in their leadership and staffing the supranational as well as the supraconfessional nature of the church; and finally let us pray for those miracles of dialogue about which Reuel Howe has written so movingly:

> By dialogue we can let God into our world because in dialogue we open ourselves to one another, and in so doing, we open ourselves to God. When man is open to man and God, miracles have to happen. But they are forged out of everyday events, the happenings between persons: the conflicts, failures, misunderstandings and tragedies of living together, as well as out of the love and acceptance that are both the source and the environment for the working of the miracles of dialogue.[21]

[20] *The University and World Affairs, op. cit.,* p. 11.
[21] Reuel L. Howe, *The Miracle of Dialogue* (New York: The Seabury Press, Inc., 1963) , p. 152.

C. FREDERICK STOERKER

10: Travel, Study, and Service as Related to the Campus Ministry

TRAVEL AND SERVICE are closely linked with study in the academic world today. Tens of thousands of students and faculty from American colleges and universities will be abroad this summer. Even more of them will travel within their own country. The staggering increase in the size of American campuses is caused not only by the baby boom of World War II but also by the increasing percentage of young Americans securing higher education. We study! And the Peace Corps has highlighted the willingness of Americans to serve!

Educational travel, serious study, willing service! None of these three requires justification; there is unanimous recognition of their overall worth. But there are many who would see these three as having only peripheral relationship to the main focus of the campus ministry. We contend, however, the relationship is integral. Travel is more than the "grand tour"; it is a means of learning and serving. Study occurs at many places other than the classroom, the study group, or the study hall. Service is more than the giving of something by "haves" to representatives of the "have nots!" The

Now the associate secretary of the National Student Christian Federation, for its commission on ecumenical voluntary service projects, C. Frederick Stoerker was formerly involved in ecumenical work camps in Holland and was director of the camp in Austria.

199

campus ministry not only finds itself consistently involved in travel, study, and service, but also has a continuing responsibility for orientation and interpretation in relation to all three.

As we begin to examine the role of travel, study, and service, it is important to share certain basic assumptions. The first of these is that faith is validated through experience. Whatever its intellectual content, its growth is the product of the totality of man's life rather than of any single aspect of it.

The second assumption deals with the nature of the church. Two diagrams are etched in my memory. They appeared in *AIYKA*, a publication of the Student Christian Movement of India, in a report of addresses given by the Reverend Mr. Hans-Ruedi Weber, of the World Council of Churches. Each consisted of an oval with a cross in the center. The oval to the left was full of dots. The one on the right showed every dot outside the oval. The left, as you have surmised, stood for the gathered church and the right for the scattered church. Thus both were diagrams of the church. They show that the mission of the church must be carried on outside its institutional walls, but in no way diminishing the importance of the gathered fellowship. The truth is that, unless the church's life is realized in both dimensions, it is realized in neither.

The third assumption deals with the nature of education. Let us return to our two diagrams — but substitute the torch of knowledge, symbolizing education, at the center of each. There is a growing realization that, however irreplaceable the academic community is, education in many dimensions occurs only as the members of that community "find" themselves outside it. There is an increasing mood, especially among an important segment of students, to measure growth in terms of the impact of involvement. This is a movement that sees facts and figures as a necessary part of the total experience. The struggle between the impossibility of gaining all that there is to gain on the campus, while at the same time acting responsibly in circles outside the gathered community, is one of the principal tensions of many superior students.

Both church and campus emphasize depth, and yet each is to some degree aware of the extent to which the accompanying lack of breadth may result in social irrelevance. In some circles of the campus ministry this danger is heightened by the current on-campus emphasis which may increase the student's separation from society in general.

A fourth assumption is that the church and the campus communities, in their scattered roles, are in the same world! There are times when this seems to be the assumption least understood.

The fifth and final assumption completes our circle. In certain respects both the gathered community of the church and the gathered community of the campus lead a fishbowl existence. Those who are not a part of either the community of the church or that of the campus are constantly looking at them. They may or they may not "come in." Educational institutions are becoming increasingly aware that those outside nevertheless exert a tremendous force on the campus community to which it must react with both integrity and wisdom. The church frequently lives under the illusion that it can choose its relationships with forces outside its door. Actually, however, the communities of both the church and the campus are judged by the action of their members as they spend much of their lives beyond the border of the gathered fellowship.

This chapter, within its spatial limits, is addressed to specific programmed aspects of the *outside* experience. Reflecting a mixture of motivations, plans, and pressures, a variety of programs located outside are being designed and packaged and sold to the clientele of the campus ministry — student, faculty, and administration. We shall look at the home front and then at the national front before turning to the international scene. These introductory paragraphs seek to sketch in, with broad strokes, the backdrop against which all that follows is to be seen.

There is one important figure yet to be sketched in. Regardless of whether he abhors or enjoys his position, there is no doubt about the centrality of the role of the campus minister in the campus ministry. This is nowhere more true than in the relationship of the ministry to outside programs. How, then, does the campus minister relate to the conglomeration of announcements on bulletin boards, the growing list of mailings reaching the desk top, the brochures, the pamphlets, and the catalogs which come to him? This writer recently looked through three bulging loose-leaf notebooks giving the announcements of fellowships and foundation studies available to the graduate students and faculty in a single academic discipline. A single bulletin board in a student union included posters from AFSC, EVS, three denominations, and the "Y"!

No one can adequately meet all the pressures put upon him, but the image which the campus minister has of himself in relation to travel-study-service is very important. There are four possible relationships which he may have to the travel-study-service information reaching him. First, he can rule all such material and all such projects out of his responsibility and ignore them. Or, second, he may be a "pusher," pushing the proper (he hopes!) piece of information into the hands of the student or staff, perhaps to get the individual out of his hair, or perhaps to bring to an end a long serious conference. Third he may be a "promoter." He knows that some of his constituency are probably interested, and that when they get into "those things" they come back with an added dimension which contributes to the total fellowship. And so he congratulates the professor who gets a Fulbright, the student who goes to a work camp, or the person who takes the grand tour. But the campus minister may occupy a fourth role. He may be a "believer." The believer will certainly at times be promoter and pusher, but he will not stop there. A short quotation, the source of which is unknown to the writer, states: "A belief is something on which we act, while an opinion is something which we merely entertain!" The believer, out of his understanding of the integral unity of the work of the gathered and scattered community, sees these opportunities as an important aspect of his campus ministry. He is a participant. And he communicates this fact, whether actually leading a project or program, as he sometimes does, or discussing its relevance with another person. Only if travel, study, and service are important to the campus minister are they apt to be integral to his ministry.

LOCAL EMPHASIS

Historically, the emphasis of the church has not been on travel or study so much as on service. Though in earlier years the condescending labels "almsgiving" and "charity" were used, there has always been an expression of that concern which we now seek to describe by the use of the word "service." There have always been elements of this concern in the campus ministry. The great push, however, in the direction of service projects by local groups is almost entirely a postwar concern. The present emphasis on the use and value of the volunteer marks a shift away from that professionalism which was the trend during the second quarter of the twentieth century.

Likewise, the emphasis on worldwide travel, on study tours and study abroad, and on international work camps is not a new one. The *increase* in such emphasis, however, began in the mid-1950's and is still growing. The weekend work camp program of the Friends Social Order Committee directed by Mr. David Richie is the only program of its kind with a continuing history of more than twenty years. Even literature specifically designed for such programs has remained scarce. In 1952 the Friends Social Committee published a small brochure entitled *Weekend Work Camping, an Opportunity.* In 1956 the United Christian Youth Movement published a brochure entitled *Community Service, a Guide to Weekend Work Camps.* And in 1963 the National Student Christian Federation published *Committed to Serve, a Manual to Aid in Developing Local Service Projects.*[1] But how are we to explain and evaluate current activities in the local area?

Knowing and serving the total community

From the standpoint of both the church and the educational community there has been a growing realization that the problems of the world are not all at a great distance from our front door. There has been a growing realization that there is much to be done in our own culture, and that we have a very limited knowledge of it. As the writer was reading Lederer and Burdick's book, *The Ugly American,*[2] and agreeing that his own observations unfortunately supported much that was being said about Americans abroad, a question came into his thinking and has remained there. Why should the American who does not understand his own culture be expected to understand another's? Is not the understanding of one's own culture a basic task of both Christianity and educa-

---

[1] *Committed to Serve* is available through the Ecumenical Voluntary Service, National Student Christian Federation, 475 Riverside Drive, New York, N.Y., 10027.

[2] William J. Lederer and Eugene Burdick. *The Ugly American* (New York: Norton, 1958).

tion? True, exposure outside one's culture usually contributes to this understanding, but in some cases one's perception may be so limited that distant exposure is of no avail.

The clue to the understanding of the situation seems to be that an individual, without his being aware of it, may live within such a narrow stratum of his own society that he cannot understand his environment. The fact that both the church community and the campus community tend to represent almost exclusively middle- and upper-class affluence strongly suggests that both may tend to suffer a myopia resulting from restricted experience. Outside programs are thus necessary for simply knowing the total community.

This insight is neither anti-intellectualism nor wild-eyed utopianism. Although intelligent action cannot occur apart from knowledge, it is generally accepted that understanding, in the area in which people may be involved, seldom if ever takes place without the emotional element of that involvement. Of course there are limitations. The illiterate and the sophisticate can never completely understand each other. The person who is primarily attached to rural life can never fully understand the urbanite and vice versa. People of one race can never actually put themselves into the skin of a person of another race. What do outsiders know about factory work? Organized labor? Local politics? The school board? The court room? And, narrowing our circle, how well are most of those who are part of the campus ministry acquainted with those churches which are not represented in either the fringe of buildings circling the campus or the circle of their immediate friends?

Universal participation

One of the greatest challenges to the campus minister is the possibility that *everyone* can be involved in the program of the campus ministry. In contrast with the few who will be able to participate in more distant programs, the campus minister can here point to a common need about which *everyone* may rightfully be expected to do something!

Common cause with education

The goals of the campus ministry need not separate the church from other elements related to education. If the educator is interested in the pursuit of truth, isn't the campus ministry also so concerned? If the sociology class is interested in better housing, isn't the campus ministry? If the fraternity is seriously interested in helping the community nursery, isn't the campus ministry? The search for understanding, for opportunities to serve — how fortunate that these are shared!

There is certainly need for the campus ministry to appreciate and maximize its areas of common experience with education. At one time the scholar who took an analytical attitude toward the role of religion in society hesitated to say very much about it because his criticism would arouse an impassioned defense of everything related to the church! Today, however, the climate of the campus has reached the point where a lecturer discussing religion — so long as he is not too positive in his attitude (thus arousing the aggressive secularist) — is apt to receive only a snicker from some listeners and a slightly confused silence from others. The need for maximizing the common experiential area of religion and education is certainly not solely the concern of staff and faculty groups. It is an ironic fact that the secular social analyst is apt to give a more important place to the church in the understanding of social and political life than many a person who considers himself a vital part of the gathered fellowship.

Forms of witness

The Christian who participates in programs directly sponsored by other groups may supplement the witness of his presence by making comments or asking questions about the role of religion in general and Christianity in particular. Thus persons related to the campus ministry who know what they are talking about and are not defensive may make significant contributions. Such witness on the outside, however, comes only through preparation within the gathered community of the church.

The second distinct area of witness is clearly seen in programs sponsored by the campus ministry and distinguished by a content directed toward either the faith, the church, or the role of these in society. The study seminar, the field trip, the weekend consultation or conference, are as important to the campus ministry as worship. In fact, in terms of those outside the fellowship, they may be more important! Naturally, everyone is invited to share in these programs who has the necessary qualifications. It is well enough to restrict meetings of the planning cabinet to its membership, but if members then are the only ones who participate in the program planned, the time has come for that "agonizing reappraisal"!

Finally, much of this outside involvement is *compulsively* service-oriented. The Christian has no monopoly on service or on motivation for service. And surely he must be involved in many things which do not constitute service. Response to human need is so central to the New Testament that it must also be central to the program of the campus ministry! At this point, it is interesting to note that the washing of the disciples' feet on Maundy Thursday takes us into the gathered community. The equally familiar story of the Last Judgment is an account of the expected concern for others in the scattered community. Unfortunately, we still tend to think of service as directed only to abject physical need. No one can overrate the importance of meeting this need in the twentieth century, but it does not provide a very complete picture, for needs can take many other forms.[3]

We must also recognize that all need to receive the ministry of service as well as to give it. A one-way concept of service can easily become the false god around which many programs are built. For this to happen is a double tragedy. In the first place, it rules out our understanding of the brotherhood which we call Christian love. In the second, it distorts service into a form of paternalism. A mutual ministry, on the other hand, includes a conscious or unconscious awareness of our own limitation, a conscious or unconscious respect for the other person, and a recognition of his respect for us. Here service gives us something which knowledge alone cannot yield.

Before turning to the topic of national concern, we must recognize the increasing complexity of the local campus (see Glen O. Martin's chapter on "Campus Culture"). The growth of numerous community junior colleges, the rise of vast commuter institutions,

[3] A personal favorite is W. A. Visser 't Hooft's *The Pressure of Our Common Calling* (New York: Doubleday & Company, 1959), affording an introduction to the demands of Christian service, witness, and fellowship in a form which can be readily shared.

the creation of an increasing number of graduate and research centers, all contribute to the bewildering variety of the American educational scene. There is widespread nostalgia for the campus in a sense that it no longer exists for many a student, professor, and campus minister. The quiet of the campus is gone — to the extent that it ever existed — and the gathered community is more constantly exposed and involved in the outside. Perhaps because of this fact, many of the most interesting and significant outside programs in the last three years have been related to schools which according to pre-World War II standards would have been designated as "anormal."

<h2 style="text-align:center">NATIONAL CONCERN</h2>

In our first section we have been emphasizing programs which may be locally sponsored and which are basically directed toward the understanding of and involvement in the total life of the community. We have stressed the extent to which these programs are an area of common interest to the church and campus communities, and the need for universal involvement. And so, as we begin a discussion of our national concern, there are certain differences which are immediately apparent: (1) Although sponsorship is occasionally shared, it is more likely to be transferred to a national organization or to a local agency located at a distant point. (2) Under these circumstances the participant has an initial degree of objectivity, because he is not so completely identified with a national program as he is with various aspects of the local home community. (3) Also, the recruitment of participants in the program from various parts of the country usually results in an even more heterogeneous group than is found in a locally-controlled and developed program.

In direct educational circles, trips and study tours usually originate with a department on a given campus, or take the form of regional or national conferences and seminars, or become further formalized through special summer courses on a given campus — but these may be widely recognized, so as to draw students from across the nation.

Summer work has long been a tradition for the American student, and the clinical or intern year is a growing pattern. Historically the emphasis on the national scene has been with the churches and voluntary agencies, and continues to be so. As far as this writer was able to determine, service projects in this country began with work camps sponsored by the American Friends Service Committee from 1934 forward. Other groups soon began to explore the use of similar projects. The result was, at the end of World War II, an explosive development in this type of activity. The churches and a number of other voluntary agencies joined in the creation of the Commission on Youth Service Projects and began publication of *Invest Your Summer*.[4] However, with few exceptions, the pattern of such projects until the mid 'fifties was almost exclusively in the area of work camps. Only since then has the concept of community service projects really taken hold. And, with the exception of the American Friends Service Committee, it is only in the last few years that a significant number of projects have actually gone into areas of political and social action divorced from rather set institutional relationships. In fact, the immediate postwar experience with the work camp technique was so uniformly significant that the pattern became almost an idol. Only gradually are the creative dynamics of a wide diversity of project types being fully developed and appreciated. But we shall have more to say of that, of longer-term service and of the National Service Corps as we move from the historical note to consideration of the present.

Americanism without chauvinism

In speaking to the idea of "Americanism without chauvinism," we need to make clear that this concept, when applied to the service aspects of the campus ministry, does not mean a departure from its central responsibility as a Christian ministry. On the contrary, this is simply a development of the point made earlier in this chapter. The average client of the campus ministry was launched as a child into a narrow segment of American society whose views and clichés he has tended to wrap around himself protectively, finding reinforcement from his close associates. Just as we spoke of his need for relating to the total community in the first section, we are now speaking of the need to identify with all elements of American

---

[4] *Invest Your Summer*, Commission on Youth Service Projects, published December 1 of each year. Address: Room 753, 475 Riverside Drive, New York, N.Y. 10027.

society. For the smooth slogans of "The American Way" tend to hide rather than reveal the conflicting and shattered elements of American society. How little we know of the whole! A brilliant high school student now on a full scholarship to a very excellent technical university reported that the most interesting experience of a summer camp was working in the vegetable garden. He had never been able to follow the growth of anything before. Yes, he lived in New York City. But the rate of urbanization is such that there will soon be as many in his situation as the now more familiarly caricatured person straining to see the top of the Empire State Building. Neither New York nor Los Angeles is America. For that matter, neither is the North, the South, the East, nor the West! The substructures within this organic whole defy census. Parenthetically, it is somewhat ironic that the mobility of the American people is perhaps doing more to contribute to the understanding of America in its totality than either the church or the educational community.

But, while affluence still dominates the campus, there are shock waves that are increasingly being felt by a sensitive minority. There is a lack of deep personal satisfaction, an awareness of the world in revolution, and a realization that we are either a conscious or an unconscious part of it. And there is the fear of the Bomb. All of these are on the campus — and the campus community, both church and educational, is either choosing the ostrich security of affluence or grappling with the question, "What can I do, if anything?" Scattered individuals have found responses which yielded them personal satisfaction. Relatively small groups have rallied to face the question of peace and the Bomb. But, with one exception, no single issue has proved strong enough or pervasive enough to be the catalytic agent necessary to mark the transition from protest to significant positive movement. This exception is race.

It is important to take a moment to look at this catalytic movement. Its leadership has been and is in the hands of the "new Negro," though both support and involvement have become increasingly biracial. The focus has been the question of the rights of the Negro as an American citizen. But this is more than a civil question; it is a religious question, a question of the nature of man. It is a "white" problem fully as much as it is a "Negro" problem. If it is fair to say that the Supreme Court decision of 1954 marked a continental divide from the legal standpoint, it is also true that the Montgomery, Alabama, bus strike led by Dr. Martin Luther King, Jr., stands as the moral and spiritual divide. Action and reaction have come from all levels of society, and surely the campus Christian community has been playing a major role. Especially in the South, both Negro and white students found a meaningful answer to the question; "What can I do?" To them involvement has meant not only commitment but sacrifice. Sit-ins furnished a first meaningful form of direct nonviolent action. Jail sentences were one result. Divided families, split churches and campus communities, and personal moral dilemmas were others. The question of moral responsibility for civil disobedience became vital rather than rhetorical. The Student Non-violent Movement was born and — finally — the Northern Student Movement took meaningful shape in 1962.[5] Headlines tended to move from sit-ins to freedom rides, and other forms of direct action followed. True, this has been a minority movement, "more's the pity!"

Affluence is for many the direct or indirect reason for adopting a chauvinistic attitude. The problem of the rights of the Negro citizens of the United States, however, has struck at both the affluence and the chauvinism. National concern comes only when both are challenged, when, in fact, the blessings of the United States are not used to hide its problems. Direct nonviolent action supports a clear claim of American citizenship, focuses on the human problem, is not restricted to any one segment of society, deals with an issue central to the entire world revolution, and forces consideration on moral and religious grounds as well as social and political grounds. The contemporary racial revolution is perhaps the most dramatic issue which the United States must meet, but it is also suggestive in many ways of the problems of housing, medical aid, education, the plight of the American Indian, and many others. In effect, it is a reminder that "faith without works is dead."

Although, unfortunately, the church as an institution continues

[5] You will want continuing information and up-to-date addresses and reports. The Department of Racial and Cultural Relations, National Council of Churches, 475 Riverside Drive, New York, N.Y. 10027, can supplement your other sources and contribute in its own right!

to lag in its own integration, nevertheless religious conviction has been an essential element not only in the leadership of the move toward the integration of American society, but also in many of those involved as followers. In this movement such people have been and are involved with large and powerful secular groups. While the long-run goals are on the whole unified and clear, day-to-day tactics involve actions on which there is a very legitimate difference of opinion. Within the campus ministry, for instance, dismissal from jobs and disassociation from group sponsorship have been frequent institutional judgments made on those who have become involved.

But here the long-run question is not one of integrity. The real danger of the future is that too many shall tire of being upset and will sue for peace "at any price." The danger here is subtle: That we shall withdraw from immersion in the total struggle in which our forces work with those of a myriad of other organizations, and that we shall then erect our own more pristine barricades characterized by "lessened moral ambiguities." Such action would constitute a retreat from involvement. If the creative and imaginative development of campus ministry programs outside the gathered community is to continue, it will be because this ministry responds to the deepest problems of our society in cooperation with the forces technically and/or actually not related to the gathered community.

It was not until Moses, in the experience of the burning bush, was convinced of God's presence where Moses himself was working, that his spiritual isolation ceased. Then his day-to-day activities began to seem relevant to his greatest hopes and dreams. Likewise, it is only as the experience of the gathered community is validated in the scattered community at work that the deeper satisfactions can emerge. The question here is one which education by itself can never adequately answer: it is one of commitment. Such commitment may be made from a secular base, but, for those with a religious faith, the issues involved stand at the very heart of it.

Again, let us not draw too sharp a line between the role of the educational community and that of the campus ministry. The way in which facts are presented and the context out of which they are presented join in making education an exceedingly persuasive force. Yet neither persuasion nor even indoctrination can be raised to the level of commitment, for persuasion or indoctrination is the act of another's will, but commitment is an act of a person's self-will.

A crucial question which the campus ministry must ask is whether it will realistically face the question of national interest and national problems, or seek the escapism of a sentimentalized rationalization of the role of religion which "shield it" from playing its normal and proper role in the daily rough-and-tumble.

New patterns

The church has always been interested in letting its constituency know about church missions and institutions. Denominational journals did the major job of sharing information, and personal visits were also encouraged. Now, however, the psychological annihilation of space and the wanderlust of our mobile population have greatly increased the amount of travel. In fact, the average individual's vacation is almost bound to take him close to one or more of the centers of church influence and activity in the United States. But increasingly the campus ministry has gone a step or two further. To the local study groups and traditional conferences and consultations there have been added tours, some serious travel seminars, and a constantly proliferating number of service projects (incorporating varying degrees of study). Service, travel, and escape from family are among the motivations of the students — but the realization of the need for broadened involvement has certainly motivated the campus ministers in their support of nationally planned and recruited projects.

The reference, *Invest Your Summer,* is a familiar friend, with listings of work camps, community service, institutional service, the working seminar, study seminars, caravans, individual service (two months to two years), and related programs. Many have watched the number of agencies listed in *IYS* grow to their present total of more than forty. Of special importance are two rather subtle changes: (1) A few years ago the listings would have fallen primarily into the category of work camps, but in the 1963 edition only six of twenty-five pages on which programs are listed fall under this heading. (2) Many still think primarily of international programs, yet there are twenty pages on which projects within the United States are listed. While lack of detailed information on overseas projects means that one overseas listing will frequently cover a number of programs, the percentage of domestic listings is still impressive. Both the growth in number and the improvement characterized by diversification and greater quality control owe much to the sponsoring groups, but they owe an equal amount to the campus ministry, through which not only project members but also a large percentage of leadership come.

The fact that a few years ago the great majority of service projects were work camps and that the pattern of work camps almost became enshrined has already been mentioned. So has the growing understanding now developing of the essential differences in the dynamics of the varying types of programs and projects. Another problem constantly faced is that of *for whom or for what* a given program is organized. At this point the tour, the study seminar, and some other types are in an unambiguous position. Like the classroom there is no doubt that they are directed toward the participants. This is excellent! Our difficulty, however, arises when we look at work camps, community service, institutional service, and individual service. The campus minister, properly aware of his responsibility for his clientele, is more or less subtly tempted to look upon their "development" as the reason for service projects. Certainly it is hoped that this is one of the consequences of participation. It would be less than honest — indeed it would be flaunting the obvious — if one failed to recognize that many outside programs are organized entirely because the campus ministry has this clientele. But if the service given is not sufficiently needed and worthwhile to justify the project, then the project or program is a phony, an imposition on the location at which it is held. Some other type of program should be designed to benefit the clientele.

This problem is far from simple, and a complete discussion is not in order at this point. Nevertheless, it is presented here for a very specific reason. The campus minister is the chief promoter of these projects all over the country. It is very important that he ask himself whether a given student has anything to contribute in a particular service project or should be directed toward another type of service project — or perhaps to an entirely different type of program. The most careful planning by a sponsoring group counts for nothing unless recruitment is thoughtfully done and references are frankly given. Surely some are screened out as a result of such care, but in most instances the participants could be more intelligently selected than they are, and the leaders could have a more adequate picture of the group as the period together begins.

The conscientious objector during World War II was primarily responsible for the beginning of the churches' development of longer-term projects. Although the C.O.'s worked under numerous agencies, it was chiefly the peace churches which accepted responsibility for them and whose substantial year-round service programs have resulted. By the middle 'fifties, some trends began to emerge: (1) Professional schools began a rapid expansion of their clinical or intern years to provide the experience which was not possible within the gathered community. This was an intensification, both in terms of time and quality, of the custom of the American student to try to find summer work in his field. (2) Church and civic institutions of various sorts, finding themselves in a very disadvantageous labor situation, began to evaluate more carefully the possibility of using one- to two-year volunteers. (3) Alumni of summer projects began to volunteer in small numbers for longer service. Obviously, training was demanded by this longer period of service. The United Church of Christ [6] was the first non-peace church to establish a center for this purpose, and the first to establish such a center exclusively oriented to preparation for a year of *domestic* church-related service, designed to supplement agency or institutional training. (4) And, as the readers well know, to the trickle of college-age and close-to-college-age persons there is added a growing number of the "untired retired" giving similar service.

On February 14, 1963, President Kennedy in a special message to Congress asked for a National Service Corps. Concerning this "domestic peace corps" there are a number of generalizations which would seem safe: There will be a genuine response to this appeal for service. The NSC will appeal economically to the college student who will see it as a valuable experience and a prestige factor while taking some financial pressure off the last year or two. The NSC will put a premium on those who are not only qualified in other ways but have the Christian understanding of service, though the adjective may never be used. The NSC will again force the student

---

[6] Address: Voluntary Service Center, R.R. 2, Pottstown, Pa.

to choose between definitely church-related openings and itself. There is no doubt about three chief goals of the NSC. One is to do necessary and desirable work which might not otherwise get done. Another is to provide involvement in depth across various social lines. The third is to arouse communities to self-help. The sponsors of NSC are aware that democracy is not only dependent upon citizens whose individual rights are respected and whose basic needs are met but also upon those whose understanding of America is as comprehensive as possible.

Again, it is necessary to recognize that if this program is enthusiastically supported only in the circle of an increasingly cloistered gathered community it will be self-defeating. This writer does not think the campus ministry can be duped in this way. We are at the threshold of a very fluid period. The interpenetration and interrelationships of the gathered and scattered communities of church and campus will be such that clear lines, where they now still exist, will be blurred at many points. This is a challenging time — a time when the experience of the gathered community must be a freeing experience, quite consciously and joyously running the risk of losing any ready identity in the scattered community, but aware that its witness is never in vain!

International Involvement

There is no doubt that, from the American standpoint, the outstanding physical event of the post-World War II era has been the destruction of space. I am not thinking of outer space, as exciting as the explorations there have been. Nor would I minimize the impact of instantaneous communication as typified by intercontinental telecasts. As you read that Mach 2.2 rocket planes are on the drawing board, remember that even the comparatively slow planes in World War II were adequate to knock the psychological props from under the isolation of the Midwest! The individual American no longer dreams, "How I wish I could go there!" Instead he begins to make plans. Along with this attack on space, most of the world has been eager also to obliterate time, cramming the work of centuries into a few years. Immediately after World War II we saw this tremendous haste focused in the supreme efforts of Europe to make a rapid economic recovery. And, much more dramatically, the newer nations are attempting to move from whatever their current developmental level is into the modern industrial world in one giant step, to be taken, preferably, in less than a generation! We Americans are part of this revolutionary world, and the obliteration of space makes possible the development of travel, of study, and of service in it — and promises to make these experiences increasingly a matter of genuine exchange, to the benefit of all.

Thank goodness the passport lines are long, the ships are filled, and the airlines are constantly stepping up their schedules. Everyone can benefit from the enriching experience of international involvement. Since this trend is the focus of much of our interest as campus ministers, why has it been delayed until the third section of this essay? The answer is clear. The basis of the life of each one, and the place where the campus ministry has its responsibility for universal involvement, is in the local community. The step from community to nation is a matter of logical enlargement within a single society. It is against the background of our understanding of both that we plunge into the once-large world which has become so small a neighborhood.

The basic outline of the story of the American churches in world involvement can be compressed into a few sentences. Most of our denominations either came from Europe or developed indigenously in relation to European churches. During the nineteenth century they embarked upon far-reaching mission programs, in which evangelism was joined by education, efforts to feed the hungry, and practical service of many kinds. This pattern continued substantially unchanged until after World War I and in great measure until after World War II. That there was often a serious confusion of western culture with the Christian faith is the cause of tragic consequences with which we must live, but these do not form the main thread of our narrative.

Since 1945, the developments in our purview have multiplied. Almost simultaneously with the outbreak of the war the World Council of Churches had been established in a provisional form. In spite of the conflict, it had functioned, and contact had been maintained. So the end of the war found the numerous members in closer and more potentially creative relationship with one another than they had been at its beginning. Of exceedingly great importance was the fact that its membership was never limited to western countries; it was truly worldwide.

One division of the World Council, now the Division of Interchurch Aid, Refugees and World Service, immediately established itself. It has done an excellent job in the area of interchurch aid, but most people think of it primarily as the relief arm of the church. This is its public image. It has become the symbol of the churches' concern for man as man. The record of response by groups not usually cordial to the church indicates that it has spoken with a loud clear voice. It continues to do so, and is now opening its ranks for highly selected volunteers to spend approximately two years in service.

Almost before the war-wearied people of Europe knew that V-E day was a reality, American Christians had been dispatched by the churches to assist not only in relief but in rebuilding. One of these, a minister of the United Church of Christ, the Reverend Mr. Joseph Howell, was serving under the former Congregational Christian Service Committee. Why, he asked, could not young American Christians come over, volunteering their own time and paying their own way, to assist in the reconstruction of Europe, with personal growth as a major by-product? As a result the first ecumenical work camp was held in 1947 at College Cevenol in La Chambon, France. This program became the first of the Youth Department of the World Council of Churches when it was organized in 1948. In 1949 the first camp in Japan was held. Now about twelve hundred people participate each year in projects, diverse in nature, whose locus has shifted from being predominantly European to covering the entire globe. In 1955, the Commission on Ecumenical Voluntary Service Projects of the National Student Christian Federation was organized to administer American participation abroad and the development of ecumenical projects in the United States. There was agreement that, insofar as possible, international programs and projects should be conducted on an ecumenical basis rather than being sponsored by individual denominations.

Not only was there a major geographic shift from Europe to other parts of the world in the middle 'fifties, but also the Hungarian revolt led to the use of volunteers for longer period of time. The emergence of new nations, as well as the recovery of Europe, led to a broadening of the type of projects from the work camp to community service and on to several others. This process of diversification continues and the development of longer-than-summer opportunities is gradually multiplying.

Meanwhile, to meet the needs of education and certain other service areas, mission boards developed short-term (usually three-year) programs. Junior-year-abroad programs developed, and denominationally-sponsored international study tours became annual program items.

Developing patterns

From the standpoint of the church, the image of the 'sixties has yet to emerge. There are signs in the sky! The beginning of year-long work camps, the use of some carefully-screened volunteers by Church World Service, the "Church Peace Corps groups" being organized and sent out by the churches in a number of nations, the appointment of Canon Chiu by the World Council of Churches to help in the exchange of information and personnel — all of these are significant. Also most important is the determination of the churches that there will be genuine exchange, with multinational and multiconfessional involvement. Impressive studies and pilot projects [7] are under way, but the "take-off point" has not yet been reached. Major attention must be given to developments in education which extend back into the early 'fifties and to the Peace Corps, this well-known child of the 'sixties!

Prior to World War II, American educational institutions were primarily concerned with individual students who wished to study abroad on the graduate level. Almost without exception, these people were directed to Europe. If they studied non-western history and culture at all, it was primarily in relation to the impact of the west upon them. The jar of World War II, however, was rapidly followed by the hastening demise of colonialism and the emerging development of newly-independent nations. The "old world" had passed, and new patterns in education emerged. The wanderlust was happily allowed to express itself at this point. Junior-year programs developed on an individual basis and then shifted to a group

[7] Paul Loeffler's *A Layman Abroad in the Mission of the Church* (New York: Friendship Press, 1962) is a particularly fine study of trends and pilot projects.

basis, some involving group enrollment in a foreign institution, and some taking faculty along. With the help of foreign lecturers, these programs constituted essentially "the American institution" abroad. Such a program frequently cost a student no more than he was already paying. The number of colleges and universities establishing overseas programs is still rapidly increasing. Meanwhile, the Fulbright program and the growing foundation-grant programs take increasing numbers of faculty overseas as part of one-way or exchange programs.

Africa, Asia, and South America began to make their voices heard. *This development was overdue!* Much of the educational leadership of America heard these voices and responded. A very different educational situation prevailed on those continents, compared with that of Europe. Except for certain specified fields of scholarship, there were few graduate programs fitting into the American pattern. Nevertheless, educators were convinced of the worth and importance of study in these parts of the world. Thus it became recognized that while some educational programs abroad are essentially academic, others should stress the value of an intercultural study and living experience.

The sum total result of these programs has been to make educational travel "big business." The new approach speaks effectively vis-a-vis tourism; not that tourism is inherently bad, but that it is (from the educational viewpoint) inherently wasteful in that tourism does not provide that depth of involvement which experience outside the gathered community of the campus should provide. With certain exceptions, these programs correctly center on their contribution to the development of the individual.

In February of 1963, the Peace Corps [8] advertised six thousand openings for service overseas. Barring catastrophe, that number will inevitably increase. The greatest number in any single profession will be the teachers, but the diversified group that can be gathered under the general title of "community development" will probably become an increasingly large segment. And, on the basis of its present orientation, there are solid reasons for the campus ministry

[8] The Peace Corps has information releases which can be mailed to you regularly, if you so request. And, of course, the information of special concern to the churches can be obtained by writing to National Council Peace Corps Office, 475 Riverside Drive, New York, N.Y. 10027.

to encourage participation in the Peace Corps. Born in 1961, the Corps is sponsored by the government, but it needs to be distinguished from other operations of the government overseas. Certainly the goals of the Peace Corps are in harmony with the concerns of the United States, yet the total picture of its functioning makes it quite unique. First, the Peace Corps goes only where asked; second, it always works under a contract approved by the host government and administered by it or by an approved organization within that nation's borders; third, the Peace Corps volunteer almost never operates in a technically supervisory position; fourth, he is present to serve in the middle-job capacity; fifth, he lives on a basis similar to his national counterparts; sixth, he has no responsibility to follow a U.S. "party line" and is specifically not on a political job or looked at as a political representative in any way whatsoever; seventh, for a variety of reasons quite clear, he represents no vested interests private or public. Peace Corps projects are, from this end of the line, frequently under the direction of private agencies or educational institutions. Their acceptance abroad has been such that, as of this writing, the Peace Corps has been invited to increase its program in each operating country. The Peace Corps clearly seems to be one of the overseas opportunities which the campus ministry would most consistently like to promote.

In short, the churches offer the major opportunity for short-term service projects, plus an increasing number of individualized highly selective opportunities of longer duration. Meanwhile, overseas educational programs are assuming mass proportions, and the Peace Corps program offers numerous openings for the development and fulfillment of Christian vocation.

World, "front and center"

But how central is all this to the campus ministry? Isn't short-term service for the affluent? Isn't longer-term service for the few? Can't one say that preparation for world involvement, when taken literally, is and should be a sideline in the campus ministry? Shouldn't much of our concern be directed toward the international student in our midst, an opportunity to which this essay does not address itself? There is no doubt about the overwhelming importance of the campus ministry's involvement with international students and with training for world citizenship. But an understanding of the extent to which this ministry is concerned with direct preparation for personal international involvement is probably one of the least appreciated of all the pressures crowding in upon the campus minister. Why?

Look at the figures! From a number of sources it is possible to reach some general conclusions: There are nearly one million persons related to our armed forces overseas and there are nearly another million living overseas in other jobs. The overwhelming majority of this second million are connected with business or government. Relatively speaking, only a few reflect the concerns of the church or of education. But the contribution of the campus ministry must be measured in terms of its assistance in the preparation to the *total* number overseas! It is not too much to say that every part of the constituency must be prepared and challenged for overseas service. Although this chapter has been directed primarily at selected programs, the responsibility of the campus ministry must be measured in the larger dimension.

The piles of announcements and brochures from educational institutions and from the various private and church-related boards and agencies are to the campus ministry tools for interpreting significant opportunities, some involving study, a great number involving service within the framework of the church. These we tend to emphasize. And yet the vast number of our clientele will, in their overseas relationship, be in an entirely different role. Their presence will have no relation to the church at all, and the witness of the Christian will be whatever he chooses, within the limits of the program or the project, to make it. One of the greatest dangers is that our concern for "special projects" will keep the campus ministry from giving adequate emphasis to preparation for witness in those overseas involvements which are totally lacking in any direct institutional relationship.

A commencement faith

If the campus ministry does not worry enough about the preceding point, it should be interesting to turn to a problem that may be overemphasized. Frequently the question is asked: "Why do so many of the finest of our young people who go into the Peace

Corps frankly say they do not wish to go overseas under the auspices of the church?" There seem to be at least three answers. In the first place they feel that the overseas missions of the church are identified too completely with the past and with western influence, rather than with the emerging nations and with the future. Every mission executive would probably admit that there has been some truth in this view but would quite properly point out the changing climate of missions and the extent to which mission personnel is already working at the direction of the national churches. Probably most important is the second point: These people in large numbers are saying that they do not know what they believe with sufficient clarity to be evangelistic — and frequently that they are not sure they believe in the types of evangelism with which they are familiar. Third and finally they say: Let us serve, and let our service speak. What is true of the Peace Corps at this point is also verified by Operation Crossroads Africa and by the strong appeal which the American Friends Service Committee has in its international program. The church can gradually live down the first problem, and no one but the young person can meet the second — so let the campus ministry be grateful for the third. Let it promote projects as wholeheartedly as its own! Overseas involvement is in many ways a beginning, rather than an end. Let it mark a commencement, and it may well be that a more solid and relevant dynamic faith will be one of the things they will acquire, rather than one which they take with them. Dr. Arnold Toynbee, in his book, *America and the World Revolution,*[9] speaks at length to the question of freedom as a root of human dignity. He has a chapter entitled: "Can America Rejoin Her Own Revolution?" He feels that, while the march toward human freedom got its major modern push in 1776, the pressures of affluence, variously described, have so curtailed our zeal as to allow communism to seize the psychological initiative in many parts of the world. Can America, he asks, shake herself from her lethargy and recapture the leadership of "her own revolution"? It can be done, he suggests, but only with a

[9] The entire volume of Arnold Toynbee, *American and the World Revolution,* (New York: Oxford University Press, 1962), is excellent, but the fourth, fifth, and sixth chapters are "required reading" for many of the concerns of this essay.

radical upheaval in our own thinking. The most positive hope for this he sees in the arising impact of the lay mission movement — the Peace Corps. It is difficult to disagree with his analysis, however much one may question the adequacy of his prescription. I mention Dr. Toynbee's point because, while the language is secular, the problem is obviously religious. Clearly, the answers to the questions of faith are determined in the crucible of involvement. The preparation and continued sustenance of the gathered community can be completed and its meaning discovered only as it participates in the scattered fellowship.

CONCLUSION

While one cannot discuss the role of travel, study, and service in the campus ministry without relating it to the educational community, there is no doubt about where the emphasis has been placed! The fundamental question faced was: To what extent must faith and theology grow from broad experience as well as be nourished from within the gathered community? The answer: Life in the scattered community is as important as that in the gathered community. The witness of the church in the college and university is limited to the extent that its witness is limited outside. If the church is not willing to lose its life, it probably will! If the church does not experience its existence as the scattered community, it is socially irrelevant as a gathered community.

There is a parallel in the relationship of education and the church to the total social structure. The interesting parallelism of these two make the role of the campus minister much more difficult in many ways, but in others multiplies the opportunities available. The extent to which the campus minister is a firm believer in the integral relationship of the gathered to the scattered fellowship will determine his understanding and use of the special programs of travel, study, and service offered in ever-increasing number to the members of the campus community.

It has been difficult at many points to refrain from the discussion of the convulsive nature of the worldwide revolution of our time. Unless the revolutionary nature of the gospel becomes an actuality to many through the campus ministry, we shall not only "lose out" in our possible role in the world's development, but we shall do so because we have lost contact with the very faith which we profess. God's love and grace are by no means limited to those who call themselves Christians, and the God of history certainly does not speak only in the still small voice. The harsh, strident, chaotic, cruel, and occasionally kind voice of the social and political realities of our day speaks of the presence of the God and Father of our Lord Jesus Christ just as surely as the hymn of praise and the reading of the Scripture. The life of the gathered fellowship and that of the scattered fellowship are neither alternating nor separated, but simultaneous and part of an indivisible unity.

11: Counseling
the College Student

JOHN R. MOTT ONCE REMARKED that if he had his life to live over again he would place himself alongside a great university because in it were the greatest needs and the greatest opportunities in the world. Anyone who works with students is aware of what he meant. They represent the top levels of the population in terms of ability and training. Their whole future is ahead of them — they have great potential for leadership and service — but they also have problems. They have far-reaching decisions that must be made, plans to be developed, tensions to work through. The very fact of being a student has some problems of its own.

Anyone who works with students in any capacity has accepted a sacred responsibility, which is never more evident than at those times when the student comes seeking personal help. Without meaning to be melodramatic, we may observe that the way the counselor handles this hour may be very influential in this student's whole future. When the student comes to face some problem, make some decision, discuss some feeling of guilt, anxiety, or inadequacy, then the pastor has a most sacred responsibility.

Charles F. Kemp is professor of practical ministries at Brite College of the Bible, Texas Christian University, and is author of six books including **The Pastor and Vocational Counseling.**

225

EARLY BACKGROUNDS OF STUDENT COUNSELING

Thornton Merriam, in one of the few studies of religious counseling of university students, says, "The question of the place of religious counseling in the total educational program of a college or university can be properly understood only in the perspective of history." [1]

When we examine the history of higher education in America we find most colleges and universities were established by religious bodies for religious purposes. The sources for counseling and guidance were twofold: the friendly teacher and the pastor whose church adjoined a campus. W. H. Cowley, in an article on student personnel work, writes of the perennial need for counseling with regard to the selection of courses, the development of social intelligence, and what to do about home sickness or love sickness, and comments: "In the nineteenth century faculty members engaged in all three of these relationships." [2]

One cannot overestimate the influence of these men. The greatest contribution some teachers have made has not been the subject matter they taught as much as it has been the influence of their lives and the friendly relationships they had with students. Harry Emerson Fosdick says that the most important single influence of his college career, especially when he was having difficulty with his religious thinking, was simply the presence of William Newton Clarke on the campus.[3] Mark Hopkins and his log would not meet some contemporary standards of good counseling technique, but he was tremendously effective.

One of the greatest sources of religious guidance with students has always been the pastor who was located near a campus, who understood students and had time to work with them. Horace Bushnell, Phillip Brooks, and (more recently), Harry Emerson Fosdick have all been men who knew personal struggle in their own lives and were able to speak with such clarity and insight that stu-

[1] Thornton Ward Merriam, *Religious Counseling of College Students* (Washington: American Council on Education, 1943), p. 53.

[2] W. H. Cowley, "The Nature of Student Personnel Work," *Educational Record*, January, 1936, p. 222.

[3] Harry Emerson Fosdick, *On Being Fit to Live With* (New York: Harper and Row, 1946), p. 190.

dents came to hear them and then sought them out for personal help. Brooks' influence became so widespread that people from all over the country would write him about students who were studying in Boston. They say Brooks took time to look up each one of them and gave him his personal attention. When he preached in Harvard Chapel, he was almost besieged afterward by students seeking interviews.

A religious leader of this previous generation who had almost phenomenal success in speaking to students was Henry Drummond. After the publication of his books, he literally became the counselor of youth by the thousands throughout England, America, and Australia. His friend and biographer, George Adam Smith, said:

> One who heard Drummond through several years of the students' movements said there was one power which distinguished him beyond every other preacher to men, and that was the power of so speaking as invariably to move from one to two hundred of his audience of seven or eight hundred—not merely to stay to an after-meeting, but to talk with him one by one and face to face. This power never failed him with the students and it was by it he left an abiding mark on many hundreds of lives.[4]

Wherever he went, students sought him for interviews. He was constantly seen walking on the campus with some students or engaging them in conversation in some dormitory at all hours.

LATER DEVELOPMENTS IN COUNSELING WITH STUDENTS

The influence of the friendly teacher and the local pastor still continues and is still valuable, but developments in the field of higher education have made their contributions alone inadequate and the development of additional resources imperative. With the rapid increase in the size of colleges, it became obvious the pastor of the local church could not meet the needs. The Student Christian Associations (both YMCA and YWCA) were the first to enter the scene. Here the great names are John R. Mott and Robert E. Speer. Like Henry Drummond, they spent much of their time in student counseling. One letter from John R. Mott indicates how common this was in his experience. This was written while he was visiting a campus on a speaking tour:

[4] George Adam Smith, *The Life of Henry Drummond* (New York: McClure, Phillips & Co., 1901) , p. 358.

I then fixed interviews in a neighboring hotel with men who wished to see me. There were so many . . . that I limited men to ten or fifteen minutes each, although in certain cases I extended the time. My interviews that night kept me from 9:30 to 1:00 a.m. On Monday morning, I devoted about three hours to similar interviews. . . . Three hours more in the afternoon were given to interviews. In all I had over forty interviews with these inquirers. . . ."[5]

With the shift from denominational to state-controlled universities, the leaders in the churches became aware that in almost every denomination there were more students attending the state universities than their own schools. To meet this need there appeared a new form of student ministry, the university pastorate. More recently, there has developed another expression of ministry to students, the university chaplain or director of religious activities. He is employed not by a church but by the administration of the university. Suffice it to say here that the church has developed a specialized ministry to students, although it has taken many forms all involving much counseling.

At the same time as the churches were becoming aware of the need for a special ministry to students, the colleges and universities were becoming aware of the need for individual attention and guidance. As early as 1905, William Rainey Harper, noted Baptist layman at the University of Chicago said, "There should be a diagnosis of each student, in order to discover his capacities, his tastes, his tendencies, his weaknesses, and his defects; and upon the basis of such a diagnosis his course of study should be arranged. . . . Every student should be treated as if he were the only student in the institution."

Through a combination of circumstances, Harper's ideas became rather widely accepted. The rapid development of the psychological disciplines, as well as the appearance and growth of the mental hygiene movement and the vocational guidance movement, served to focus attention on the problem. The increased interest in testing and counseling provided methods and techniques that could be used in understanding the student and helping him with his educational, vocational, and personal problems.

The phenomenal growth in college and university attendance

[5] Basil Mathews, *John R. Mott, World Citizen* (New York and London: Harper & Brothers, 1934), pp. 160-161.

made some program almost a necessity. From 1890 to 1924, while the general population was increasing by 78%, the number of students increased 445%. As late as 1920, only two schools claimed more than 2,000 students, but many now have more than 20,000. The old concept of the informal, friendly relationship of professor and student has almost disappeared. The curriculum has expanded almost as rapidly as the enrollment, making the choice of a course of study and a vocational plan increasingly complex.

To meet this need a new area of specialization was created, that of the university counselor or personnel worker. This new field has developed rapidly; it already has specialists within its own ranks. Universities have an extremely wide variation in the amount and quality of such services available. Some use psychiatrists on their staff; some use psychologists; most have psychometrists and depend strongly on batteries of tests. Some conduct study-habit clinics; some use group guidance; some include speech therapists, reading specialists, etc.

These men are in a unique position to help. They are usually well trained in personality dynamics and in counseling methods and techniques. They have available information for understanding the student, drawn from a battery of tests, grade averages, etc. They have the symbolic role (which may help or hinder) of a psychologist and a counselor whose main function is to offer guidance.

The Pastor's Unique Opportunity

The pastor has a unique opportunity, too. It might seem that, with the appearance of these specialists in counseling, his responsibilities would be diminished, but such has not been the case. There are still far more needs on the campus than any one group of counselors can meet and some which are a primary responsibility of the pastor.

The two groups should be working in closer cooperation than in most cases they are now doing. The university pastor has a distinct advantage over the pastor in the average community by virtue of the fact these other specialists are available. Here is a referral resource he can use if need be for special problems or needs. Here is an invaluable source of information concerning a student's aptitudes, intellectual capacities, interests, and personality — one that can help tremendously in understanding the individual student. One survey we conducted indicated that university counselors would welcome cooperation with university pastors at such points but that the pastors seldom request it.

The university pastor also has some opportunities that other personnel workers do not have. He has a naturally informal relationship with students that the professional counselor cannot be expected to maintain. Much effective counseling is done in informal conversations, over a cup of coffee, on a retreat, or after a discussion group.

The religious worker has a natural group to which the students can relate themselves and which can be used for group guidance. Much has been written on group dynamics, the need of feeling accepted by and belonging to a meaningful group. This is a very powerful resource.

The pastoral counselor is not identified with the administration of a college or university. He does not make out grades. A student can tell him a story of misbehavior without the threat of any disciplinary action. There is no embarrassment about going to a pastor's office or study as there sometimes is in going to a counseling center.

The religious worker, too, has a symbolic role. This can be a help with some students, a hindrance with others. He has had special training which qualifies him to help with spiritual and religious concerns.

WHO IS THE STUDENT?

We have said enough about the counselor. Who is the student that he counsels and what are his problems? The religious worker on a campus is working in a distinctive atmosphere and with a select group of people. A college or university has a society all its own; it has its status systems, in-groups and out-groups, cultural and vocational interests, its own folkways, customs, traditions, and taboos. The one thing that ties all these things together is that it is an academic institution, organized and maintained for educational purposes.

All counseling must be seen in terms of the framework of the institution in which the counselor works. (The methods, techniques, referrals, etc. differ according to whether one is the chaplain of a mental hospital, the pastor of a rural church, or a campus minister.)

So, first of all, the pastor must know the world of the campus. This is the world in which the student lives. This is where his problems arise and where they must be worked out. To know it is not easy. Campuses differ. There is quite a different atmosphere on a state university campus from that of the campus of a small denominational college, an Ivy League school in the East, a junior college in the Southwest, a municipal university, or an agricultural college campus. There are even great differences among colleges on the same campus, or departments within one college. The variation in attitudes, interests, and behavior between the students in the department of physical education and the department of fine arts is one example. The difference can be very great between philosophy majors and business majors, between engineers and theological candidates. Each pastor must know his campus, its mores, its own patterns. As much as possible he must maintain a relationship with all students.

The pastor on a campus is working with a specific age group, whereas the pastor of a church works with all ages. The campus worker deals with later adolescence and young adulthood. His is a select group intellectually, for it comprises only those who continue their education beyond high school. A gradual screening has been going on since the primary grades, continuing through college entrance exams, and the freshman year on the campus. Those who are left are, to a considerable degree, the ones at the top of the curve intellectually.

The first-year student is living in a new environment; very often he is away from home for the first time. Moral restraints of home, church, and community are gone, and homesickness may be a real factor. If he comes from a small town and a small high school, he may find more people in the freshman class than the entire population of his home town. He is confronted with a wide variety of social, athletic, and cultural activities outside the classroom. The pressure for a student's time can be terrific and many face this problem with no previous background of organizing and disciplining their time.

It is no wonder that students are often a bit bewildered and confused. Chad Walsh, who as a professor has a chance to observe students firsthand, describes the modern student this way: "He is confused, well-meaning, likeable, quietly wistful for something — he isn't quite sure what." [6] This picture does not mean to imply they are any more confused than the rest of the population. Many are mature and well adjusted. It simply is to recognize they do have problems and great possibilities, and they benefit from a face-to-face relationship with some one with whom they can talk.

THE COMMON VENTURES OF YOUTH

Student counseling is vital because this is the age when the young person is making decisions that will affect his entire future. His own happiness, his vocational and professional achievements, his contribution to society, are all being determined by the choices that he makes here. In the main it is during the student years that one makes the choice of a life partner, a life vocation, and a life philosophy. The student determines what educational goals he will pursue, how he will invest his time and talents. He determines those values and commitments by which he will live.

Some students make these choices without much tension, but for others it may be a very difficult and trying experience. To aid even one student in making one of these decisions is a most sacred task.

It is commonly recognized that religious problems are accentuated on a college campus. Some students are faced with the necessity of completely reorienting their thinking. In many cases it may be the student's first contact with points of view other than his own. It may be the first time he has heard his home church or the church of his parents challenged or debated. This crisis is further complicated by the fact that so many students come to the campus with very limited background and training. Thornton Merriam says, "What religion they have is sometimes chiefly a body of sentiments, prejudices, and conventional behavior. . . . The scanty deposit of ideas from childhood training is insufficient capital for the intellectual market of the campus." [7] This generalization may be unfair

[6] Chad Walsh, "Flat Minds, Kind Hearts, and Five Arts," *The Christian Scholar*, June, 1953, p. 100.

[7] Merriam, *op. cit.*, p. 40.

to some students, but the circumstances are so common that every campus religious worker will recognize its truth.

Such problems can cause great stress which is often accompanied by anxiety and guilt. The pastor is the one who is in the key position to render a service at this point, for this is an area which the professional counselors, as a rule, do not wish to enter. Here they want the pastor to be the specialist to whom they can refer. During an entire academic career the satisfactory working through of such issues may well be the most significant thing that the student accomplishes.

While the pastor or religious worker is concerned primarily with religious matters, he is working in an academic atmosphere and will be confronted with academic problems. Many professional counselors feel that the religious worker should move with extreme caution in the fields of educational and vocational guidance; some would prefer that he not attempt it at all. They have reasons for their words of caution. Educational guidance is a highly complicated field and involves many specialized skills. Correctly carried out, it requires a knowledge of psychological tests and their interpretation and a thorough acquaintance with the curriculum both as to specific courses and to fields of study. It is concerned with educational techniques such as study habits and reading abilities. It demands an acquaintance with scholarship sources, speech clinics, school practices, rules, and traditions.

The religious worker must recognize his limitations and work with those who have skills and resources he does not have. At the same time he cannot completely separate himself from responsibility for educational guidance. Because of his relationship with students, some come to him who cannot be persuaded to go to a school counselor. Some of the problems he deals with that are of a personal or religious nature may have educational implications. It is very common for a student to come to his pastor with a problem of dissatisfaction with his educational plan or vocational goal, with feelings of inadequacy and discouragement that have an important relationship to his educational progress. Many things hinder optimal educational achievement other than ability or study habits, such as worry over finances, social or family conflicts, adolescent revolt against authority, anxiety or guilt over moral questions, emo-

tional conflicts over religious or philosophical questions. These are
as likely to be brought to the pastor as the university counselor.
Here the pastor can be of service both to the student and to the
personnel service of the university.

Closely related to educational matters is the whole area of vocational choice. The significance of this is obvious. The student's
entire future career is concerned. His personal happiness, his economic well being, his place in society, and his contribution to his
generation all depend upon his making this decision wisely and
well. The fact that many people have a difficult time making a
decision is evidenced by the fact that so many students change their
majors while in college. The intensity of the struggle that some
students face is recorded in hundreds of counselors' files. The fact
that many do not make the decision wisely is revealed in a number
of surveys which point up the amount of vocational dissatisfaction
that exists in our society. The number of people who dislike their
work, or just plain endure it, is one of the tragedies of our generation. The student is at the age when these questions are being
faced and these decisions are being made.

The same precautions mentioned about educational guidance
also apply to vocational guidance. On the other hand, the same set
of circumstances also indicate that the religious worker cannot escape this responsibility. There is one area of vocational guidance
in which he is looked to as a specialist, namely the counseling of
those who are considering one of the many church vocations. Professional counselors are not aware of the different opportunities
such as religious education, missions, campus ministry, religious
journalism, the military and institutional chaplaincy, and many
others. They do not know of the different denominational requirements, the seminaries that are available, scholarship opportunities, etc. They do not feel comfortable in discussing the religious
motivation for such a career and often do not understand the meaning of a "call" to the ministry. In these areas, the religious worker
is looked to as the specialist. More and more, these decisions are
reached at the college level. Many candidates for the ministry
begin as pre-med, pre-law, business, or liberal arts majors. Here
is one of the religious worker's greatest opportunities and most
significant responsibilities. It involves not only the guiding of

potential candidates but also the rerouting of those who are not qualified. Both the welfare of the student and the future of the church are involved.

All of the problems of courtship and marriage are present on the college campus. Premarital counseling has been discussed so thoroughly in so many places it need not be repeated here except to point out that it will, of necessity be a major responsibility of the university pastor. More and more students are married during their academic careers, especially at the graduate level. This practice presents further problems of early adjustment in marriage, reversing the roles of wage earner for awhile, with accompanying problems of adjustment and understanding. Since the pastor is the one who usually conducts the wedding, he is also in a natural position for premarital and family counseling.

To summarize this section, the university pastor inevitably must do a great deal of counseling and in very vital areas. (1) Some areas he must handle alone. In working with religious problems, premarital counseling, and counseling for church vocations he is probably the most qualified. (2) In some areas he works with other counselors. When questions of educational or vocational decisions are brought to him, he may consult with the testing service, speech or reading clinics, other faculty members, or university counselors. (3) In some cases of severe educational problems or very emotionally disturbed students he may refer to the health service, the counseling center, or some other specialist who takes over the counseling completely. In any of these three areas, he has an important role to fill.

The Need for Closer Cooperation

All that we have said points up the need for closer cooperation between the religious worker and the university personnel. This is evident from the literature in the two fields. In recent years a whole new kind of literature has developed in two different areas — one in pastoral counseling, the other in student counseling. The field of pastoral counseling grew up around the hospital: Men like Russell Dicks, Carroll Wise, Seward Hiltner, and Wayne Oates have made a splendid contribution. Their references are primarily to the doctor and the psychiatrist; only occasionally is there a chapter or even a paragraph on the school and the educational counselor. The field of student counseling has an equally impressive bibliography. A study of these volumes finds only an occasional reference to the significance of religious values and the pastor as a counselor.

It is our feeling that the problem is primarily one of neglect. It is a lack of awareness rather than suspicion or opposition. Most school counselors and most pastors will welcome cooperation. What is needed is a stronger emphasis in seminaries on the need for deeper understanding and cooperation. The same need is present in schools of education and psychology.

Basically the final test is on the campus itself in work with the individual student. When pastors and university counselors work together for the welfare of one student and do it in a mature and professional manner, it does more than anything else to foster the further cooperation that is needed and makes for closer relationships with other students.

TRAINING REQUIREMENTS

One cannot stress too strongly the significance of such a task. To accept the responsibility of guiding one student in educational, vocational, or marital choices is to accept responsibility for his whole future. To sit down with one troubled, discouraged, anxious student is to deal with him where life is most difficult. This demands the best training of which one is capable.

What training is required for one who would assume such a responsibilty? (Here, we are talking only of his counseling responsibilities, not his total training.) First he should have a basic B.D. degree or its equivalent. Since he functions as a pastor, he should have the background of a pastor with thorough familiarity with the biblical and theological fields. This is considered his specialty. Since he will serve within the setting and framework of higher education, he should also have some specialized training in the field of religion and higher education. In addition, he should have some special training in the dynamics of personality and counseling techniques and procedures. This should include a knowledge of his own limitations and the principles of referral. Finally, since he is on a campus, he should have some acquaintance with the specialized fields of educational and vocational guidance and family life counseling.

When it is possible to secure such specialized training in seminary, this is desirable. In the future, this must be done. Provision should be made to provide training for those who plan to specialize in a student ministry. They simply cannot be considered prepared for their task without education in counseling. When such training has not been available, the pastor can often take advantage of opportunities which the campus offers to improve his effectiveness in these areas.

In either case, he should attempt to keep abreast of all these areas. If he does so, in the course of time he will be increasing his effectiveness and multiplying his influence many times, and the contribution he can make to individual lives in this way is without limit.

By Way of Illustration

In conclusion, by way of illustration, let's take an actual case which summarizes, in terms of one student's experience, what we have been saying. We will call him Del. He went to the university counseling center because he was having some problems, and he heard they might help. Many of his questions were of a religious nature, so the university counselor called a university pastor to see if he would be willing to talk with Del.

Del was a young man from a small town and a small church. In the university his courses in philosophy, psychology, etc. were confusing to him. He was reading William James, *Varieties of Religious Experience* and he found some varieties he had never heard of. They discussed his religious problems, but in the midst of the discussion Del said, "Now about my girl."

It turned out he had some problems that were not religious, at least not theological in the conventional sense. They discussed these too. In fact, there were more problems than could be included in one hour, so Del agreed to come back. Two or three interviews later he said, "Of course I have been drinking too much." This took the conversation into another area.

As the interviews went on, Del continued to grow in his capacity to face himself. One day he said, "I'm only half a man." It was then the pastor discovered for the first time Del had a slight limp. It was too small to be noticeable, yet a defective knee was sufficiently serious that it prevented his participating in athletics and kept him out of the army. Although it did not impair him academically or vocationally, it had a real influence emotionally. It created deep feelings of inferiority. While many would have appreciated avoiding the army, for Del the fact that he was not eligible made him feel inadequate.

In the course of the conversations Del became so moody that the minister to students suggested it might be well if he consulted the psychiatrist at the university health center. This Del agreed to do. After examining him, the psychiatrist sent him back with the report that Del was not sick, and that the university pastor had the best relationship with him of any one on the campus and should continue with him. This the minister was glad to do.

Some of his earlier problems having been worked through, Del began to discuss some of his vocational plans and aspirations. Although taking a business course, he really was interested in something like social work where he could help people. A check of his orientation tests indicated that he had the mental ability to handle any course he really wished to, but there was another problem. He already had accumulated several hours toward his business degree. Most of these would not apply to social work. Should he continue in an area where he had lost interest, or change his major and take prerequisites for no credit? His situation was further complicated by the fact that he was working his own way through school, and there was the question of expense, etc. to be considered.

What can we learn from this case that relates to what we have been saying thus far, or about counseling with students in general?

(1) It points up the fact of the strategic position of the university counselor. The fact that he was there, available and qualified in a certain field, gave the university counselor someone to whom he could send this student. Of course, he was also available to many other students who voluntarily came to him.

(2) It also points out that the university pastor may be called upon to counsel in any area. It so happened that Del had religious problems, premarital problems, educational, academic, and vocational problems. The only thing unusual about this combination is they all appeared acutely at the same time. All students have them to some degree or other.

(3) It emphasizes the importance of the counseling ministry. Del's problems couldn't be solved in a class or meeting. They could only be solved when one person could sit down with Del, face to face, and help him confront his own problems and his own needs.

(4) It also emphasizes the importance of the pastor's having a working relationship with the personnel staff. It was a counselor who sent Del in the first place. The university psychiatrist helped with an evaluation that gave the minister a sense of security. He then knew what conditions he was dealing with. The counseling center gave him information about Del's mental abilities, scholastic aptitude, etc. which helped to understand him better. The pastor, then, wasn't guessing about Del's abilities or expectations.

(5) If the pastoral counselor was to help Del, he had to understand him — not only his abilities, grade average, and such matters, but how he felt about all of these matters that were discussed. Del had to express his feelings of doubt, inadequacy, and at times guilt. The pastor's task was to listen and understand. This is a tremendous service and met one of Del's greatest needs.

(6) It also illustrates the fact that one never knows, when a student presents a problem, what the problem really is or where the discussion will lead. Del came to talk about a religious problem. True, he had religious problems. However, the fact that he was met with understanding and acceptance led him to reveal many other problems that even he didn't realize he wanted to discuss.

(7) This case also makes clear that such counseling takes time — a great deal of time. A basic quality of student counseling is patience. Such things cannot be done in a hurry.

(8) This case also illustrates that it is the relationship that is important. Counseling techniques are important and should constantly be improved, but the relationship is more important than the techniques. The psychiatrist sent him back because the pastor and Del had a good relationship. Without a good relationship he would have been of little help.

(9) The pastor's purpose was to help Del help himself. He could not make the young man's decisions for him nor live his life for him. The pastor's task was to create the atmosphere in which Del could think through his own situation, his own problems, and his own needs clearly and maturely.

(10) All such illustrations remind us that people can be helped. Del had a multitude of problems, complex, interrelated, real, but he was able to work most of them through. In every case the counselor must maintain an optimistic attitude, a realistic optimism that grows out of the fact that people have grown, matured, and gained understanding and self reliance in the past and others can do so in the future.

(11) Such work requires training, skill, patience, and faith. To consider one such person as Del is to see how important it is for the counselor to train and develop himself. This student's future adjustment and his contributions to society depend on how well these conversations were handled. So it is with every student who seeks the pastor's help.

GEORGE L. EARNSHAW

12: The Implications
of Church and State
in Public Higher Education

SINCE THE DAYS FOLLOWING THE SECOND WORLD WAR a great deal of interest and discussion has centered on the American public school system as it pertains to the question of religion.

Because of pressures exerted from the outside by an aggressive Russian Communism, the American people have been forced to reevaluate their own heritage and tradition. In this process many have looked to the state-supported educational systems and found them failing to give our young people an adequate moral basis for meeting the complex problems of twentieth-century life.[1] The various efforts to remedy this deficiency have brought into focus a reconsideration of the First Amendment of the United States Constitution, and a further question of the meaning of "the separation of church and state." This is not a small problem when one considers all the ramifications. Living in a nation whose people embrace many points of view in regard to the meaning of "religion" further complicates the task.

This chapter is an attempt to show that the men who framed the Constitution and drafted the First Amendment (as interpreted by the courts) intended them to protect individual civil liberties

[1] See Phillip E. Jacob, *Changing Values in College* (New York: Harper & Row, 1958). See also Alexander Miller, *Faith and Learning* (New York: Association Press, 1960).

241

and to provide a permissive atmosphere where the government and voluntary and free religious organizations could grow and prosper alongside one another. Although the state can never give its sanction to any kind of official religious orthodoxy, it was meant, by design, to be friendly and encouraging to those who give allegiance to a Supreme Being. This chapter will also strive to show that there is a major distinction between the state-supported education at the university level and that of the primary and secondary level. The state universities are therefore at liberty to contribute to the religious life of their students without violating any of the prohibitions posed by the Constitution so long as the principles of voluntarism and equity are followed.

The conclusions drawn from one's interpretation of the legal limitations placed upon the state by the federal Constitution play a large part in the determination of crucial questions in regard to religion and the state universities: Can tax-supported property be utilized by sectarian religious groups? Can the state require compulsory worship on the part of its students? Can courses in primary religious content and theology be taught and included in the curriculum?

DEFINING THE PROBLEM HISTORICALLY

In order to give a rational answer to the above questions, it becomes essential to have an accurate historical perspective. The whole question of church and state rotates around America's constitutional form of government, especially that section of the First Amendment which is designed to safeguard religious liberty from infringement by the government and vice versa, namely, "Congress shall make no law respecting an establishment of religion, or prohibiting the free exercise thereof. . . ." The word "establishment" means that the state will use the force of law to give financial support to a favored church through taxation and give legal support to that church's doctrines and public worship. The other part of the First Amendment's phrase, "free exercise," implies that an individual or church should have the freedom to worship and to attempt to convince other people by *persuasion* of the truth of their beliefs.

Space does not permit a detailed historical account of how the old-world patterns of establishment were brought over to this country during the time of the thirteen colonies. Suffice it to say that, by the time of the American Revolution and the Constitutional Convention and ratification of the First Amendment (1776-1791), all the states had moved in the direction of "separation."[2]

It should also be said here that the federal and state constitutions are not fixed and rigid when it comes to the separation principle. They are flexible and malleable documents which accommodate themselves to public opinion and changing practices in our society, and these elements are important in judicial interpretation. This principle is, in fact, the genius of our American constitutional system!

In July of 1869, the final step was taken in this historical evolution with the incorporation into the American constitution of the Fourteenth Amendment, whose words read, in part:

> All persons born or naturalized in the United States, and subject to the jurisdiction thereof, are citizens of the United States and of the State wherein they reside. No State shall make or enforce any law which shall abridge the privileges or immunities of citizens of the United States; nor shall any State deprive any person of life, liberty, or property, without due process of law; nor deny to any person within its jurisdiction the equal protection of the laws.

Beginning in the 1940's the Supreme Court began to apply and enforce the provisions of the First Amendment (which up to that time had not been applied to the states) in such a way as to protect the civil liberties of individual citizens guaranteed in the Fourteenth Amendment.

Several historic and important cases will be cited to illustrate the point and further clarify the meaning of the phrase, "separation of church and state." The first case in 1940 dealt with the sect known as Jehovah's Witnesses. Jessie Cantwell and his two sons were ordained ministers of the sect and had violated a Connecticut statute of law which prohibited solicitation of contributions to any religious cause without the approval of the secretary of the Public Welfare Council. In declaring this statute unconstitutional, Mr. Justice Roberts, speaking for the Court, wrote:

[2] See my article in *Foundations*, a Baptist Journal of History and Theology, "The Problem of Church and State in Public Education," January, 1961, pp. 18-38. See also R. Freeman Butts, *The American Tradition in Religion and Education* (Boston: Beacon Press, 1950) .

In the realm of religious faith, and in that of political beliefs, sharp differences arise. In both fields the tenets of one man may seem rankest error to his neighbor. To persuade others to his own point of view, the pleader, as we know, at times, resorts to exaggeration, to vilification of men who have been, or are, prominent in church or state, and even to false statement. But the people of this nation have ordained in the light of history, that, in spite of the probability of excesses and abuses, these liberties are, in the long view, essential to an enlightened opinion and right conduct on the part of the citizens of a democracy.[3]

This historic case was followed almost immediately by many other cases involving similar groups and their difficulties with society. Not all of the Court decisions were favorable to them, but it was apparent that the Court was supporting the individual's right to the "free exercise" clause.

Six years after the Cantwell case came another which dealt with the legality of transporting children to and from school at the taxpayers' expense. New Jersey had a statute authorizing district boards of education to make rules and contracts for the transporting of children to and from schools other than private schools operated for profit (*New Jersey Laws,* 1941, c. 191, p. 581). The School Board of the Township of Ewing, operating under this provision, was reimbursing the parents of parochial school children who rode highway busses to school but would not do the same for parents whose children rode busses to attend private schools operated for profit. A citizen named Everson sued the Board for unfair practices. His case ultimately was brought to the United States Supreme Court. In a 5-4 decision, it was ruled that this particular statute of New Jersey did not violate the United States Constitution. Mr. Justice Black delivered the majority opinion. He stated:

> The First Amendment has erected a wall between church and state. That wall must be kept high and impregnable. We could not approve the slightest breach. New Jersey has not breached it here.[4]

There was no disagreement whatsoever on the plain meaning of the First Amendment. The state must not grant direct aid to religion.

Justices Jackson, Burton, Frankfurter, and Rutledge dissented.

[3] *United States Supreme Court Reports,* October term, 1939, *Cantwell v. Connecticut,* U. S. 310, 84 Law. Ed., p. 310.

[4] *United States Supreme Court Reports,* October term, 1946, *Everson v. Board of Education,* U. S. 330, 91 Law. Ed. p. 18.

In one of the dissenting opinions, Mr. Justice Rutledge, recognizing the subtle dangers involved in declaring the principle of complete and uncompromising separation of church from state and then yielding support to their commingling in educational matters, declared:

There cannot be freedom of religion, safeguarded by the state, and intervention by the church or its agencies in the state's domain or dependency on its largess. . . . Public money devoted to payment of religious costs, educational or other, brings the quest for more. It brings too the struggle of sect against sect for the larger share. . . . That is precisely the history of societies which have had an established religion and dissident groups. It is the very thing Jefferson and Madison experienced and sought to guard against, whether in its blunt or in its more screened forms.[5]

While there was disagreement as to the meaning of "auxiliary services," there was complete agreement by the entire Court that church and state are to function side by side and each is to have its own area of competence, but that neither has the legal authority to interfere or control the other's operation. Religious life, they contended, is at its healthy best when completely divorced from the coercive control of the state.

Soon thereafter, in 1947, another case came before the Court which has subsequently caused a great deal of discussion and controversy. In this case a local board of education in Champaign County, Illinois, agreed to give "released time" religious instruction for those in the public schools who had secured parental permission. The important feature of this case was that the instruction was to take place during school hours *in the school buildings* by outside teachers furnished by a religious council representing the various faiths. It was contested and brought to the highest court of the land on the grounds that it constituted a divisive element in our society. The Court ruled, in an 8-1 decision, that the Champaign statute was contrary to the Federal Constitution as expressed by the First Amendment. Mr. Justice Frankfurter, concurring with the majority opinion, wrote the following words:

Separation means separation, not something less. Jefferson's metaphor in describing the relation between Church and State speaks of a "wall of separation," not a fine line easily overstepped. The public school is

[5] *Ibid.,* pp. 53-54.

at once the symbol of our democracy and the most pervasive means for promoting our common destiny. In no activity of the State is it more vital to keep out divisive forces than in its schools, to avoid confusing, not to say fusing, what the Constitution sought to keep strictly apart. "The great American principle of eternal separation"—Elihu Root's phrase bears repetition—is one of the vital reliances of our Constitutional system for assuring unities among our people stronger than our diversities. It is the Court's duty to enforce this principle in its full integrity.[6]

The Court stood firm against direct cooperation between church and state in the instance of using tax-supported public buildings in the secondary schools to foster sectarian religious instruction.

Almost the identical case reached the Supreme Court in 1951 with the important difference that the "released time" religious instruction was held during school time but *outside* the school buildings. In a 6-3 decision the Court upheld the New York Court's decision approving the practice as it operated in Brooklyn. Mr. Justice Douglas delivered the majority opinion. He stated,

We are a religious people whose institutions presuppose a Supreme Being. . . . When the state encourages religious instruction or cooperates with religious authorities by adjusting the schedule of public events to sectarian needs, it follows the best of our traditions. For it then respects the religious nature of our people and accommodates the public service to their spiritual needs. To hold that it may not would be to find in the Constitution a requirement that the government show a callous indifference to religious groups. That would be preferring those who believe in no religion over those who do believe. . . . But we find no constitutional requirement which makes it necessary for government to be hostile to religion and throw its weight against efforts to widen the effective scope of religious influence.[7]

The wording in this decision, it seems to this writer, appears to be much more in accord with the common understandings and practices of our history. It moves the separation principle out of the dogmatic and absolute language and brings the theory more in line with practice. Religion and the state have always been officially enmeshed since the inception of our nation. Tax moneys pay our armed forces chaplains; they help to build sectarian hospitals; they sent our World War II veterans to denominational colleges; they

[6] *United States Supreme Court Reports*, 1947, *McCollum v. Board of Education*, U. S. 333, 92 Law. Ed., p. 231.

[7] *Zorach v. Clauson*, 72 Supreme Court 679, Oct. term 1951, U. S. 431, p. 7.

have given and continue to give tax relief to religious institutions. Furthermore, our presidents have established religious holidays and made religious proclamations. The feelings of our people and those who have been in positions of leadership in the past have established precedents which contradict the absolutizing of any ironclad meaning of separation.[8]

All of the above that has been cited from the Supreme Court has to do with the public school system in the primary and secondary level. It is important to understand that the nature of our pluralism in a *compulsory* public educational framework has exposed the nerve of sensitivity to any subtle or overt infringement of the First Amendment.

One more case illustrates what is being implied. On June 25, 1962, the Supreme Court of the United States, in a 6-1 decision, (two justices not participating) reversed the State of New York's program of opening its public schools with an officially prescribed prayer. The Court said that, since public education at the primary school level was compulsory, any prayer composed by a state body and sanctioned by public officials was, in the words of Mr. Justice Black, "no part of the business of government." Furthermore, because attendance was required of all the students, any religious act of worship was inherently coercive, at least in a psychological sense.[9]

Should Courses with a Primary Religious Content Be Included in the Curricula of State Universities?

We must remember that universities were founded by the church in the Middle Ages as an extension of the medieval church school. Traditionally, there were four faculties within the university: theology (regarded then as the "queen of the sciences"), law, medicine, and the arts. Interestingly enough, in spite of this heritage, very few universities today (including those which are state supported) have theologians on their faculty, or departments of religion, or courses that deal with theology. Why?

A quick look at history will reveal that most of the institutions

[8] Much of what has been written is based on Paul G. Kauper's very helpful and authoritative chapter entitled "Law and Public Opinion" in the volume *Religion and the State University,* University of Michigan, 1955.

[9] *New York Regents' Prayer Case, Engel v. Vitale,* U. S. 370, p. 421. See also the Lord's Prayer and Bible Reading Decision of June 18, 1963, footnote 11.

of higher learning in this country were started by the church. Out of 207 colleges established before the Civil War, 180 were denominationally sponsored, 21 were state universities, and 6 others were under public or semipublic auspices. Even when the state-supported schools began, they were patterned after their church-related sister institutions. Many older men on the faculties of the state universities today can still remember "back when" they had compulsory chapel or Sunday church, and when such courses as Biblical Hebrew and New Testament Greek were included in the curriculum. However, the pendulum swung back to the other extreme as a result of the industrial revolution in our country with its accompanying urbanization and secularization. Concern for religion waned, and most of its vestiges on the state university campuses were dropped.

It was not until shortly after World War II, when Americans began reflecting upon the vacuum created by the influences of scientific humanism and the nihilism of Nazi Germany, that they once again felt an honest need for the spiritual roots and moral support which could be provided by a deep religious faith. The concern has centered its attention on the American public school system.

In the last decade or so, many prominent religious leaders and educators have challenged the university to engage in some serious soul-searching as to its mission. Is it really educating its students? Are its graduates being equipped to meet the crucial issues of a nuclear age? Is the state university's function merely to provide, for those who seek it, a professional training in technology, or does it have a broader responsibility?

Many responsible voices are saying that it is the duty of the academic community to provoke students to think about the really fundamental questions of life. One such educator has written:

> Most students go through our universities without ever having been forced to exercise their minds on the issues which are really momentous. Under the guise of academic neutrality they are subtly conditioned to unthinking acquiescence in the social and political *status quo* and in a secularism on which they have never seriously reflected. Owing to the prevailing fragmentation of studies, they are not challenged to decide responsibly on a life-purpose or equipped to make such a decision wisely. They are not incited to disentangle and examine critically the assumptions and emotional attitudes underlying the particular studies

they pursue, the professions for which they are preparing, the ethical judgments they are accustomed to make, and the political or religious convictions they hold. Fundamentally they are uneducated.[10]

Although in the liberal tradition of education it is not the task of the university to force any specific answer upon a student, many are saying that he should have the opportunity to be exposed to a variety of life's answers and values so that he can make his own free choice. Unless the student has this opportunity to be exposed to philosophic and religious answers and to make up his own mind as to which is *the* truth for him, the university is actually forcing a subtle, but nonetheless alternative answer upon him — a neutrality which is the essence of the "religion of secularism." This is exactly what the highest Court of the land has condemned. In a decision ruling out Bible reading and the Lord's Prayer in the elementary and secondary public schools in June of 1963, Mr. Justice Clark, speaking for the Court, wrote:

> We agree of course that the State may not establish a "religion of secularism" in the sense of affirmatively opposing or showing hostility to religion, thus "preferring those who believe in no religion over those who do believe." [11]

Religion — and Christianity in particular — has occupied an essential place in western civilization. It has provided the people in our society with a high sense of purpose and motivation. It has been a stabilizing influence in our culture, and it certainly has exerted a powerful force in the shaping of the policies and philosophy of our government. The moral and spiritual values generated by the various religious groups have had a tremendous impact upon our character and public life. By means of its theological insights it has stimulated Americans to open up new frontiers of truth and beauty. It seems, therefore, then that in no sense could any reputable academic institution of higher learning omit offering courses in primary religious content. The question at hand is whether or not this kind of education is possible in a university supported by public tax moneys.

Two important points must be made at this point in regard to

[10] Sir Walter Moberly, *The Crisis in the University* (New York: Macmillan Company, 1950) , p. 70.

[11] *School District of Abington Township, Pa. v. Schempp*, 83 Supreme Court, 560.

religion and the state-supported colleges and universities: (1) There are virtually no judicial decisions to give any legal precedent or rulings in this regard, and not one single case has yet come up before the Supreme Court of the land. This is indeed a most significant fact with important permissive overtones. (2) It is essential to realize that there is a *basic difference* between discussing religious matters at the elementary or secondary level of the public schools and doing so at the university level. Two salient facts lend weight to this argument, and, according to the opinion of this writer, change the whole complexion of the subject. One is the maturity of the student and the other is the compulsory nature of the secondary school attendance laws. Religious exercises and instruction do not lend themselves to the charge of "indoctrination" when college-level courses are optional and are taught to students of mature years in an atmosphere of intellectual free inquiry. So long as more than one religion can be studied and so long as the course is entirely optional, it can be argued that the teaching of religion in the curriculum of a state university would not violate the freedoms in the First Amendment, even though public funds were used.

The Supreme Court ruled in the 1952 Brooklyn "released time" decision that the Constitution does not require the state to be hostile or even indifferent to religion; therefore the state universities might well agree to give students a chance to study religion taught by teachers who are academically qualified and religiously committed.

The late Alexander Miller succinctly summarized this thesis by saying that the universities must pay more attention to "values," and that they need to equip students not only with an abundance of data but with the makings of a philosophy of life. He says that the main job of the university is to cultivate the intellect — not to inculcate morals but "to equip men and women destined for responsibility with the knowledge which is power." Continuing, he declares: "To refuse to help them find the will or the way to use it, is a species of irresponsibility in itself, and in human fact, a refusal really to *educate*." [12]

The fact of the matter is that recently in many of our state universities certain courses in religion have been added to the cur-

[12] *Faith and Learning* (New York: Association Press, 1960), p. 52.

riculum in the various academic disciplines, to supplement the long-accepted courses in comparative religion and psychology of religion. In particular states where their own constitutions specifically prohibit the use of public moneys for "sectarian instruction" (such as Michigan, Missouri, Colorado, South Dakota, Wisconsin, Nevada, Wyoming, and Nebraska) several of the state universities have set up credit devices for courses taught by academically qualified teachers supplied and paid for by outside denominational groups. The University of Kansas at Lawrence and the University of Illinois at Champaign have this pattern.

The State University of Iowa at Iowa City has set up a "school of religion" as an integral part of the university, although it is supported by private funds and has teachers supplied by the three major faiths.

Other denominations have established Bible colleges adjacent to state university campuses and have arranged with the administration to offer courses on a voluntary basis for university students. The Disciples of Christ have done this at the University of Missouri and the University of Nebraska.

To summarize this section it appears that the state universities, in an attempt to offer their students an adequate and well-rounded education dealing with the whole man, and in response to the felt need of its people, may legally offer courses in primary religious content without violating the intent of the constitutional restrictions so long as their offerings are optional and no discrimination is made with respect to any one recognized religious body.

RELIGIOUS ACTIVITY ON CAMPUS — IS IT PERMISSIBLE?

In recent years, in an attempt to meet the changing religious atmosphere of the state university, denominations have followed their young people to the campus and experimentally tried to fashion a strategy to meet religious needs while they are away from the home church. This operation has taken many forms, from acquiring modest off-campus dwellings to serve as religious centers for study and fellowship, to erecting very elaborate club-like structures. In addition to these, new churches have been founded. The existence of religious centers or church-related student foundations with full-time denominational "chaplains" bears witness to the church's conviction that students, administrators, and faculty members in a state university need to live by some basic loyalty to God and neighbor.

In the state university, with its fragmentation of both studies and community, there is a real need for cohesion and wholeness.[18] When a student leaves home for college he has dramatically cut the psychological and sociological "umbilical cord" which had previously bound him to the authority and security of the home and family. In part, the mission of the church on campus is to help him make the transition from infantile spiritual dependence to responsible freedom — from youth to adult maturity.

Most of college activity is centered on campus, and if the work of the chaplain is to be effective he must go where the students are. If he is to counsel, teach, and also be a friend to those in the academic community, he must spend a good share of his time where his constituency studies, eats, and lives. The question to be raised and answered primarily in this section is whether or not sectarian religious activity on campus violates the separation principle.

It seems clear that, so long as all religious groups are dealt with in a non-discriminatory way, there is no legal problem with church and state. Most state constitutions spell out rather specifically that "no religious sect or sects shall ever control any part of the common school or university funds of the state" (using the Constitution of Kansas as an example, Article VI, section 9). In a few cases there are prohibitions against "sectarian instruction," but (as experience has shown) no amount of religious activity on campus has ever been construed to violate these provisions, and most state university administrators welcome the counseling, guidance, and undergirding that is given by the various campus denominational chaplains and workers.

A perfunctory survey of what is currently happening on the various university campuses will substantiate the above statements. It is difficult, of course, to put down at any one time specific examples that will be accurate ten years later. Because of the experimental nature of campus ministry, what is happening in specific state universities is subject to change, but the general pattern remains fairly stable.

[18] See Chapter 5.

In most state universities there is some kind of official recognition and stature given to off-campus denominational churches and foundations and their workers. In some places the university provides a building or land (or both). For instance, the University of Connecticut has set aside a block of its land on a strategic section of campus for religious centers. In some schools such as Minnesota, Ohio State, Michigan, and others, the administration of the university, in recognition of the need for inclusive cooperation of the total spiritual community, has provided a nonsectarian religious officer or coordinator to carry out the liaison between the various activities of the "recognized" religious organizations. At the Pennsylvania State University this job has been handled by the office of the University Chaplain. In many places these off-campus religious bodies reflect a long history of responsible relationships and cooperation between university and campus.

Traditionally the Religious Emphasis Week or Religion-In-Life Week has been a focal point for on-campus interfaith activity. In most schools a student-faculty committee composed of representatives from the various faiths plans a specific program for a set number of days, usually headlined by an outstanding denominational "name speaker." Representative clergymen and students are also invited to participate. The members of this team are invited to speak and lead discussions in dormitories, fraternity houses, and perhaps in classes themselves. In recent years some state universities have dropped the Week of Religious Emphasis, not because of constitutional prohibitions, but because of student disinterest.

At the University of Wisconsin, for instance, where Religious Emphasis Week has been discontinued, it has been replaced with a quarterly lecture series sponsored by the major faith groups and held in the Student Union. Here instead of a once-a-year "nod to God" (as one student termed it) there is an opportunity provided throughout the academic year for those on campus to grapple with the theological answers to the great social and political issues of the day.

Then there is the question of worship. Many of the state universities in the pre-"post-Protestant era" had their own either nondenominational or nonecclesiastical chapel services led by faculty members or visiting Protestant clergymen. In the last part of the nineteenth century, for an example, the Illinois Supreme Court upheld compulsory chapel at the University of Illinois. However, with the tidal wave of student population inundating our campuses in the first two-thirds of the twentieth century and bringing with them a new religious heterogeneity, all the former practices of compulsory worship and chapel were dropped. (Oddly enough this pattern seems to be followed everywhere except in the tax-supported service academies of West Point and Annapolis). With the recent Supreme Court decisions ruling against prayer and Bible reading in public secondary schools it would seem that the intent of the First Amendment is clear. Neither the state nor its officials may sponsor or conduct under its auspices any sectarian worship. This would be a state invasion of the domain reserved for voluntary religious groups. However, in an attempt to provide opportunities for its students to deepen their religious life, many state universities have recently erected new chapels on campus. In all such cases the funds for these buildings have been carefully obtained from private sources and thus have avoided any church-state entanglements. Pennsylvania State, Kansas State, Cornell, and Maryland are four such institutions which have followed this pattern. The chapels mentioned above are interfaith in philosophy and can accommodate all of the major religious groups by a changeable altar and liturgical appointments in order that each campus church group may worship according to its own tradition and custom. These examples substantiate the thesis of this chapter that our Constitution guarantees freedom of worship and insures the integral religious function in the university.

Let us, in summary, restate the thesis and the arguments and examples marshaled in support.

It was said that while the state cannot support or give its sanction to any kind of religious orthodoxy, it is by constitutional design meant to be friendly and encouraging to those who give allegiance to a Supreme Being. This was expressly stated by the majority opinion in the 1952 Zorach case.

It was also contended that, although the Court has placed strict controls on any religious innuendoes in the primary and secondary public schools to prevent any subtle form of sectarian control or indoctrination of "young tender minds," these constrictions do not necessarily apply at the state university level. Two main reasons were cited to support this contention: the age difference plus the voluntary nature of higher education. When a student of mature years voluntarily elects a college course in theology or religion, he does so well within the bounds of law. The fact that no case to date has ever been brought up before our highest tribunal is in itself evidence to this point.

It was argued further that, because religion has played and continues to play such an important part in western civilization, and particularly in our American democratic heritage, it should be included in the curricula of all the state universities, not only tangentially as part of history and sociology, but centrally as primary content courses either through a department of religion or in the separate disciplines by those academically qualified, theologically trained, and religiously committed. The only limitation is that no one religious group be discriminated against and that there be no overt proselytizing.

And finally, it was shown by present practice that the state universities are able to provide a great deal of hospitality and encouragement to on-campus religious groups and activities without violating any church-state restrictions, so long as they do not favor any one group over the other. As a matter of fact most of the administrations in the state institutions of higher learning, because of their concern for the total educational task, welcome the voluntary religious groups and value the contribution which these groups make to student morale. The philosophic interrelatedness of the community of faith and the community of learning, guarded by clear-cut limitations, is an essential aspect of academic excellence in higher education.

RICHARD R. BROHOLM

13: Campus Evangelism

HARVEY COX IN AN ARTICLE on "Biblical Evangelism in the Twentieth Century" gives sharp focus to any thinking on the question of contemporary evangelism when he declares that biblical evangelism "requires first a disciplined and informed basis in the Biblical revelation. But it also demands a thorough awareness of the particular character and ethos of that specific age in which it lives. . . . For the God revealed in Jesus Christ is One who has committed himself to the particularities and ambiguities of all human history. . . . Evangelism which could not speak to its own particular age is therefore not just bad evangelism; it is not evangelism at all." [1]

Thus any attempt to speak about the scope and nature of the evangelistic task on the college and university campus today must certainly come to grips sooner or later with the fact that we are moving into a radically new age.

Romano Guardini is one of the many prophets of our time who have attempted to give some shape to this awareness of an emerg-

[1] Harvey G. Cox, "Biblical Evangelism in the Twentieth Century." *Foundations*, April, 1959, p. 101.

Richard R. Broholm is program associate of the Division of Evangelism, American Baptist Home Mission Societies. He was formerly chaplain to Baptist students at the University of Wisconsin, and director of the community of life and faith, a residential lay study center for undergraduates.

ing new world order. In his book, *End of the Modern Age,* Guardini speaks about the emergence of the "fourth man." He suggests that this "fourth man" is the symbol of a new era which differs as much from the modern era as the modern era has differed from the middle ages, and the middle ages in turn from the ancient era.

C. Wright Mills attempts a description of this "fourth man" in his book *White Collar,* in which he says this man "seems to have no firm roots, no sure loyalties to sustain his life and give it a center. He is not aware of having any history, his past being as brief as it is unheroic; he has lived through no golden age he can recall in time of trouble. Perhaps because he does not know where he is going, he is in a frantic hurry; perhaps because he does not know what frightens him, he is paralyzed with fear." [2]

Whether this new man of whom Guardini and others speak is the *product* of our scientific and technological era or has *produced* this new age is difficult to say. Yet we cannot afford to ignore the fact that man increasingly does view himself and his world in a radically different way from the self-image of earlier generations. This does not mean that there are not vestigial remains from earlier epochs which continue to influence our thinking and which make it difficult for many people to grasp the new shape of things. In fact these holdovers may well constitute one of the major problems confronting the church in our time. The church is living in the twentieth century as if the world remained that of the eighteenth and nineteenth centuries.

Though in many ways we still are in a transitional period where the shape of things to come is blurred, this emerging new man may be seen most clearly on our college and university campuses. His outlook might well be characterized by describing him as both postreligious and postmoral. Rampant atheism is a rarity in our time, but agnosticism can be observed on every hand. This generation of students (and in all likelihood many to come) appears to live in a state of perpetual, yet creative, doubt in which everything is under radical reexamination. Religion is only one of many areas in which this agnostic state of mind finds expression. True, it can be argued that student years have traditionally been a time of

[2] C. Wright Mills, *White Collar* (New York: Oxford University Press, 1953), p. xvi.

questioning and radical doubting; that it is only a matter of time until these students become parents and community citizens who gradually cease to question and begin to affirm. However, the condition which I have been describing appears to be of another sort. There is strong reason to believe with Dietrich Bonhoeffer that we are seeing a "man come of age" who is seized by something far more profound than the normal questioning and doubting of youth. Exactly what this postreligious label means is not clear, but it would indeed be unfortunate if we treated today's students as if they were just passing through a religious phase, the outcome from which is already certain and clear to their elders.

To describe the student of the mid-twentieth century as also being postmoral is not to suggest that he does not have ethical and moral convictions, but rather to point up the fact that his ethics and morals are privatized: Each man to his own code. All is relative, he believes; what is seen as good for one individual may not at all be good for another. Today's student is reluctant to be caught "with his absolutes showing."

The fact that we are still in the midst of this revolution means that no easy conclusions can be drawn concerning the task of evangelism. At the same time, it is of critical importance to understand that any evangelism which takes its roots in the biblical understanding of the gospel must address itself both to the meaning of the gospel and to the nature of the contemporary world.

What Do We Mean by Evangelism?

The very definition of the word "evangelism," as well as its implications for contemporary life, is under close scrutiny in our time. It would be difficult, indeed, to obtain a consensus from the many diverse theological positions within Protestantism. Yet, again and again, in any attempt to speak about the meaning of evangelism we find emerging certain similar ideas — though expressed in various forms and dissimilar language:

(1) Evangelism is the presentation of the good news of God in Jesus Christ to the end that men may accept Jesus Christ as Savior and serve him as Lord.

(2) Jesus Christ is himself the Evangelist who has come to redeem the world. Men witness to the Evangelist, but it is always a

misnomer to speak of men as the evangelists or to imply that men "save" other men through their witness.

(3) Evangelism is concerned with the *whole* person and the *whole* world. Any attempt to "spiritualize" the evangelistic task into otherworldly concerns is ultimately an effort which will lead to its distortion or total destruction. The declaration that "God so loved the world" calls us to the proper arena for our work and the proper perspective for the thrust of the gospel. It means that evangelism is concerned with the social patterns of human existence and any attempt to separate social action and evangelism into two spheres springs from a false understanding of the way in which God moves to redeem his world.

Thus evangelism is not a peripheral function nor an optional choice, but rather the central task of the church. In fact, it is correct to say that the church exists for mission — for proclaiming in word and deed the gospel of reconciliation in the world over which Christ is Lord. Obviously, then, much that has gone under the name of evangelism both in our churches and on the college campus is a flagrant denial of the wholeness of the gospel. Those Christian groups which have talked most often about "the full gospel" can well be criticized for their failure at this very point.

If the gospel speaks to the whole man in the whole world and therefore is concerned with every aspect of life, then many of our evangelistic methods also stand under radical judgment as being inadequate, if not totally unfaithful to God's redemptive purpose in history. One example is the emphasis upon "personal decision" in such a way as to deny any possible social implications. It seems somewhat anachronistic that some denominations which pride themselves as being "strongly evangelistic" should at the same time studiously ignore the social implications for Christian decision-making in the fearful sore of racial segregation. To make this statement does not in any way diminish the importance of individual decision, but such decisions must be regarded in proper perspective, for there can be no such thing as a privatized Christian existence.

PROBLEMS OF EVANGELISM ON THE CAMPUS

The evangelistic task on the university and college campus in our time is difficult. Most of the problems stem from our cultural exposure to institutional Christianity along with the unspoken and fuzzy assumption that America is a Christian nation. In many ways our thinking in this country has been conditioned by a medieval mindset which implies that to be a citizen is to be a Christian.

Therefore we need to face the fact that our principal efforts in evangelism will be conducted among those who believe themselves already to have been "evangelized." These include, on one hand, those "Christians" who have obediently given their loyalty to a gospel and a church which are foreign to the biblical understanding of the gospel and the church, yet whose religious language is so filled with biblical expressions that their ears have been deadened to hearing the authentic word. "Hearing they hear not." On the other hand there are a growing number of students and faculty who feel they have been exposed in full to what the gospel has to say, that they have given it a fair hearing, and yet have found it lacking and irrelevant. We may rightfully applaud their discerning rejection of a spurious gospel (and wish that many more Christians would follow in their path) but our feeling of approval in no way diminishes our consequent difficulty of getting them to listen openly to what the gospel is really about.

As we face the apparent fact that Christianity has become the "cultural religion of America," we cannot help being deeply disturbed by the vast number of thoughtful and sensitive students who rightly reject such a religion; neither can we avoid being troubled by the even greater number who dutifully give the Christian faith a voice vote, all the while failing to grasp its relevance for their lives.

A second problem which confronts us in evangelism is the ineffectiveness of many of our more traditional evangelistic methods on the campus. For example, any attempt to "blitz" the campus with visiting firemen who come and go in a week's time is a less-than-adequate way to present the Christian faith. For all the good that is accomplished (and there is some of this) in the long run, the Religious Emphasis Week or Campus Crusade only serves to solidify the false notion that faith is an aspect of life which one must attend to at certain infrequent intervals and at certain inappropriate places. These "nod-to-God" weeks usually serve further to deepen the gulf that already stands between the self-conscious

Christian community on campus and those who profess no faith or are in the process of thoughtful reexamination. There are some variations of the Religious Emphasis Week which may not justifiably bear the full weight of this criticism. Certain schools have dispensed with the practice of having visiting theologians deliver all-school lectures (usually attended only by the religious community anyway) and have sought to use these men in classroom lectures, relating theology to the particular academic discipline studied in that class. This approach, of course, depends upon finding Christians who are trained in more than the discipline of theology. Perhaps the most effective type of personnel for use in this strategy may be the faculty member whose academic competence in a particular field serves as an entree to the classroom and at the same time provides the bridge of correlation between his concerns as a man of faith and the subject at hand. Such laymen, of course, need to be theologically alert and articulate. Thus one of the central tasks of the church within the university may well be the theological training of those members of the faculty who are self-conscious Christians.

A third problem in campus evangelism is the "ghetto nature" of much of our present ministry. Far too often the campus ministry is captive to a particular geographical plot of ground on or near the campus. These religious ghettos, rooted in wood and concrete, are often totally peripheral to the fabric of campus life. The captivity of student centers and foundations is not primarily due to the fact of a building which restricts the reaching out of a ministry, but rather to that framework of *thinking* on the part of campus ministers and students which leads them to live and move as if they believed the life and mission of the church were bound within the four walls of their edifice. Unfortunately, even when the Christian student fellowship discovers a world beyond its walls, there still is a real sense in which it is building-oriented, both in thinking and in economics.

The recognition of this problem should not lead us to an adolescent anti-institutionalism, but rather should cause us to be radically open to new ways of thinking about the use of structure, both in program and building, for our ministry and mission to the world of the campus.

In addition to the problems of our cultural situation, outmoded programs of evangelism, and our ghetto frame of thinking concerning the locus of our mission, there is also the problem of inadequate understandings which continue to plague us.

For example, though the church has moved beyond the unfortunate implications inherent in the phrase "full-time Christian service" (used in the past to refer to those persons engaged in professional church work), it still has not faced the profound meaning to be discovered in the biblical understanding of the idea of vocation. If all Christians share the same vocation — that is, to be a minister of reconciliation — then how do we most adequately express this vocation in the daily round of teaching a class in property law, serving as president of the student union, or working as a secretary in the office of the dean of men. One of the critical tasks of the campus ministry is to help faculty, administration, and students to explore the dimensions of their vocation as Christians.[3] This exploration cannot be made apart from their sharing fully in a covenanted community of fellow Christians who together share and reflect on their attempts to be ministers of reconciliation in the world. Our problem, then, is to grapple meaningfully with the implications inherent in the idea of the "priesthood of all believers," so that no longer will the layman conceive of his role as "the pastor's helper" in the program life of the church, but rather as one who himself has a ministry to fulfill. At the same time we must attempt to explore the possibilities in a campus Christian community (in effect we must discover what it means to be the church when gathered together), recognizing the need for a fellowship of persons who know each other well enough and at a deep enough level that they can share their problems and frustrations and find help and support. Any man is reluctant, if not unwilling, to expose himself at that level of deepest need unless there is some certainty that those who stand by will seek to understand him and are committed to the same purposes. In too many cases the institutional church's life is too superficial to allow this kind of openness to take place. Yet it is only where the church becomes a body of believers who can "speak the truth in love" to each other that we can have

[3] See Chapter 1, "A General Philosophy for a Relevant Campus Ministry," especially pages 28-30.

any hope of facing the challenging *and* threatening implications inherent in the idea of the Christian's vocation.

A second inadequate understanding which plagues the life and mission of the church is the unresolved dichotomy which still exists in our thinking concerning the nature of the world. In spite of our biblical heritage we continue to move and think as Greeks who believe that there is a basic division of the world into the sacred and secular realms. God is believed to be lord only over that sphere of life which we call sacred. Increasingly as the world becomes more and more secularized, the Christian appears to be in constant retreat, claiming less and less of the world as God's kingdom. God becomes a God of the gaps. We use him to explain those areas of life which still remain mysterious and unknown to us. Unwittingly, therefore, we move into the trap of trying to preserve some spheres of life where we can still claim God's sovereignty. Thus for many sincere Christians the battleground of faith today is in attempting to hold onto Sunday as the "Lord's Day."

Thanks to the careful scholarship and bold writings of biblical scholars and theologians today, we are being made to recognize that the "earth is the Lord's and the *fulness* thereof." The world is one and Christ is lord over this one world. The growing secularization of the world thus may be looked upon as a good rather than an evil. As the so-called "sacred realm" becomes smaller and smaller, we may discover the sense of liberation and joy in proclaiming once again that God is concerned with the whole of life and not just the "religious" sector. Politicians and others may then be less inclined to make such statements as that attributed to one of the presidential candidates during the height of the 1960 campaign: "A man's religion has nothing to do with his being a good president. The only important thing is that he have one."

Many of us have been strongly attracted by Dietrich Bonhoeffer's call for a non-religious interpretation of the gospel. Just what this concept means, no one yet has fully revealed, but it suggests that we are moving toward that day when secularization may well be seen as a gift of God; a gift which frees the world to recognize once again its Lord and Creator.

Within the campus ministry the impact of this idea of the oneness of the world has already led us into heretofore suspect areas of life and work. Such so-called secular concerns as jazz, the theater, and modern art have become vehicles in and through which the gospel has been preached and revealed. Worship services using jazz as the musical medium can no longer be looked on as impious meddling with the "sacred" but as an authentic attempt to express the fact that Christ is lord over the whole world. The fact that so many biblical themes are now being dealt with in the "secular" theater is cause for rejoicing by the Christian community, not because it is a sign that people are becoming more religious, but because it is an indication that the gospel is inextricably bound up with the whole of life.

Thus the sooner we in the campus ministry, as well as the whole church, accept the fact of the growing and inevitable secularization of the world, the sooner can we get about our business of effectively proclaiming Christ's lordship over the whole of it.

A third area of inadequate understanding which radically hampers effective evangelism on the campus is the church's failure to distinguish between religion and faith. We have come to the place where we use the two terms interchangeably. Nothing could be further from the truth! Both serve an important function, but religion can never be a substitute for faith.

Religion serves as the memory of faith. Without the Christian religion we would be a people who have no identity, no sense of history to give shape and direction to the way in which we move in the present. I need the story of Jonah to reveal to myself the ways in which I attempt to escape the call of God and the ultimate foolishness of such attempts. Without Jonah, the parables, the letters of Paul, and the exhortations of the prophets, I would indeed be a poorer man. Yet these stories and this history can never become an adequate substitute for my having to live as a man of faith who "goes out not knowing to what country I am going."

Whereas faith is a particular posture from which to live, religion too often becomes a particular position to be defended.

The problem of religion for many persons is that it tends to identify faith with the mores and patterns of thinking of a particular time in history. We then so easily move to the place in our thinking where we believe that we are being most faithful to the gospel only when we use biblical expressions and categories of thinking in our attempts to witness to the faith. Is it any wonder, knowing nothing of the Jewish system of ritual sacrifice, that modern man, has so much *honest* difficulty with the meaning of the cross when we talk about the "shed blood of the Lamb which takes away the sins of the world"? What else can we expect but confusion and open rejection? For Paul the most meaningful and logical way he could get at the truth of the cross was to interpret it in terms of the religious customs and rituals of his day. This was the mark of his faithfulness to the meaning of the gospel. For us to continue to do so is more a mark of our faithlessness than our faithfulness. Thus the man of faith living in the twentieth century must seek to find those categories of thinking and acting which are most real to modern man, and then through these categories express the living power of the gospel so that its relevancy can no longer be ignored or misunderstood.

Religion is the embodiment of faith in words, rituals, and symbolic actions. It is inevitable and necessary. But this embodiment can easily smother and strangle the dynamic and fragile life of faith. For example, we can perform the ritual of prayer in such a way as to deny its power and reality. Faithful to the form, we smother the spirit.

If students and faculty could be helped to understand this distinction between faith and religion, they would be much more likely to come to grips with the real Christian message and at the same time to value its historical expression in religion. To blur the distinction is to lose both our religion and our faith.

When we take seriously the task of finding new and relevant ways of witnessing to the meaning of the gospel within the academic community, we may well discover that many of our present forms, rituals, words, and programs are wholly inadequate to the task. Do we then demonstrate our faithfulness by moving out into those uncertain areas of life which we have not trod before and where there are no clear road signs — discovering, at times, that the path we have chosen is no broad highway but a dead-end street? Such is the call of the campus ministry today: a call to walk in faith, not knowing with any degree of certainty how it is we are to move. To make the distinction between religion and faith is to free us for this awesome calling. A very helpful booklet, in this regard, is William A. Clebsch's *Contemporary Perspectives on Word, World, and Sacrament.*[4]

TENTATIVE GUIDELINES FOR THE EVANGELISTIC TASK AHEAD

The sooner we all recognize that we are living in a transitional era in which there can be little certainty about methodology and programs, the sooner we may begin to demonstrate in action what it means to live in the uncertainty of faith. To make this discovery does not mean that we are to drift to and fro in a vacuum, but it does imply a certain tentativeness about all our efforts and ideas which will leave us open to the searching judgment and leading of the Holy Spirit.

1. In many ways our day calls for a "tent ministry." We need to grasp the fact that we are being called into a wilderness of uncertainty which demands a kind of mobility of the church, to which it has not been accustomed. We have been too quick to build elaborate structures which root us for time and eternity to a particular spot or a specific kind of programming. We have become captive to our ideas, our structures, and our ways of doing things. Now that God is calling us to a journey through new and uncharted territory, we find the old houses cannot be carried along. We must learn to travel light, equipped with a minimum of paraphernalia.

Every foundation board or directing committee for the campus ministry should be in and of itself a community of Christians who are willing to walk in faith and take risks, anticipating the wonder of God's movement in their history and feeling both free from the necessity of justifying their own actions and yet responsible to the needs of the campus and the world around them. For a foundation board and a campus ministry to live provisionally in this emerging new world is not to imply that what they do takes on the tentativeness of experimentation. The church has no right to experiment with people's lives nor in any way to see its efforts as only being tentative. This is serious business which demands that what we do and say must become the expression of our faith, not merely of our

[4] William A. Clebsch, *Contemporary Perspectives on Word, World, and Sacrament* (Chicago: Division of College and University Work, National Lutheran Council; New York: Division of College Work, Protestant Episcopal Church).

willingness to try the new and the novel. When we discard old forms and structures and venture into new paths of thinking and acting, we must move as those who receive life with trembling hands — who are cognizant of the profundity of this gift and the fearfulness of this responsibility. Thus the church within the academic community is called to move out in faith not because it enjoys the exhilaration of the "new" but because it seeks to be faithful to the Lord of life who continually frees us all from our bondage to old captivities. Whatever we do, therefore, must be done with real seriousness. The fact that we may be called upon to discard even our new methods and programs within a relatively brief time is not so much a sign that we have been merely experimenting in an effort to find that which will last but rather that we are learning to live as men of faith who know that "all things pass away."

2. The second guideline which must be important to those who are concerned about the mission of the church within the academic community rests within the theological task itself. We are discovering that theology is not a rigid, static discipline immobilized by past formulations, but rather an alive and dynamic attempt to speak about God's present activity in the world as well as what he has done throughout history. Thus we can never be content with simply clarifying and updating old ways of speaking theologically. It is important that we study and understand our theological past, but it is also imperative that we be willing to find new ways of discussing and describing God's redeeming acts in our present history. The Christian of today cannot ignore the fact that modern man can only understand himself within the setting of a vision of his own world — which differs profoundly from the world in which the ancient theological pronouncements of the church were formulated.

There is perhaps no place more important for this new theologizing to be carried on than in the campus community where the man of tomorrow is presently emerging and taking shape. What the campus Christian community does in this regard should have significant and lasting importance for the local parish church.

In his book, *Growing Up Absurd* [5] Paul Goodman, a non-religiously-oriented psychoanalyst, suggests that the two central questions for contemporary man are the questions of *justification* and

[5] Paul Goodman, *Growing Up Absurd* (New York: Random House, 1960).

vocation. Certainly these two ideas are far from being foreign to biblical categories. Yet, as we leap to the task of attempting to communicate the biblical message in relation to these two central questions, let us not presume that our traditional ways of thinking about justification and vocation will be relevant or clear to the post-modern man. We must be willing to sweat and dig and even fail in our effort to find those categories of thought and image in and through which the gospel may be most meaningfully declared in our time. All Christians are called upon to be theologians in this regard. Theology cannot be left to the professionals but is essential to the luggage of all who are willing to live in the "tents" of the Christian ministry in our time. Thus we need to encourage faculty and students in all fields to avail themselves of theological training and study, and not to see this discipline as relevant and essential only to the professional clergy. Thus one of the primary functions of a campus ministry may well be that of providing serious theological education for the Christian community within the university or college. The role of the campus pastor must increasingly assume the responsibility of training the laity for their witness in the world.

3. A third guideline for our task in evangelism is concerned with the relationship between our work and our worship. I received a letter a few months ago from an unusually sensitive and intelligent graduate student who attempted to reflect the feelings of his generation concerning the church and worship. In the course of the letter he said:

> My generation is caught up in a struggle with a part of the life of the church which has always been central to its existence—worship. If we could worship with meaning in our institutional churches, much of our present disenchantment might well be worked out. But, to be honest, we can't. And here I suspect the cause is not so much with a lack in the church as a strange kind of spiritual frigidity among us.

However accurate this student's analysis of the problem of worship for young people, it is becoming increasingly apparent that the church in our day has all but lost any sense of the interrelationship of our work in the world and our worship in the church.

Much scholarship today is calling us back to a fresh and challenging understanding of the biblical roots of the idea of worship.

270 · THE CAMPUS MINISTRY

At a meeting of the Faith and Order Commission Professor Leonard Trinterud is reported to have bluntly stated:

> Our English word "worship" misstates the whole content and significance of that which in the New Testament is called "the service of God," i.e., *leiturgia, latreia, diakonia,* and their respective related terms.
> In the New Testament these terms refer normatively to "serving God"; "doing the will of God," in a great variety of ways most of which are *without* cultic significance or form, and which refer principally to that which is done for and among men . . . not to something done to and for God in a sanctuary. The New Testament knows nothing of a *leiturgia, latreia, diakonia* which is localized in an edifice, or to fixed times of occurrence. These terms refer to the whole round of the Christian's ordinary life as people.[6]

This understanding of the roots for the cultic act of worship suggests that one of the central concerns of the campus ministry may be to discover anew the ways in which our liturgy of worship may express and enrich our liturgy of work. If and when we can demonstrate to students and others that worship is directly related and intimately tied up with our day-to-day life in the world, we may well have bridged the present gulf which seems to separate so many young people from the institutional church as well as to enable the church to discover the wellsprings that reside within its own forms and structures.

The end result of this third guideline may well force the campus ministry to see its responsibility for the local parish church. If it is true that we are standing on the growing edge of an entirely new world which is most clearly visible within the academic community, then whatever forms and shapes our ministry takes will ultimately serve to influence the forms and shapes of the ministry of the church at large. There must be a greater degree of helpful communication between the church within the university and the church at home for the mutual benefit and enrichment of both. For too long this communication has only been one-way — from local parish church to the campus community.

SOME EXAMPLES OF AN APPROACH TO THE EVANGELISTIC TASK

Any attempt to suggest examples of campus evangelism is in real danger of perverting the entire task, because so few approaches are

[6] Joseph Sittler, "The Shape of the Church's Response in Worship." *Motive,* Nov., 1957.

applicable to every situation — plus the fact that we are not called to find the "right technique or approach" but rather to depend in faith upon the leading of the Spirit. Thus it is critically important that those who are charged with the responsibility for a campus ministry take the time and effort to think about and discuss the unique character of their own situation as they try to discern the specific way in which God is calling them to be faithful.

The primary purpose, then, of suggesting any concrete examples is not to provide models, but to stimulate creative planning in any given local situation.

The covenanted community

In recent years, following the leading of the Faith and Life Community at Austin, Texas,[7] a number of similar residential communities have sprung up around the country on college and university campuses. In most such communities one of the primary concerns is that of providing a setting in which students may seriously examine the meaning of the Christian faith and its relationship to life. Some of these communities are geared to those students who have already made a commitment of faith and who wish to "add meat to the bones" of their own Christian self-understanding. Oftentimes these groups continue to live together for more than one year and conceive of their function as the gathered expression of the church. However, in light of the changing temper of today's student and his growing agnosticism, it may well be that the character of these residential communities will take the shape of a middleground between the church and the world; a setting in which the seeking student can explore the Christian faith without having to make a commitment of faith as a prerequisite for joining. The students coming together will covenant themselves not to a particular faith position but to the disciplined attempt to examine the Christian faith as it relates to their own lives. Thus the agnostic, the seeker, the overseas student from a different culture and religious background would all be able to participate in this inquiry without any feeling of losing their integrity or of being pressured into a position with which they may have little accord.

At one university where this purpose has become realized, the

[7] See Chapter 6 and Appendix.

makeup of the residential community of life and faith has served increasingly to attract students who feel they stand outside faith and yet who are concerned about the ultimate questions of life. These students meet together for a weekly lecture, study seminars, daily worship (which oftentimes takes the form of a sincere sharing of one's hopes or problems and bears little resemblance to any traditional understanding of Christian worship), corporate work, and fellowship. The year's experience is directed toward an honest facing of doubts and questions as well as an open presentation of the meaning of the gospel. As such it becomes an important approach in evangelism on the campus and may well become a kind of lay seminary for theological training.[8]

Due to the cost of buying and maintaining property, an important variation on the residential community has been a community of faith and learning which involves students in a similar study and discussion of faith and life but which entails no living quarters. Under this plan, students continue to live in university dormitories, fraternity houses, or other residences, and come together regularly as a community to share a meal, lecture, discussion, etc.

The covenanted community is more than a glorified study program. It insists that students be committed not only to the disciplines of work, study, and worship, but to each other as well. Thus the community is not only a place where faith and life are discussed but where they are experienced as well. One of the dangers of such an experience is that it becomes a ghetto where the participants are in fact closeted from the rest of the university. For this reason many of these communities have limited participation in the program to one or, at the most, two years. The community of life and faith is thus not an end in itself, but the means toward the end of demonstrating the relevance of the Christian faith and its relationship to the whole of life.

Drama

Our time is seeing an increased use of literature and drama as a means of communicating the meaning and power of the gospel as

---

[8] Further information on this topic can be obtained by writing to the Commission on Higher Education, National Council of Churches, 475 Riverside Drive, New York, N.Y. 10027.

well as dealing with the central questions of man's existence. We are hearing with increasing frequency the declaration that dramatists and writers are dealing more honestly with the problem of human existence than is the church. Certainly such works as Albert Camus' book *The Fall,* or Jean Paul Sartre's play *No Exit,* or Elia Kazan's movie treatment of Tennessee Williams' *Cat on a Hot Tin Roof* are exciting and powerful media for raising and focusing on the central themes of the Christian faith. Thus the arena of the arts becomes an important middle ground for dialogue between the church and the world.

At the University of Wisconsin the various Protestant religious centers joined together a few years ago to establish the Mime and Man Theatre. The purpose of this amateur group was to present plays within the academic community as a means of stimulating conversation and reflection on the basic issues of life and faith. Following the presentation of such plays as Pär Lagerkvist's *Barabbas* or Camus' *Caligula* the audience would be invited to join in a discussion led by the director of the play, together with a theologian and a faculty member whose discipline was concerned with the problem at hand. Oftentimes the discussion would hold audiences for more than an hour beyond the conclusion of the production itself. The Mime and Man Theatre has drawn many students and faculty into an open dialogue with the Christian faith who might not otherwise have been reached through more traditional approaches.

Many campus groups have developed play-reading seminars, art exhibits, non-credit courses in literature, etc. as means of establishing conversation with those who feel themselves outside the Christian faith. In the very process of ministering in this fashion these groups are declaring an important cornerstone of their faith: that Christ is lord over the whole world and concerned with every sphere of life and activity. Many persons have been drawn into a dialogue with the church on this point alone. Asking the question, "Why is the church interested in the works of non-Christian writers and artists?" they have been confronted by a new and challenging view of faith as being inextricably bound up with the totality of life rather than only a religious segment. The establishment of dialogue by this technique is a significant ministry.

Academic disciplines

There is a growing recognition among Christian leaders that the church for too long has been unrelated to those centers of influence and areas of life in which most men live and work out their daily existence. This feeling has been no less prevalent within the university community. Today there is a growing concern that the campus ministry should work more directly with the academic disciplines of the university. Groups of faculty and students are now meeting regularly to discuss and explore the relationship between the natural sciences and the Christian faith, between psychology and faith, law and faith, etc. Readings from both theology and the specific academic discipline become the basis for probing discussion by the participants. Students and faculty alike have been amazed that the church was interested in their research and study, and doubly amazed that the questions they were dealing with in their specific discipline were often directly related to Christian faith.

Any such attempt to work with an academic discipline must not be seen as a technique to get the ear of the non-Christian in order that he might be "converted," but rather a serious attempt to relate to those areas of knowledge and truth — and the persons involved in them — which are a part of the whole world. The insights and understandings that emerge out of such discussions may well reshape the ways in which we understand and articulate the Christian faith. We, as the church, cannot move boldly into this dialogue presuming that we have all the answers and that our problem is simply that of gaining the hearing and consent of the other participants. Such a stance would be grossly naïve and dishonest. Our concern and interest in any area of thought and research, as well as in any person, must be predicated on the basis that we both are children of God seeking to discover the truth of God in whatever way or fashion he seeks to reveal himself. Neither Christians nor non-Christians can assume that they have a corner on the market of truth. Both can enter into meaningful communication only insofar as they humbly take each other seriously.

Existing groups

It is becoming increasingly apparent that the most effective work of the church may well be done through already-existing groups and organizations rather than by setting up new structures in the church to which people must then be attracted. In an otherwise overly-organized society we must ask whether the church does anyone a favor, least of all itself, by establishing new groups which simply make an additional time demand on persons already driven by the pressures of many commitments. Why is it not possible in most instances for the church to make use of already-existing groups to raise and speak to the ultimate questions of life? Thus our primary task in the campus ministry may be that of helping students and faculty to make more effective and creative use of the various committees and organizations to which they are presently committed rather than attracting them to the ghetto-like existence of so many of our church groups. How can we help a faculty member, for instance, to participate in his faculty committee assignments in such a way that his involvement becomes a catalyst for significant facing of the meaning of the gospel (albeit in non-religious terms)?

Another facet in this concept of a campus ministry is to develop study groups concerning the Christian faith as it relates to existing needs. Thus a natural grouping for the exploration of faith might well be a group of couples who are engaged to be married, and who are facing some of the problems and anxieties of the engagement period as well as the uncertainties of marriage. One campus ministry had a weekend retreat for a small group of engaged couples along with the staff members and their wives. The agenda for the weekend included those problems of finances, sexual adjustment, vocational concerns, in-laws, etc. common to all marriages. The end result of this weekend was to make far more relevant the meaning of the gospel for marriage and for life in general than ever might have been the case in a study group on theology alone. By making use of existing situations and problems as the context for a discussion of faith there is a greater likelihood of initial interest as well as vital communication.

A great number of other creative thrusts might well be mentioned at this point, but all could perhaps be summed up in the one central theme that the evangelistic task must take the structures of the university with greater seriousness than we have been inclined to do in the past. Thus the church must more and more become a church *within* the campus community rather than a church *alongside* the campus community. If faith is to be demonstrated as inextricably bound up with the whole of life, we must address those areas of student and faculty life which already consume so much campus time and energy.

An Indian student on an American campus made this pertinent comment: "The church in America seems to be greatly concerned with whether or not it is proving successful. Yet as I read the Scriptures I am struck by the fact that the central concern for the New Testament church was not whether it was successful but whether or not it was being faithful." As we set about the task of being the church within the university we might do well to remember the admonishment of the young Christian from India. Our call is not so much to be successful as it is to be faithful to the One who is Lord over the whole world. It is to this end that we in faith accept the responsibility of campus evangelism which looms so large before us, conscious of the frightening demands of an emerging new world but also aware of wherein lies our strength and hope.

VERLYN L. BARKER

14: The United
Campus Christian Fellowship

We, the delegated representatives of the Disciples Student Fellowship of the Christian Churches (Disciples of Christ), of the Student
Fellowship Council of the Evangelical United Brethren Church, of
the United Student Fellowship of the United Church of Christ, and
of the Westminster Student Fellowship of the United Presbyterian
Church, U.S.A., believing that we are called to unite our campus
Christian movements to carry out this mission in our campus life,
do now declare ourselves to be one movement, and do take as our
name the United Campus Christian Fellowship.[1]

WITH THE OWNING OF THIS COVENANT at Stephens College in the
fall of 1960, a new expression of Christ's mission within the college
and university communities in the United States was founded.
Viewed from one perspective, the United Campus Christian Fellowship (UCCF) is a union of several student Christian movements. Seen more broadly, it is a response by the participating

[1] United Campus Christian Fellowship, *A Statement of Commitment and Covenant, Basis and Aims, Articles of Operation* (St. Louis: UCCF Publications
Office, 1963), p. 7. Documents related to the merger discussions which evolved
into the United Campus Christian Fellowship, as well as other UCCF materials,
are on file in the UCCF Publications Office, 1720 Chouteau Avenue, St. Louis.

Verlyn L. Barker is the secretary for campus ministry of the Division of
Higher Education and American Missionary Association of the United
Church Board for Homeland Ministries, United Church of Christ, and was
at one time the campus minister at the University of Nebraska.

communions to the changing scene within this nation's colleges and universities as well as to the new currents of theological understanding found within the contemporary church. A statement about UCCF, therefore, necessitates more discussion of its background and context of work than of its history or organizational developments.

THE CHANGING SCENE IN HIGHER EDUCATION

Higher education has always been an important factor in American society, but at no time has its role been more influential and had a more immediate and direct bearing on this culture in particular or the world culture in general. The critical role of the educated man is universally recognized, for he is the one who will assume the burden of responsible leadership in every avenue of human endeavor. In the colleges and universities are the men and women who are receiving the basic education and training which prepare them for positions of responsibility in the laboratories, the halls of justice, the diplomatic posts, the classrooms. In these institutions something of the future is being molded as creative and imaginative minds work with ideas, some of which are so powerful as to change the direction of human history.

External changes

What is happening within these institutions? Externally, the situation is well known. It is common knowledge that five to six times as many high school graduates are entering college as in 1958, and that the present enrollment of nearly four million will reach seven million by 1970. As the United States enters the age in which nearly every qualified student will have the opportunity for a college education if he so chooses, the implications are staggering with regard to additional needs in facilities and teaching personnel. A college education in the United States no longer is a luxury, but an essential for the new world which is emerging. Most institutions of higher education in America are now struggling to adjust to and be prepared for this new and rapid development.

Secondly, this is a day of great state university complexes (some with enrollments reaching the 50,000 figure), a day in which the former teachers' colleges are broadening their courses of study and attaining university status, and a day when the junior colleges are emerging as a very significant development in American higher education. In some states, for example, it is projected that a junior college might be established in every county seat. There is every reason to believe that the junior college development will increasingly be related to higher education rather than to secondary education. Thus the state universities may concentrate increasingly on upper division, graduate and professional instruction.

Parallel with these developments is the fact that the church-related colleges now are assuming a smaller proportion of the educational responsibility. They are no longer the pacesetters in the total higher education scene, though their task is no less important in American higher education. Only a short time ago the church-related colleges had sixty per cent of the college enrollment; now the figure is approximately forty per cent and it is expected that the percentage will decrease within the next decade.

Thirdly, today's student population is a mobile population. In some of the larger urban universities, there are as many as nine transfer students for every ten freshmen. There is, in general, a high percentage of students transferring from one institution to another as, after receiving general and basic course work, they find it possible to gain entrance into institutions which they consider better or which offer particular specializations. This mobility will increase with the junior college development, particularly (as in California) when the course of study in the junior colleges is geared into the state university system.

The mobility is also noticed among the administrative and teaching personnel. There was a time when the tenure of these persons sometimes extended over several decades, if not the whole, of their professional life. Today, a glance at the faculty turnover ratios indicates that the college and university communities are no longer characterized by this continuity and stability. Professors leave for better positions as readily as students leave for better schools.

Fourthly, it is estimated that within the decade the commuter-type college will accommodate seventy per cent of the students. Already one hears of the "lunch box" student in contrast to the "dormitory" student. These students arrive at the beginning of the day's classes and leave the campus immediately at the end of the last class, often leaving for a job in order to have the finances for their education and their families. They do not identify with the university as a community but retain an identification with a small circle of persons in their own area of study and with the home community. If they are related to any campus group, it is likely a professional group, not a social or religious group.

Fifthly, the colleges and universities have greatly extended their services for the student. For instance, most schools have well-equipped and well-staffed infirmaries, many with medical plans for students and staff. Student personnel offices with trained counselors have been added in most schools. The newest and most modern building on campus is often the campus center, in which are facilities for eating, listening to music, reading, dancing, movies, lounging, small and large group meetings, and often bowling alleys, game rooms for table tennis and billiards, and even barber shops. In many ways, campuses are becoming more self-sufficient and thus less related to the life of the larger community and less dependent on the services heretofore provided by non-college and university groups and institutions — including the church.

Lastly, the youthful, energetic lad in loafers and a sweater who is usually "off on a spree" is not a typical picture of the contemporary student. The student population is a more varied group. It is not unusual for as much as thirty per cent of the student body to be married, living in apartments throughout the college community or even in a married student complex provided by the college. Too, from twenty to twenty-five per cent of the graduates enter graduate or professional schools; hence, an increase in their numbers on campus. Nor is the campus as "American" as it once was. There are many thousands of students from other countries studying in the United States.[2] The emerging world culture is a part of the everyday experience on the campus.

Externally, then, the college and university campus is not the same as it was even a decade ago. The school of four to eight thousand students is no longer considered large; the campus where most students are in residence becomes rarer; the profile of the

[2] See Chapter 9.

student as an undergraduate, single, American man between eighteen and twenty-one who stays his four years in the same school is shattered. The question for the church is this: Might not all these circumstances indicate something to the church and its campus ministry, particularly the ministry whose main emphasis is on a weekly fellowship meeting directed at single undergraduate students living in campus residences? Being relieved of providing social and recreational opportunities and, thus, of the need for facilities now found in the campus center, the church may now be free for a mission of extraordinary significance.

Internal changes

The internal changes within higher education are equally astounding. It is well known that the university is becoming increasingly specialized and diversified, expressing in the several schools of the university or in the several departments of the college separate interests and skills which are developed to a degree heretofore left for the specialists themselves. As a result the schools find it increasingly impossible to transmit a coherent view of human culture to the student. The attempt to provide a general educational curriculum in all schools has not kept pace with the more specialized movements within the university. Just the increase in the amount of knowledge in any one area of study poses the dilemma of choosing between an inadequate education in a particular area in favor of a general education on the one hand, or specialization at the expense of general education on the other. This is a severe problem for the educator. Some have suggested that the college course should be extended to a five-year program for the bachelor's degree, but even this, according to certain faculties in the technical and scientific fields, would only mean that the student would be able to devote more time to advanced studies in his own area.

With this development has come a constant raising of the educational standards. This is possible because many students now arrive at college with an educational background comparable to that of a student of a decade ago with two years of college study. Increased competition within the schools and a growing motivation among the students are also contributory. Added to the quantitative factors, these qualitative standards pose difficult problems for the dean of the faculty or president as he searches for competent teachers. More than a few educators are faced with the question of whether the quality of education can maintain pace with the quantity of knowledge and numbers of students.

At the same time the utilitarian function of education has been intensified. In the public mind education is linked with the national security and with overall national growth and development. In our society the quantity and quality of a person's education are directly related to his job opportunities and personal job security. A philosophy of education which speaks of "liberating" the person has perhaps always been more an ideal than an actuality in American higher education; the present empirical goals and objectives of students and educators speak loudly. At the present, most students view study as a means for acquiring knowledge and skills that will provide them with an academic degree which, in turn, will assist them in finding employment. Better grades from the better institutions mean a better chance in the job market. It is not surprising, then, that the contemporary students take their studies quite seriously amidst the severe competition they face. The night air is less filled with carefree episodes and the days are less given to the nonsense of floats and parades. Campus organizations and activities, including religious organizations, have had their day of prominence. The glory that these activities used to bring some individuals, which was regarded as a mark of "leadership," is now viewed as bothersome and trivial. A new pattern of life has emerged on the campuses, and to understand this may help to interpret the general decline in religious groups and activities.

A discussion of the internal changes could be expanded to include such factors as the motivation of the faculty and their relative devotion to teaching, to research, and to writing. Or it could take up the role of the administrator and his tensions in being both an educator and a public relations expert responsible for finding the resources for new buildings and larger operating budgets; or the discussion could comment on the administrator's role of pacifying the alumni in order to retain their support or on his relationship with the legislative bodies which have a decisive voice in policy and educational philosophy. All of these factors have important implications for what is happening inside the college and university.

Perhaps of most importance for this particular discussion is mention of the changing context within which the church's mission is now cast, especially the changing relationship between the church and the university. Certainly, there are many indications that the acute separation between the church and the university is passing. To be sure, there is yet considerable apprehension regarding the church in higher education, for it is still easy to recall the day when the work of the scholar was restricted and directed by the church. As Professor Dirks of Yale has said, "The regimentation and restriction were so outrageous to academicians that some of them went into such profound shock from which even now their entranced successors have hardly emerged."[3] But at least the day has arrived when many in the church would agree that if its presence meant a policy of dictating to the universities, the church would do better to remain outside and beyond these institutions of higher education. The church needs the confidence of the educator that it will not seek to dictate the content and methodology of education: "When it comes to facts, the Christian has no new facts to press upon the educators. . . . When it comes to training the intellect, there is no particular skill of faith which adds to reasoning, nor are there religious methods of turning out new facts."[4]

Surely the church has come to the point where it is not seeking to tell the artist what to paint and the writer what to write, but rather is wanting to share in interpreting what has been painted and written, what has been expressed by and about man and his culture. In like manner, certainly the church no longer seeks to tell the scientist what to discover in the laboratory and no longer instructs the scholar what should be found in the archives. The church must now be interested in and prepared for discussing the significance of the scholars' findings for mankind and for man's

[3] J. Edward Dirks, "The Mission of the United Presbyterian Church in Higher Education," p. 3. An address presented to the meeting of the Synod of New England at Northfield, Massachusetts, June 13, 1961. The writer of this chapter is immeasurably indebted to Professor Dirks' teaching and guidance, both in the classroom and through his writings. Used with permission.

[4] *Ibid.*, p. 6.

destiny. The church must attend the forum of discussion, but it must arrive as a listener and learner, as well as a teacher.

There are signs which point up the changing context. There is a new outlook by the scholar as he engages in his work. No longer are research and teaching conducted in such a naïve fashion as to imply that the scholar believes he can finally ignore his finiteness or exclude himself, his passions and biases, from his work. The new methodology of seeking to be as objective as one's understanding and information permit is much different from some of the former claims of total objectivity. Today's stance implies that the man of faith recognizes he is just that and, further, that he cannot disengage his faith-commitment as he steps onto the campus or into the classroom. While he does not use this relationship as an excuse for prejudicial or inadequate treatment of material and concepts, his awareness of a faith-commitment allows him more freedom and objectivity than the man who claims no faith position. More than this, he does not remain blind to who he is as a man.

Another sign is the emerging climate for dialogue. One need not circulate long within a campus to realize that there are those eager for study and discussion of the theological dimensions and perspectives in their work. Volumes of Tillich and the Niebuhrs are found on the professors' shelves and in the libraries — probably more read in these settings than in our church study groups. No one needs to convince the nuclear physicist that America's 7.6 overkill capacity, possible because of his work, has certain crucial implications for mankind. Nor need the church send a special messenger to the laboratory of the life biologist to warn him of the significance of his passing remark about creating life. And it was before articles on contemporary art appeared in our church literature that artists realized Picasso had something rather incisive about man and society to communicate through his painting. All of this is to say that there are those within the campuses who understand Professor Dirks' way of speaking about the truth of the Christian faith. This statement can be understood by the Christian and the non-Christian:

> The truth of Christian faith is not literary; it is personal, relational. It is not a statement, but the way things really are, how God and man and the world stand to each other, what we have to do with each other. All the statements we make, the myths we use, are attempts to give a

THE UNITED CAMPUS CHRISTIAN FELLOWSHIP • 285

picture of the way things really are and where we fit in—the context of our lives.[5]

These signs indicate that a new moment for the church's presence has arrived. There is emerging a new language within the academic world which encompasses the theological; a new mood which encourages the question about man and his destiny. In response, the church has greater tasks than big building projects (in the shadow of the campus center) and recreational tournaments. Its all-too-common posture of sitting across the street while dreaming up religious questions, in which college and university people ought to be interested, must change. It is time that the church became a participant in discussing the questions already being asked.

Externally and internally, institutions of higher education in the United States have changed and are changing. The question before the church is whether it is sufficiently concerned about higher education to consider these changes and sufficiently free from present patterns of work and ecclesiastical structure to find effective ways of engaging in a ministry which is relevant to the daily work and life of the institutions of higher learning.

THE CHANGING SCENE IN THE CHURCHES

To characterize the way in which the church has viewed its mission in higher education within any one time and any one place is to risk certain inaccuracies, but for the purposes of perspective there may be some value in stating a few generalizations. One is that Christian education and evangelism have sometimes been seen as among the tasks of the church-related schools by assigning to these schools certain objectives and goals which were taken from the church rather than from education itself. Some church-related schools use "church criteria" in evaluating their usefulness and their Christian character, such as the number of Christian professors, the range of courses in the department of religion, the extent of participation in religious activities, and the attendance at required chapel. The stronger of the church-related colleges have, of course, seen themselves first as institutions of higher learning rather than church institutions and have seen their Christian vocation to be that of education itself.

[5] Ibid.

Starting from the same frame of reference as the church-related college which is primarily concerned about its church-relatedness, the campus ministry (or student work, as it was formerly called) has often been seen as a necessity for the "godless" public universities in which the church was not able to exact the same controls in faculty and staff, curriculum, and campus activities. The expectations of these ministries have often been to preserve the students "by protecting and guarding them from the corrosive acids of rationalism" as well as from the more liberal practices commonly associated only with these institutions. Stated differently, campus ministry has been seen as a way in which the "religious" part of man is nourished even as the college or university cares for the intellectual, physical, and social needs of the student. Too often the view has been that, since the students in the public institutions were not so fortunate as to be able to attend a church-related school or not so wise as to choose one, the next best course for the church was to follow them to these public institutions.

Institutional relationships

Whatever truth there is in these general characterizations has been challenged as the church continues to determine the nature of its mission and responsibility in higher education, whether in the church-related college or in the private and public institutions. First of all, the church no longer sees its responsibility as that of making colleges or professors or students Christian by providing "Christian" activities for them. Rather, the church considers that it is called to recognize study, teaching, and research, as all areas of work to which the Christian must bring to bear the best efforts of a critical, imaginative, and creative mind. The day is passing when the church can look upon its own colleges and universities as especially precious in the sight of God; the day is likewise passing when the colleges and universities of the so-called secular order are seen as outside the bounds of the churches' concern.

The pertinent concern no longer is that of who controls the institution or how many are attending fellowship groups, but rather what is the meaning of one's life and work within the academic community when he believes he is called to obedience to Jesus Christ. The concern is thus for the person engaged in the work of the university, for the challenge and encounter he finds in study and research, for the personal relationships he has there. Does the Christian faith have any word for the nuclear physicist concerned about America's overkill capacity — something, that is, other than a response of placid avowal that he should never have made it possible? Dare the church risk coming out of its building, crossing the street, and being encountered by the life biologist's postulates? Do matters of academic freedom basically concern the Christian? If the answer to these questions is in the negative, then the church has no "mission" here. If, however, the church affirms that Christ is Lord of all of life, then it must necessarily affirm the meaning of his lordship within the life and work of the campus.

In this instance, what the Christian has to contribute in the area of education is a point of view about the world and man, about life and destiny, about the Creator and his relationship to his creation. The Christian affirms that the "one thing needful" for man in fulfilling the divine purpose of his life is to enter into a redeeming, reconciling, personal knowledge of God through Jesus Christ. This stance is at the heart of the truth proclaimed in the Christian faith. Standing before the God of Truth who revealed himself in Jesus Christ, the church is free to exhort the communities of learning to be faithful and rigorous in their pursuit of truth. Perhaps this position is at the center of the church's mission, the essential meaning of the oft-used phrase, "supporting the university."

> The Christian will covet truth, pursue truth, make it his own as an act of worship, for his God is the God of truth. Every effort after every kind of truth—scientific, artistic, political, economic—is an obeisance before the God of all truth, a doing of honor before Him, an act of worship. This discovering and transmitting of true knowledge is not something casual or professional or merely interesting; it is part of the worship of God, the Christian's off-the-knees devotion. To pursue knowledge is like the pursuit of righteousness—it is man's duty to God. The late Archbishop of York observed in this connection: "A sound Christian theology insists that the love of truth is as important as the practice of truthfulness."[*]

This point of view does not permit the conclusion that the church no longer has a critical role to assume within the university, but

[*] Ibid., p. 8.

it does mean that such criticism must be rooted "in the full belief that the university has a lofty purpose to serve, that it is responsible to God and to man for serving well, and that only to the peril of culture can the university turn aside from its high purpose and be content with irresponsible learning or with irresponsible technical competence.'" Sir Walter Moberly is said to have stated: "Only the person who loves the university well should venture to tamper with it."

There is one particular area in which the church in this day needs to emerge with constructive criticism, namely that of the teaching of theological studies in the university. Because of confused thinking about the church-state problem, and because of an inarticulate delineation between Christian nurture and education and teaching about religion, public colleges and universities have, for the most part, ignored this area of teaching. As a result, Islamic and Hindu studies, for example, have been included, but the Hebraic-Christian tradition which is so much a part of western civilization is excluded. The fact that Islamic and Hindu studies are included is not cause of alarm, for indeed they belong within the total offerings of a university curriculum. The time has come, however, to question the institution which purports to offer instruction in all areas of human knowledge and yet omits the theological discipline as an historic element in the academic tradition, a discipline which has been one of the principal intellectual activities of mankind throughout the whole evolution of western history and thought.

Scholarly instruction in the Bible, history of Jewish thought, history of Christian thought, and other similar subjects can be given for enlightenment without the necessity of indoctrination. Further, the colleges and universities should not be so timid about challenging the scholarly quality of much of the off-campus "credit" religion courses which the churches devise and offer by their appointed teachers. To include many of *these* courses in the curriculum would raise some legitimate church-state issues. Nevertheless, there is a growing conviction that we are hiding behind a mythical legal barrier which in reality does *not* prevent public institutions from including the discipline of theology within the curriculum,

⁷ *Ibid.*

taught by scholars selected by the institutions on the same basis any other faculty appointments are made.

The teaching in the area of theology is just one example of the important issues to which the church should address itself as it seeks to "help the university be the university." This approach, of course, does not mean that the church "tells" the university, but rather engages in conversation on this or any issue with the hope that new understanding will emerge on the part of both the church and the college or university. On many issues and problems there will remain divergent opinions, but sterile and backward is the college and university community which is not constantly struggling for new light amidst diverse convictions and perspectives. Through enlightened and imaginative interchange, both the church and the institution of higher education can find new directions as each seeks to discharge its unique tasks.

Initially, then, the church is beginning to see its task in campus ministry differently. The mission is not essentially that of keeping track of students while they are away from home, nor that of providing a "religious" house with a hand-holding pastor. Rather, it is primarily that of professing the Christian faith amidst a community which has a common vocation of study, research, and teaching — a vocation in which the church believes firmly. This mission includes the critical function, but this is for the purpose of helping education to fulfill its functions, not that of promoting special interests of the church.

Personal relationships

Secondly, for campus ministry the relationship between the church and higher education is increasingly one between two communities of persons rather than between two institutions. The community of the people of God and the community of learning are not distinct in membership, as has so long been presumed, but distinct in task; the memberships overlap. Gone forever, hopefully, are the days when the most common encounter between the church and the university was the encounter in which the church made its demands on the university, when the joint religious groups arrived at the president's door with the demand that Wednesday nights be left open for religious activities, that the Greeks stop rushing and socializing from five to seven on Sunday evenings, and that the university grant credit for religious courses devised and taught by the church foundations. And may the days soon be gone when the university welcomes the presence of the "foundations" only as the moral police force within the campus or as an excuse to show the public that the university cares about religion. The courteous bow of respect and the subtle use, or abuse, of the other fails to recognize the integrity of either the church or the university and precludes the dynamics of a creative interchange between these communities.

More specifically, the meaningful relationship is not between institutions but between persons. To recognize that administrators and faculty do not lose their humanity by assuming particular tasks in the academic community is to assist in breaking down the depersonalization and ghettoization within schools and departments. To be sure, there are categories of persons: administrators, faculty, students; Greeks and independents; residents and commuters; undergraduate, graduate, and professional students; American and international students. There are ranks: professors, associate professors, and assistant professors; deans and assistant deans. Likewise there are disciplines and there are colleges in which persons seem to have their principal identity. But there is also a human aspect. These are persons faced with the experiences of any man — love and hatred, acceptance and rejection, jealousy, envy, and pride; sorrow and happiness, sickness and health, life and death, belief and doubt. These are husbands, wives, fathers, mothers. They, too, are affected deeply by the power structures and struggles, even (or especially) within the universities themselves. In all, these are persons for whom the message of love and reconciliation is no less significant nor the truth of God's revelation in Christ less meaningful because they live within the community of learning.

Among these persons are devout Christians and many non-Christian allies. Among them also are those who are not in sympathy with the philosophy of education which modern society has thrust upon the institutions of higher learning, too heavily emphasizing the functional, nor with a new intellectual climate which cares too little about the creative and imaginative work of the mind. These persons need encouragement as they strive for the rebirth of humane learning and culture. They await counsel, guidance, and colleagues for the battle against the vulgarization of the educational enterprise.

To have stated so briefly and with so little discussion these comments about the changing scene in higher education is only to emphasize the fact of change in the colleges and universities. One is not so sure about the change within the life of the church and its campus ministry for there is yet much "stability" which provides an effective challenge to the thesis presented. At most, it is a changing, not a changed, picture, a part of which is the ministry expressed in the United Campus Christian Fellowship.

UCCF and Campus Ministry

Simultaneous with the changing scene in American higher education and the changing relationships between the church and higher education have been certain vital currents within the life of the church which have contributed to the new direction of campus ministry as expressed in UCCF. Of particular significance has been the emerging ecumenical movement and its focus on the unity of the Christian mission and the reaffirmation of the meaning of the ministry of the laity in the life of the church. With these currents there has also been a growing emphasis upon the mission of the church directed in the world, an emphasis which, to some degree, has shifted the church's focus to a concern for the world in which the church has its life rather than on itself.

Perhaps the most important characteristic of UCCF is that it is an expression of the ecumenical church. UCCF affirms clearly the belief that the day of denominational competition and duplication of efforts must pass, that the ring of denominational "student centers" which surround so many of the college and university campuses is a mighty witness to the brokenness of the body of Christ, a witness that too much lifts high the denominational banner at the cost of Christian mission.

UCCF had its inception, historically, with the United Student Fellowship of the Congregational Christian Churches and the Evangelical and Reformed Church, now the United Church of Christ. In a student study conference in 1953, this student Christian movement discussed the subject, "The Nature and Destiny of United

Student Fellowship." The result of their discussions was the declaration which follows:

> The outstanding facts of our existence as a USF have been the awareness of our unity in Christ Jesus and our failure to proclaim Him as the one Lord of the Church and the world, of the university and of our common lives as Christian students. Therefore, we dedicate our life as a United Student Fellowship to the end that a united student Christian movement might emerge in this country. We have neither the wisdom nor the purity to know how or when this will happen, but we do know who is calling: Jesus Christ, our Lord.[8]

This statement provided an occasion for the various segments of the student movement in the United States to consider the meaning of Christian mission and the implications of this meaning for their lives. It was clear from the beginning that UCCF was to be some new expression, that the existing movements and organizations would die in order that something new might arise. Too, there was no equivocation about its being a uniting effort in response to a conviction that Christ's call was for a visible expression of the unity of his church as his body. This statement from Lesslie Newbigin was perhaps quoted more than any other:

> Her [the Church's] life is precisely life under the sign of the Cross, which means that she desires to possess no life, no security, no righteousness of her own, but to live solely by His grace. When she becomes settled, when she becomes so much at home in this world that she is no longer content to be forever striking her tents and moving forward, above all when she forgets that she lives simply by God's mercy and begins to think that she has some claim on God's grace which the rest of the world has not, when, in other words, she thinks of her election in terms of spiritual privilege rather than missionary responsibility, then she comes under His merciful judgment as Israel did.[9]

To those engaged in the UCCF discussions, Newbigin specifically meant that United Student Fellowship, Disciples Student Fellowship, and the other participants had served their day and it was time to strike these tents and move on. The conviction was strong that the event of Jesus Christ was so decisive that the deepest divisions among men were now transcended and that no tradition or precious organization could be exalted above the unity found

[8] United Student Fellowship, Minutes of 1953 Study Assembly.

[9] Lesslie Newbigin, *The Household of God* (New York: Friendship Press, 1954), p. 149. Used by permission.

in Christ. Further, there was and has been a conviction that this affirmation necessitates a single Christian witness. UCCF began with the belief that the church's mission was not to keep the communion's own students safely within the fold of that communion, nor to prove that intellectuals believe in God, nor to acquire control of the campus in a struggle with the so-called secularist; stated affirmatively, it began with the belief that the mission was to express God's love in the world, in the university. Given this understanding and confession, why should there be a sectarian witness on the campuses?

Through biblical and theological study of the nature of the church and its mission, the participants in the earliest discussions agreed that Paul was talking directly to the contemporary church when he wrote about the churches in Asia Minor and elsewhere. The early church included Jews like Priscilla and Aquila, Greeks like Luke, and persons of mixed origin like Timothy — all knit together into one fellowship, all drawn together by him who was the Good Shepherd. Likewise, Paul spoke clearly to reproach the church in Corinth wherein some divisively had taken the name of Paul, or Apollos, or Cephas, or even the name "Christian." UCCF is based on the conviction that the church of Jesus Christ is called to express visibly, as well as invisibly, the unity which is in Christ Jesus.

> We affirm that in the church of Christ we are members of one body, and we believe we are called to the organic union of our campus Christian movements as a more adequate expression of our unity in the Church, that we may better proclaim the gospel in campus and community life.[10]

In a sense UCCF is one response to the continuous "ecumenical discussions" which have found it difficult to move beyond concentrating on why a common witness is *not* possible and on a study of traditions which often has strengthened existing structures rather than fulfilling the hope of bringing the resources of various traditions into a common movement. It has been difficult for many to recognize that present structures and patterns represent a change from those of the past and that the mission of the church might now be demanding a further change from the present.

[10] UCCF, *Statement*, p. 7.

The intent of UCCF as a united effort has sometimes been mis-understood as a move to combine present groups into one large group and under one roof. This is not the objective so much as to be engaged in a common ministry based on a common understand-ing of the mission. Where present locations permit a greater out-reach, UCCF may operate out of two or more centers, each of which may concentrate in different areas of the campus community. On some smaller campuses, sometimes campus ministry personnel has been made possible by the unified approach. On other smaller cam-puses no full-time leadership has been possible, but a common ministry is expressed through the combined leadership of local pastors or faculty personnel.

Beyond the theological factors there are other reasons which have made this new direction imperative. It is not possible for each communion to provide a ministry which can reach into every facet of the university community, the different dorm complexes, the graduate and professional schools, married students, faculty, even into the new campus developments which are emerging. Together, there is a possibility of greater outreach and effectiveness.

Secondly, UCCF is a ministry which seeks to encompass the whole of the campus community in contrast to the time when the church saw its mission to be that of working only with undergraduate stu-dents. UCCF is a ministry of and with the total Christian com-munity.

Sometimes the intent of a "campus" movement has been inter-preted as an attempt to bring together faculty and students into a single fellowship. The endeavor, however, is not to bring anyone into a group but to do that which will assist these persons in their Christian witness so that they become a part of the Christian out-reach. UCCF has stated it in this manner:

UCCF affirms that the *koinonia* of the church is one. Students, faculty, administrators and campus ministers may hold what are somewhat dif-ferent offices (positions) or stations (areas of responsibility) within the *koinonia,* but they are not independent of one another. UCCF believes that if there is to be a visible Christian community within the campus, the wholeness must be manifest in unity of purpose, common under-standing and shared mission. This understanding of mission will reveal tasks which can be carried out best among undergraduates within their own circles of living and working. There will be others demanding expression within the milieu of graduate students and within the professional schools. There will be some meetings and projects among faculty members and administrative officers. Among the campus ministry there will be specific functions and commitments to counsel and work together in their mission. There will be times when the communions' representatives will need to meet among themselves to work at their assignments. Numerous tasks will require participants from two or more of the states and offices. Most important is that all of these efforts and structures necessarily be kept flexible, dependent upon the leading of the Spirit and prepared to function as God's servant in behalf of the world.[11]

No longer is the term "student work" descriptive of the ministry, nor is the term "student worker" accurate in the portrayal of the role of campus ministers within this ministry and movement. The campus minister is no longer the "director" of the ministry; he is not hired to "do" the ministry but rather is the one essentially responsible for enabling the Christian community as a whole to be engaged in the ministry. His task is that of an "enabler" or that of the teaching elder. He assists by preparing others for their mission in their daily life and work. Rather than drawing university personnel into "programs" in the belief that this is the manner in which they witness to their faith, he recognizes that university persons are responding to their Christian vocation when they are engaged honestly and openly in study, research, and teaching, and when they are faithful in expressing the power of God's love and reconciliation in their relationships with others. The campus minister seeks to be the theological teacher for those earnestly seeking an understanding of the Christian faith as it is addressed to the ultimate questions being raised in study and research.

These statements suggest that campus ministry personnel must come from the best trained men in the ministry. It is increasingly apparent that the need is for those competent in biblical and theological thought, those whose standards of scholarship will make possible an imaginative and creative interchange with persons in the academic community. The day for the recreational leader and the popularizer of the faith has gone forever; the day has arrived when the church must raise up men who can participate in the battle of ideas.

[11] *Ibid.*, p. 3.

Implied in this discussion is the idea that there has been a change in the locus of the campus ministry. Formerly, there was considerable concentration on the gathering of the students, on the group itself. The programs and publicity focused on the weekly meeting which became the "religious activity" of the week. Presently, there is an increasing emphasis on the rhythm of the gathering of the Christian community and its dispersion into the community for the task of sharing the faith in the daily routine. The gathering is not so much an entity in itself as a time to prepare the Christian community for the task of witness and to experience the strength which Christian fellowship provides. The concept does not minimize the importance and power of Christian fellowship, but it does acknowledge that the church has often been guilty of equating the "group" with Christian fellowship, when in reality it was little more than a ghetto of self concern and escape from the real world. There have been times and places where the so-called Christian fellowship has been more difficult to enter than the hardest of the Greek systems, so ingrown had the religious groups become.

Just as the locus of the ministry is shifting from the "center" to the campus, so is the focus. The center is little more than a place of contact for the campus minister, the place for study, the place to gather those persons responsible for strategy of the mission. The center is the place from which the ministry stems, the place out of which the campus minister works.

Likewise the emphases of work are changing. Greater time and energy are now devoted to study, discussion and dialogue, and Christian social action, than in a former time. Little emphasis is given to recreational programs and social affairs, which at one time were so prominent. This is true not just because the church has found areas of greater need, but because the colleges and universities have, themselves, provided for the recreational and social needs of the students. Campus life committees and campus centers with a variety of activities provide a variety of opportunities for the students, a variety which the church could not offer even if it cared to continue this emphasis.

Lastly, UCCF is definitely a part of the life of the parent communions; it is a mission of the church which sees itself related to the broader life of the church as well as to the life of the local congregations. Though administratively apart from the local churches, more and more the campus ministry and the ministry of the local congregations are seen as a shared ministry. There is a mutual grappling with the nature of the church's mission within academic communities in an effort to destroy the common image of the church as being "intellectually lost in an obscurantism with a nineteenth century theology contending with nineteenth century science of evolution." Too often the university town churches have seen little more in their relationship to the academic community than a scrambling to lure the new president, dean, or faculty member into the church for questionable reasons or an attempt, by scores of devices, to get a good turnout from the students on Sunday morning. The time has come to listen to the student who wants nothing to do with the church because he sees so little relationship between its affirmations and its actions, and to listen to the faculty who would like their children to benefit from a sound Christian education but care little about the quality of teaching or curriculum which is found in the Christian education program in many churches. A relevant and effective ministry within the college and university communities demands the best efforts of both the campus ministry and the ministry of the congregations; together, they must share in this ministry with mutual understanding and endeavor.

In summary, the campus ministry expressed through the United Campus Christian Fellowship is a ministry of a Christian community within the life and work of the communities of learning. It is a common witness of four communions which is shared with the local congregations and a witness which seeks to include the whole of the campus community.

UCCF AND STRUCTURES

UCCF is more than a merger of several student Christian movements. A precise separation of a campus movement from campus ministry is not possible. To be engaged in a common mission, through UCCF, is to become involved in a common philosophy and strategy in campus ministry; a philosophy and strategy which could not leave intact the structures of campus ministry agencies at the local, state or regional, and national levels. Nor does it leave unaffected such areas as budgeting or personnel standards.

Increasingly the communions have become aware that each cannot separately develop campus ministry philosophy or strategy, for these elements directly affect the other communions with whom the UCCF covenant has been made. Each year the number of campuses on which any of the UCCF-related communions are individually engaged in denominational campus ministry decreases. In fact, there are many states in which these communions have no separate work. Hence, it is not uncommon to find joint or united campus ministry boards being formed at the local and state levels, agencies with representative membership from the parent communions. These united boards assume responsibilities for campus ministry philosophy, strategy, personnel, budget, facilities, and interpretation.

At the national level, there is now a proposal that the UCCF Commission for Church Relations become the single advisory committee for campus ministry for the higher education agencies of the four participating communions. This commission is composed of representatives from these agencies as well as the national officers of UCCF. The fact that such a proposal is under serious discussion indicates that, at the policy-making level, most work and recommendations will be determined jointly. For the most part, the national campus ministry staffs of the four communions function as a single staff, frequently consulting together and increasingly representing each other in the field.

In selecting campus ministry personnel, the four communions fully recognize the recommended candidates from any of the four communions. The common advice to personnel committees is that the best qualified candidate should be called, regardless of the communion in which he holds membership or his ecclesiastical standing. Once a campus minister is called, he becomes the campus minister of each of the participating communions.

These more structural changes are mentioned only for the purpose of illustrating some of the organizational implications which are emerging as these four communions discover what it means to own the UCCF covenant. At a time when the church has been made aware of its "establishment" and "institutionalism," it should also take note of those areas of work where ecclesiastical structures are being recast in order that its mission might be extended.

It would be presumptuous to postulate what will become of UCCF. It lives dedicated to the hope that other communions will find it possible to "own the covenant" in order to strengthen the Christian mission and the witness to the common lordship of Jesus Christ. New participation might mean some changes in UCCF, but ingrained deeply within the very formulation is its dedication not first to traditions and structures or patterns, but to mission. If UCCF becomes enamored with its own existence, likely it will become known more for its organization than for its missionary life and work. If it is faithful to that which called it into being, it will become only another tent which will be struck down and set in another place in another form as these people of God travel within the world.

LeROY S. LOATS

15: The Church Alive
in the University

Now TO ACTUAL MINISTRY! What form does the church take as its members live out their days in a modern college or university? The purpose of this chapter is to describe a variety of campus ministries. What should you anticipate these days when you seek to discover what men and women of the church are doing in the academic community? Obviously, there are many forms, a variety of ministries, and divergent expressions as the gospel of Jesus Christ is taken seriously in individual localities and in the wide range of vocations within the university itself.

If you are over thirty-five years of age you are likely to anticipate a campus Christian ministry similar to that which you knew when you were a student. Even if you were not active yourself in a student Christian group or program, you may harbor a concept of their activities. For most of us the very name "student work" conjures up a series of images similar to the following: a Sunday night supper with many wholesome teenagers devouring hot dogs, casseroles, and ice cream; a "student worker," young, handsome, likable, and pop-

LeRoy S. Loats has been the university pastor and an instructor in the department of religion at Oklahoma State University. He is now area secretary for the north central area, Division of Higher Education of the Board of Christian Education of the United Presbyterian Church in the U.S.A.

ular, who is milling about meeting newcomers and sharing the good time with the regulars; a songfest with teenagers gathered around a piano singing "Jacob's Ladder" and, "Lord, I Want to Be a Christian"; a hay ride; a weekend retreat; and a remodeled nineteenth-century house on College Avenue which serves as a "denominational fellowship center" equipped with a hi-fi set, ping pong tables, a small shelf of books, and the inevitable soft drink dispenser. These are the marks of the Student Christian Movement as we have known it in America.

If you were involved in such a group, you fondly remember the fun and fellowship which enriched your life as a student, and you expect a similar experience for students in college and university today.

What is described in this chapter is quite different, only because a silent revolution has been in progress for more than a decade now. Since World War II, and particularly since the early 'fifties, campus ministry has undergone extensive change, and new patterns of Christian ministry have emerged or are in the process of emerging in the colleges and universities of our time.

The most obvious evidence of change is the presence of faculty who, in many universities, have become participants in ministry in recent years. Secondly, the students in our time attend colleges and universities under conditions which have been altered considerably by recent world history. Generally, they come to campus better prepared than their parents were for involvement in higher education. They are vocationally oriented. They are more concerned about achieving success in the classroom and less inclined to be involved in extracurricular activities.

For these and other reasons, what is described here with brevity will perhaps not fit the familiar stereotypes of "student work," but we hope is a reliable account of what is happening in our time.

Although this chapter does not report on the work of local churches in college and university communities, let it be said early that the life and work of countless congregations has been, and remains, extremely important to campus ministry. The steady, reliable, continuing, and often unsung witness of pastors and members of these churches with students, faculty, and administrators continues to be strategic. Worship opportunities here, as everywhere, are central to life and mission, and who can possibly know how many persons have discovered the profound meaning of life because Christians who are the community of faith in college and university communities involved them in their endeavor.

What follows is not an attempt to describe campus ministry apart from the local church, but rather an account of a wide variety of patterns which emerge within the university itself, frequently as the result of the experiences and insights which campus pastors and local churches have discovered as they live and work together in the common task.

Perhaps it would be helpful to look to Herluf M. Jensen who, until recently, served as executive secretary for the National Student Christian Federation. In a comprehensive report to a NSCF General Assembly, he observed recent trends in campus ministry which are quite helpful. Permit this rather lengthy but worthy quotation which follows from his report:

> I should like to suggest several campus trends which I believe are clearly discernible since they may affect our understanding of where we go. The first several I would identify as *receding trends:*
>
> A. I believe there is today less and less interest in the nod-to-God and all that which passes as Religious Emphasis Weeks. Does this mean that massive assaults on the campus are out? If so, is it related to our apologetic inabilities?
>
> B. Surely today there is less concern for social life and recreation in our student Christian fellowships. Perhaps this is because of the development of social life available, *e.g.* in Student Unions and the generally more permissive attitude and ethos of the campus.
>
> C. There is less interest on the part of students in what goes on in Student Christian Centers and Foundation Houses. In many campuses these buildings have become almost "white elephants."
>
> D. There is less interest in the campus Christian Community in the mass rally, speaker type program. In a large number of places the weekly meeting with a main speaker has virtually ceased to be of any significance numerically.
>
> E. There does also seem to be less interest in rigid program separation along denominational lines. Perhaps correlatively there is less concern for the church as gathered community and more concern for the church scattered in the world, but yet corporately engaged in the life of the university and the world.
>
> F. There seems to be less interest than ever among Christian students in World University Service.

On the other hand, I believe it is also possible to identify certain *developing trends,* which I believe are of interest and concern to us.

A. There is a growing interest in serious efforts of study. Study groups, retreats and conferences seem to be increasing.

B. There is a growing development of small group work organized along lines of intellectual interest frequently on a disciplinary basis, and of small groups gathered around social and political concern. It is also interesting to note that many of these are organized on an inter-denominational basis.

C. There seems to be a growing interest among students in various forms of individual voluntary service. Our own voluntary service projects program gives us some evidence of this as does the interest in the Peace Corps.

D. There is a developing trend toward greater corporate or team ministry efforts by the campus ministry staff. Not only do they more and more meet regularly together; they also share common responsibilities, notably for work among students in graduate and professional schools and for work with faculty.

E. There is a growing interest and attention being paid to the ever increasing students from other lands.

F. There is a rebirth of interest in social and political issues. This became apparent with the advent of "sit-ins," but is also discernible with reference to the problems of peace, arms control, nuclear disarmament, the House Un-American Activities Committee, civil defense, Operation Abolition and the growth of political clubs.

G. There is a seemingly greater interest in ecumenical contacts and relations both on the campus and in intercollegiate affairs.

H. There is certainly a growing interest in international travel among students generally.

I. There is, I believe, a major trend in interest and development of Koinonia Houses, Faith and Life Communities, and in a disciplined involvement in Christian intentional community.

J. There is, I believe, a growing willingness on the part of campus Christian staff to accept ecumenical responsibility and to exercise leadership in behalf of attaining greater knowledge and understanding of ecumenism.

K. There is a continued strong interest in accentuating participation in the World Student Christian Federation.[1]

These general observations from one who has provided leadership in the contemporary Campus Christian Movement are similar

[1] *Some Thoughts About the National Student Christian Federation as Community and as Organization,* a working paper prepared by Herluf M. Jensen for the III General Assembly, NSCF, Lake Geneva, Wisconsin, September 3-10, 1961, pp. 19-21.

to those which many would make. These changes are quite remarkable and they have occurred largely within the space of a decade. Wherever campus ministers and campus ministry boards have been alert to these changes, equally remarkable changes in ministry have emerged. Those who were not alert have continued traditional programs and are today usually quite out of touch with the university and frequently unable to communicate with students.

FACULTY IN MINISTRY

Ten years ago it was rare indeed to encounter a campus ministry in which faculty and administrators were participants. Campus ministry was understood as work with students only. Today it is as rare to discover one which does not include teachers, administrators, research persons, and graduate students. In some instances secretaries, house mothers, hostesses, and janitors are also involved in the ministry of the church within the university.

One example of faculty involvement in campus ministry is a group of professors from various disciplines who are concerned about the relevance of the gospel to their life and work within the university. Each Wednesday morning they meet for breakfast at 7:00 A.M. to enjoy the culinary art of one of the group. Their primary purpose is not food and fellowship, however! They congregate to read and discuss papers which have been prepared by members of the group. Usually these papers deal with the problem of relating Christian faith to one of the academic disciplines. It is interesting to note the role of the minister in this group. He is not the organizer, the prime mover, nor the one who is expected to assure success. He is merely a member who takes his place with other men in a vital search for meaning. He neither dominates nor controls the group, but is free to participate in open and animated discussion which is never dull, though not always comfortable to one who expects easy answers.

Then there is the university pastor in a large city whose apartment near a large metropolitan campus serves as an informal gathering place for graduate students and faculty. Here a continual conversation seems to be in progress. Again, he does not control or manage or manipulate the dialogue. Rarely do such informal discussions over coffee avoid theology. This university pastor concentrates on faculty because he is convinced they have been neglected, that they are human beings, and that they have special needs which cannot be met by local church pastors, primarily because such pastors do not have time.

In this instance, informal conversations have led to other kinds of involvement within the university. A university-sponsored faculty forum has now been instituted. During one year respected members of various disciplines were asked to respond to one question something like this: "How do you in your discipline regard the nature of man?" This vital question was discussed with vigor.

Also, there have come into being faculty dinners where Christians and non-Christians were involved in conversation about the great issues of our day. While there was disagreement at many points, the very fact that there is conversation is most rewarding and promising.

Another pattern of faculty in ministry has evolved on a campus where one campus pastor is charged with this responsibility on behalf of the whole Protestant community. He has been freed of all other responsibilities in order to devote full time to this aspect of the university community. He has discovered a community of Christian and non-Christian scholars who are eager to work with him in raising the human and theological issues which plague every scholar.

On this campus a faculty committee has been formed to counsel with the university pastor. For several years they have been holding faculty conferences which again are raising the issue of relating theology to a particular discipline. A committee of faculty members discuss issues which are of the utmost concern to them; they choose the subject and sharpen the questions which are to be discussed. Then a theologian, who also knows the discipline, is invited to spend several days or perhaps a whole weekend with them on campus. Sometimes papers are written and discussed preceding or following the conference, and occasionally the faculty members involved have invited the mature students within the discipline to their own homes to discuss with them the questions which have come out of their own experiences.

Other patterns abound. Faculty retreats, faculty forums, Faculty Christian Fellowship groups, and informal study groups are in progress across the country.[2] The Episcopal Church has been con-

² See Chapter 7.

ducting summer sessions for faculty for several years now. These summer schools are in session for six weeks. Visiting theologians from all parts of the country meet with faculty in a concentrated program of lectures, reading, and discussion which are intended to equip the laity for ministry within the university.

Thus we see emerging a new dimension in campus ministry. As faculty and administrators continue to share in the work of ministry, we can be sure that the community of faith and the community of learning will be bound together in what is seen increasingly as a common task.

STUDENTS IN MINISTRY

What we have been describing above marks a new concept of ministry which has altered work with students considerably. During the period when "student work" was understood as the work of the campus minister, it was quite naturally limited to the persons whom he could reach. Today the emphasis is upon the ministry of the whole church which includes faculty, students, and administrators, as well as the ordained staff. As all these persons become conscious of their calling, we should not be surprised to observe a changing pattern and a changing program among students.

In some situations the Sunday evening fellowship has disappeared, but this is not an indication that campus ministry has gone out of business. It merely points to the fact that other occasions for meeting have been discovered and that the purpose for holding meetings at all has been clarified. Indeed, the church is very much involved with students in ministry. However, we believe that they share in the *work* of ministry rather than being the *object* of ministry.

Perhaps this change can be illustrated best by recounting the experience of one university pastor and the members of the advisory committee who were courageous enough to recognize that their work was ineffectual and that the university deserved a fresh approach.

The "student program" had all the earmarks of tradition. It included a Sunday night fellowship with name tags and fellowship singing, a Wednesday forum with outstanding speakers but only a handful of students, several study groups, occasional parties, and the usual stream of campus mailings.

It was decided that all of these had to die; that it was not merely a matter of rejuvenating old forms, or pouring new wine into old skins. This pastor and committee proposed that for one year they would allow these programs, structures, and habits to slip silently into oblivion. During this time they would study new ways and means of ministry and explore a fresh approach to the work of the church.

Only one innovation was introduced. Sunday evening prayers were conducted in a chapel. It was a rather formal service, with no greeters, and no one present to be certain that each worshiper was introduced to everyone present. All of this was deliberate.

Soon there emerged a worshiping community. These persons had come not to meet and greet others but to worship God. These worshipers were not the regular Sunday nighters, or Wednesday nighters, but they were vitally interested in many issues related to the gospel, the church, and ministry.

Within a year a whole new campus ministry program had emerged. It centered on worship and involved well over 150 students in faculty-led seminars on subjects which were the natural concern of students. These faculty members were anxious to invite students to their homes for dinner. Discussions followed which were relevant to life. Real personal relationships developed. What is happening today on this campus is utterly different from the ministry a decade ago. It has few of the trappings we have come to expect. It does show that the church can be integral to life without employing many of the standard gimmicks in which some have placed their trust. This is one illustration of a different kind of ministry with students.

Or consider the commuters. Many of our college and university enrollments include from forty to ninety percent commuting students. In these situations new approaches are absolutely necessary and creative patterns have emerged.

Imagine yourself walking into a large church basement room on Tuesday evening and finding cots arranged for sleeping, tables prepared for study, and a worship service in progress in a nearby chapel. This is one commuter student group in a large Big Ten university. Here commuters constitute sixty percent of the student body. They stay overnight near the campus, rather than going home, in order to worship with others, to study, and to enjoy a sense of community which is so difficult to experience while living in their situation.

Such groups meet typically at 5:30 P.M. for worship. They enjoy dinner together, which is followed by an hour or more of rather intensely disciplined discussions of materials which have been read previously. The rest of the evening is left for personal study and preparation for the following day in the university. Following study, the improvised sleeping accommodations eliminate the long trek home for the student.

Such experimental groups are now developing in several communities. Many large city universities find it possible to make economical arrangements with hotels for such an evening with commuters. Endless opportunities for encounter and study exist in our large cities and can be easily integrated into such a program. To cite one example: Theaters welcome groups at reduced rates to see certain excellent and provocative films, and some will even provide discussion rooms following the film. If such a room is not available, the group may return to the hotel for discussion and study.

As our commuting population grows, more experiments similar to these will be attempted if students are to be reached.

On a given Friday night it is possible to sit in with quite another group in a large city medical school complex. In this area there are over 6,100 persons involved in the study, teaching, and research programs related to medical science. This particular group has been carefully selected and personally invited to a dinner, following which they will spend a long evening with the selected scholars. These "invitational dinners" are infrequent and are carefully planned. Men of science, philosophy, theology, or literature are chosen and expected to relate as persons with those who have been invited. These rather informal gatherings have provided stimulating "starters" for continuing conversations among the medical people.

Quite another encounter has emerged in a more rural setting. In this community, local pastors were concerned about the changing nature of a normal school which is becoming a liberal arts college. In their opinion, religion was being edged out of the college calendar. The university pastor became acquainted with college administrators and the local pastors. To the amazement of everyone, the college administrators invited the pastors to a series of meetings during which the administrators would discuss the philosophy and aims of higher education if (and this condition is interesting) the pastors would discuss the philosophy of the church. The mutually informative discussion continued for a year and has set a new tone for ministry on the campus and in the community.

Perhaps the most serious criticism to be leveled at the church and particularly at those of us who are campus pastors is that we do not know or really care about the college or university to which we are called. Are we sensitive to the cutting edges of each discipline? Are we alert to research in progress in fields ranging from nutrition to psychology to nuclear physics? Do we know the persons who are making the important decisions which affect the lives of thousands?

One campus ministry group evaluating its own life and work concluded that its members were spending all their time talking to each other, and no time listening to persons outside the group but involved in the university. They decided that their typical Sunday evening program was neither vital nor particularly relevant and that it could be much more strategic in their total ministry. Thus it was that Sunday evening was set aside to listen to the members of the university. Each week a competent scholar was invited to discuss one question: "What is the most vital frontier in your discipline today?" They were not expected to be "religious" about it or to theologize. The group felt that this was their own responsibility. While these encounters were threatening to some, these weekly sessions served to raise real questions about life that would not have been faced otherwise.

In such encounters, theology becomes a necessity, not merely a luxury for the religious elite. What contemporary scholars are learning has far-reaching implications and may actually alter our own patterns of study and worship.

Another new feature in campus ministry in our time is the visiting theologian who is in residence on a given campus for a time. Usually, these men are invited jointly by ecumenical or interdenominational religious councils and the university. They usually lecture in classrooms and to the public, meet with campus ministry groups, and may even participate in research within the university. Although this practice was largely unknown twenty years ago, such lectures are now contributing to the enrichment of the university curriculum. Indeed, in some universities funds for visiting lecturers are occasionally combined with funds secured from ecclesiastical or other sources to bring a noted scholar who is known to relate his faith to the particular discipline.

Visiting lecturers of this kind are secured for varying lengths of time. In some cases he may come for a week or a weekend. He may address the art classes or the history department or the physical science students, as well as lecture to campus ministry or local church groups. In other cases, he may actually be in residence for a semester or for the entire academic year.

The Christian Faith and Life Community in Austin, Texas, has been mentioned elsewhere in this volume.[3] This "Austin experiment" has definitely influenced campus ministry developments across the country. In some universities the Austin pattern is emulated in amazing detail; in others the basic philosophy of the Faith and Life Community is more carefully scrutinized and a pattern of disciplined life and study and worship is designed on similar lines but with quite different goals and objectives.

One such experiment is well known to the author. It is reported here because, in this instance, the experiment actually altered the whole approach to campus ministry on that campus.

The original experiment included a selected group of upperclassmen in good academic standing, several graduate students, faculty, and two university pastors. Each signed a covenant which committed him to a year of study, worship, discussion, and one common meal each week. Individuals committed themselves to devote five hours per week to assigned study, to worship with others each week at the university chapel service, to worship each Thursday when they met together, and to pay for their own meals which were served in the student union.

The study curriculum included a series of papers in four areas: "The Nature of Man," "The Nature of the Gospel," "The Nature of the Church," and "The Nature of Mission." Seven weeks were devoted to each area of study.

[3] See Chapter 6.

Each Thursday the group met from 5:30 to 8:00 P.M. A 30-minute worship service was conducted. Discussion during the common meal was completely structured. As the group gathered at table, intercessory prayers were said. Food was served and eaten in silence while one member read aloud from the Scriptures, the church fathers, or contemporary authors. Following the first course a question or concern was addressed to the group. This might come from university life, politics, social issues, art, or from any of the disciplines. Each person was expected to respond to the question. During the dessert free conversation was held.

Following dinner the theological paper was discussed. These papers were carefully criticized and the implications openly discussed. These discussions were vital and heated and related to life as it is actually lived. To the amazement of the group, a real community emerged. Students became real persons, faculty members were called by first name, the content of the study became relevant to academic life. Fears were exposed, prejudices revealed, and hates were ventilated, but each person discovered that a more profound relationship with fellow students and faculty was a real possibility unknown to him previous to this experience.

Today, there are at least four such groups meeting on that campus. One rooming-house now includes a group of men who committed themselves not only to live together but to attend daily corporate worship and weekly study akin to what has been described.

The university pastor participating in such encounters with students and faculty must of necessity become a "teaching elder" in the Reformed sense. He can no longer be content with merely organizing programs where others speak, or with promoting religion in general. He now enters the arena dialogue with persons who expect him to take the scholarly pursuit of theology seriously. He must serve as theologian as well as pastor. He is expected to be as well informed in his discipline as the other scholars are in theirs.

This experiment illustrates clearly that the witness, if we may still use the word, of the church is exercised not apart from, but within, the structured life of the university. Each participant had a legitimate vocation within the university. He was performing a function which contributed to the life of the whole community.

His witness to Jesus Christ could not be isolated from his real-life involvements as a student or faculty member, or as a person sharing in extracurricular aspects of university life. What was experienced together in worship, informal conversation, and theological discussion was somehow very real and very vital where life was lived.

This experience transformed the whole concept of ministry. Where there had previously existed a typically successful "religious" group with all the familiar earmarks, there now emerged a community whose concerns and cares were quite different. Where once they had gathered for mere refreshments and fellowship, they now conceived of gathering for being equipped for their ministry as students and faculty in the university. What had once been a chummy group who enjoyed each other, now resembled a task force gathering to be fed and forgiven and sent forth to labor and live authentically in the world. Perhaps you are asking, "What do you mean by living authentically in the world? Just what is the ministry of students, faculty, and administrators within the university?" While this is not the place for an exhaustive treatment of these questions, the issue is so important to understanding campus ministry that we should not avoid it.

Let us commence with asking what most of us have understood to be the ingredients of a successful campus ministry. We have accepted the following criteria quite readily: A successful campus ministry is determined by the number of people who enter the building, and who are involved in what transpires there. This may include worship, discussion groups, luncheons, playing games, listening to music, attending cabinet meetings, and counseling with the campus pastor. What happens in the building and the number who participate in those happenings determine largely the opinions we have about a campus ministry. At times we have been guilty of perverting the word "witness" to mean "being faithful in attendance at our functions."

While some of these activities are good, and some necessary, we cannot avoid asking the questions, "But what about the world beyond our doors? Is the gospel addressed only to the church, or is it meant for the world which 'God so loved'?"

To live authentically is to enter the world outside the church as a human being who seeks to express his real humanity. It is to love the world which God loves and not to fear it, abhor it, or deny it. Sometimes it is difficult for us to confess that God loves the world as surely as he loves the church. He cares for all creatures.

To be a minister, as every Christian is called to be, is to care about the world. To enter the ministry is to involve oneself authentically with all manner of men and women in the joy, the struggles, the tensions, and the pressures of the common life in the world. The church was never called to be a retreat from real life in the world. We gather, not to escape life, but to be equipped for life in vocation, home, neighborhood, and society.

Students and faculty encounter the real world in the university — in dormitories where they live with others, in libraries where they discover the wisdom and knowledge of the ages, in classrooms where new information about the world is presented and evaluated and where all world views are expounded. The university also includes many communities which are non-academic. In the fraternity, sorority, student government, and countless societies, the real life of student and faculty is lived. These are the structures of the university, the built-in patterns of order which every person on campus encounters and about which he must make important decisions.

Here is the arena where witness takes place, if it has any meaning at all. The church's ministry is expressed here as members individually and collectively live their lives with others. In a real sense this is the silent ministry, the unsung ministry, the servant ministry which is not paraded and lauded but like salt and yeast is most effective in its hiddenness. It is to care about others, to be kind and forgiving in the arena where man's inhumanity to man often takes most subtle forms. To fail there is to fail utterly. When we understand this principle, we have begun to appreciate the meaning of being forgiven, and we know how gracious are the words of the gospel. The student and the faculty member sensitive to God's redeeming work will be witness to God's working *in* the vocation to which they have been appointed, in ways which can not be determined by others, and for which they require support and equipping from the community of faith.

This authentic, honestly human endeavor does not assume to desecularize the world, nor to convert the university into a church-related college, but is an expression of love and concern within the structures which have been given, and in which all men live. Success in this kind of witness cannot be measured readily, nor can our effectiveness be easily charted or described, nor can our ministry be predetermined by denominational promoters. Our life and mission grow out of the daily demands of the situation. Christians respond because they believe that here God is at work as he has always been at work in history.

Working Within the Structures of the University

One final illustration of a new pattern in campus ministry must suffice. It is so utterly different as to be frightening to traditional church people. Whether or not this pattern succeeds depends almost entirely upon the competence and commitment of the university pastor, and on his ability to gather a group of faculty and students who are themselves free enough and mature enough to participate without the support of, and involvement in, a traditional religious group. In fact, this pattern presupposes that the persons involved are worshiping in local churches and understand their own ministry to be within their vocation in the academic community.

In this metropolitan university there are 10,000 students, all of whom commute to the campus from a radius of fifty miles each day. In the typical pattern, they work part time, live at home, drive in car pools, and are on campus only for classes. Campus organizations of any kind are limited.

The campus ministry in this university has no student or faculty organization of any kind. The total ministry is conceived and manifested in working completely within the structures of the university. This means that there is no fellowship group, there are no study groups sponsored by the campus ministry cabinet, no programs are sponsored by a self-conscious group. All ministry is performed by working with people in the university, within patterns of the university.

This strategy takes seriously the belief that Jesus Christ is at work in the university in the persons who are of the church, that their mission, their ministry, is exercised in their vocation, and that the university pastor understands his ministry as equipping them and supporting them in their God-given vocation.

In everyday life this university pastor is quite unattached, unrelated to a building or to a formal group. He is free to respond to the church within the university in the person of students, faculty, and administrators as they express a need for his help or support.

All "programs" are jointly sponsored by a division or college within the university, and are usually integrated into the very curriculum or class of that division or college, thus avoiding the connotation of being extracurricular or not integral to the study at hand.

This approach to campus ministry, while utterly different from prevailing patterns, does suggest that we must continue to explore new approaches to campus ministry. We dare not be content with traditional patterns when these are obviously outmoded and largely irrelevant in the contemporary scene.

The Ecumenical Dimension

That which has been implied throughout this chapter will be stated here specifically; namely, that a relevant campus ministry must of necessity be ecumenical. There is one Lord, one faith, one baptism; and to witness to any other conviction is to be unfaithful. A community which refuses to face the sin of its own division has nothing to offer a world rent with divisions. Our ministry commences with confession of sin, and moves toward proclamation of oneness in Christ Jesus.

In the opinion of this author, ecumenical commitments are no longer electives; they are urgent necessity.

The great issues of our time cannot be catalogued denominationally: The scientific revolution, international tensions, the race issue, rampant secularism, technology — these great concerns of the century cannot be approached from individual denominational centers, nor can they be dealt with under denominational banners. It matters little whether we have large or small buildings, or whether or not we develop a successful "religious group" as it has been conceived historically. Our world is crying for insight and examples to deal with the forces that are separating man from man and nation from nation and literally tearing the world apart.

It is interesting to observe that the universities and colleges in our time are willing to consider seriously the theological implications of what they teach and do. At the same time the university is becoming more intolerant of individual denominational programs which express concern only for "our religious preference students" and seem to give little or no thought to the world beyond.

Today, there are new opportunities for work with students, faculty members, and administrators on an ecumenical basis. The university has no administrative procedure to cope with denominations. Fraternities, sororities, and dormitory councils, as well as student senates and other groups, find it difficult to invite a Presbyterian or Baptist or Roman Catholic clergyman into their houses or organizations without being subject to criticism from those religious groups whose pastor was not invited.

But when campus pastors and campus ministry committees are willing to work together on vital issues which lie quite beyond denominations, these nonreligious organizations are anxious to join the venture. They are eager to discuss pertinent issues! The same can be said for faculty groups and professional clubs.

The question we face is this: Must we provide a religious organizational structure in order to proclaim the gospel or are we expected to proclaim it within the structures and organizations which already exist within the university?

This author maintains that a relevant campus Christian witness will not come about unless we Christians recognize that the social and academic structures which already exist are gifts from God and not necessarily the work of the Devil. Why a separate "religious structure"? Why separate religious clubs? Is not the Christian life to be lived in the world? When these queries are taken seriously, a wholly different kind of program may emerge on a given campus.

Wherever the church is located, in whatever circumstance a Christian community discovers itself, it must always dare to ask the most basic, elementary, and crucial question: "What is God calling us to be and do at this time in this place?" To ask this question requires real courage. To begin to answer it is to live by faith and therein lies the essence of the Christian life. We cannot predict where we will be led, but for faithful people this does not matter.

It may be that God is leading his church into the heat of battle or to a ministry of real service to others — the dimensions and depth of which we have not yet experienced in campus ministry.

Appendix:
Study Curricula

Perhaps the most influential of contemporary attempts to "equip the saints" for better performing their roles in church and society is the Christian Faith and Life Community at the University of Texas in Austin. Begun in 1952 under the direction of a Presbyterian campus pastor, Jack Lewis, it has developed a thorough study-in-depth program. The formal course of study developed at Austin has been the basis for dozens of similar undertakings (most of which are non-residential) around the country. The Austin curriculum is roughly equivalent in time demands on the students to one course in the university. It runs for one school year and is divided into four terms, two semesters.

FALL SEMESTER

First Term: *Theology*. Selfhood and human existence, or the faith of the church.

Second Term: *Biblical Studies*. Selfhood and the Bible or the Scriptures of the church.

SPRING SEMESTER

Third Term: *Church History*. Selfhood and Community, or the life of the church.

Fourth Term: *Ethics*. Selfhood and Responsibility, or the mission of the church.

THE METHODIST CHURCH'S GUILD OF LAY THEOLOGIANS

One of the attempts to adapt the curriculum of the Austin experiment along with the idea of its discipline (without the residential aspect) is the Methodist Guild of Lay Theologians. The corporate discipline has been set down as follows:

Our Corporate Study

1. Our discipline is to be present at the weekly study and discussion at [time and day stated].
2. Our discipline is to give the necessary time each week to the study of the material assigned for the following meeting.

Our Corporate Worship

Our discipline is to attend the service of worship at the beginning of each meeting of the group on [day and time], either as a self-conscious participant or as an empathetic spectator.

Our Corporate Mission

Our mission is openly and honestly to strive to discover anew and in depth what it means to be genuine free men in action — responsible, critically intelligent persons — in a university situation, in our family relationships, in our friendships, and in all the orders of social existence.

SAMPLE CURRICULUM

The following is a sample of their curriculum entitled, "Life and Mission of the Christian Church":

Part One — The Situation of the Post-Modern Theologian

A. Theologizing in a personal vein (two sessions). Franz Kafka, Roger Hazelton, Earl A. Loomis, Erich Fromm.

B. The situation of post-modern man (two sessions). Will Herberg, Paul Elmen, Otto Butz, Glendon Swarthout.

C. The task of the post-modern theologian (two sessions). Rudolf Bultmann, Paul Tillich, Schubert N. Ogden.

D. The recovery of the symbol "God" and the renewal of the God-relationship (two sessions). Rudolf Bultmann, H. Richard Niebuhr, Karl Barth.

E. The recovery of the symbol "Christ" and the hearing of the Good News (four sessions). Paul Tillich, D. M. Baillie, Fyodor Dostoyevsky, Edward Hobbs, Terence Rattigan, Jean-Paul Sartre.

F. The recovery of the symbol "church" and participation in the community of faith (two sessions). Alexander Miller, Robert M. Brown, John Knox, H. Richard Niebuhr.

Part Two — The Heretofore Life of the Christian Church

A. The scriptural records of the life of the church
  1. Introduction to biblical exegesis
    a. Recent history of biblical exegesis (two sessions)
    b. Biblical exegesis in a personal vein (two sessions)
  2. The life of Israel, the pre-Christian church
    a. The constitution of Israel: the exodus-covenant (two sessions)
    b. The life of Israel over against the Constitution: the prophets (two sessions centering on Hosea)
    c. Israel's image of beginnings; the faith of Abraham (two sessions)
    d. The suffering of Israel under the constitution: the writings (two sessions, centering on Job)
  3. The Life of the church, the New Israel.
    a. The constitution of the church: the *Kerygma*
    b. The *Kerygma* of the church according to Paul (two sessions)
    c. The *Kerygma* of the church according to Mark (two sessions)
    d. The *Kerygma* of the church according to John (two sessions)

B. The post-biblical life of the church
  1. The early church
  2. The medieval church
  3. The Reformation church
  4. The modern church

RESIDENTIAL SEMINAR AT BROWN UNIVERSITY

At Brown University there is a study seminar similar in approach to that of the Austin Christian Faith and Life Community. At Brown, the students live in a section of the regular university housing and they covenant to attend the regular 8:30 daily chapel services of the university. This covenant group meets together for a Friday dinner, with each denominational chaplain associated with the Student Christian Association serving as a small group tutor.

The curriculum is built around the study of eight books: *The Brothers Karamazov,* by Dostoyevsky; *I and Thou,* by Buber; *God Was in Christ,* D. M. Baillie; and the writings of Kierkegaard; plus four biblical texts: a prophet, a Gospel, Genesis, and Romans.

UNITED CHURCH STUDENT FELLOWSHIP, IOWA CITY, IOWA

Individual denominational groups have also used the curriculum idea. The following example is a short-term study course based on the Austin study material, adapted for use at Iowa City by the United Church campus pastor, the Rev. Philip Shively. The description reads:

Many are searching for an opportunity to grapple with the basic issues of life. Many are aware of a loneliness that diversions and tranquilizers cannot reach. Many are demanding an opportunity to think creatively, to worship meaningfully, and to act courageously in the midst of a frightening world. Toward these reflective men and women our study group is directed.

In carrying out this basic idea, the group organizes its study as follows:

1. Introduction and Orientation
2. Where do I stand in relation to the faith and to God? to the failure of other gods?
3. Why can't I just live naturally?
4. How am I to live my life?
5. Where do I see the mission of the church in the world?
6. How do I see the mission of the church in its scatteredness?

To these ends, the group studies a variety of writings, including those of Will Herberg, H. Richard Niebuhr, Rudolf Bultmann, Reinhold Niebuhr, Paul Tillich, Dietrich Bonhoeffer, John Knox, Joseph W. Matthews, Hendrik Kraemer, Richard Shaull, W. A. Visser 't Hooft, and H. B. Sissel.

Bibliography

BIBLICAL MATERIAL

Anderson, Bernhard W., *Rediscovering the Bible*. New York: Association Press, 1951.

Anderson, Bernhard W., *Understanding the Old Testament*. Englewood Cliffs, N. J.: Prentice-Hall, Inc., 1957.

Anderson, Bernhard W., *Unfolding Drama of the Bible*. New York: Association Press, 1957.

Brown, Robert M., *The Bible Speaks to You*. Philadelphia: Westminster Press, 1955.

de Dietrich, Suzanne, *The Witnessing Community*. Philadelphia: Westminster Press, 1958.

Johnson, Robert C., *The Meaning of Christ*. Philadelphia: Westminster Press, 1958.

Kee, Howard and Franklin W. Young, *Understanding the New Testament*. Englewood Cliffs, N. J.: Prentice-Hall, 1957.

CHURCH HISTORY

Bainton, Roland H., *Early Christianity*. Princeton: D. Van Nostrand Co., 1960.

Bainton, Roland H., *The Reformation of the Sixteenth Century*. Boston: Beacon Press, 1956.

323

Butterfield, Herbert, *Christianity and History*. New York: Charles Scribner's Sons, 1950.

Fosdick, Harry Emerson, ed., *Great Voices of the Reformation*. New York: Random House, Inc., 1952.

Hudson, Winthrop S., *The Story of the Christian Church*. New York: Harper & Row, 1958.

Marty, Martin E., *A Short History of Christianity*. New York: The World Publishing Company, Meridian Books, 1959.

BASIC THEOLOGY

Finegan, Jack, *Beginnings in Theology*. New York: Association Press, 1956.

Finegan, Jack, *First Steps in Theology*. New York: Association Press, 1960.

Halverson, Marvin and Arthur A. Cohen, eds., *A Handbook of Christian Theology*. New York: The World Publishing Company, Meridian Books, 1958.

Hamilton, William, *The Christian Man*. Philadelphia: Westminster Press, 1956.

Harkness, Georgia, *Understanding the Christian Faith*. Nashville: Abingdon Press, 1947.

Hordern, William, *A Layman's Guide to Protestant Theology*. New York: Macmillan Company, 1955.

McClendon, James W., *Pacemakers of Christian Thought*. Nashville: Broadman Press, 1962.

Miller, Alexander, *Renewal of Man*. Garden City: Doubleday & Company, 1955.

Niebuhr, Reinhold, *The Nature and Destiny of Man*. New York: Charles Scribner's Sons, 1941-1943.

Phillips, J. B., *Plain Christianity*. New York: Macmillan Company, 1954.

Spurrier, William A., *Guide to the Christian Faith*. New York: Charles Scribner's Sons, 1952.

THE CHURCH

Baly, Denis, *Chosen Peoples*. Philadelphia: United Church Press, 1956.

Bonhoeffer, Dietrich, *Life Together*. New York: Harper & Row, 1954.

Brown, Robert M., *The Significance of the Church*. Philadelphia: Westminster Press, 1956.
Handy, Robert, *Members One of Another*. Valley Forge: Judson Press, 1959.
Hunt, George L., *Rediscovering the Church*. New York: Association Press, 1956.
Kraemer, Hendrik, *Theology of the Laity*. Philadelphia: Westminster Press, 1959.
Newbigin, J. E. Lesslie, *The Household of God*. New York: Friendship Press, 1954.
Winter, Gibson, *The Suburban Captivity of the Church*. Garden City: Doubleday & Company, 1961. New York: Macmillan Company, 1962 (paper edition).

ECUMENICAL MOVEMENT
Minear, Paul S., ed., *The Nature of the Unity We Seek*. St. Louis: Bethany Press, 1958. (An official report of the North American Conference on Faith and Order.)
Newbigin, J. E. Lesslie, *One Body, One Gospel, One World*. New York: International Missionary Council, 1958.

HIGHER EDUCATION
Beach, Waldo, *Conscience on Campus*. New York: Association Press, 1958.
Cantelon, John, ed., *A Basis for Study — A Theological Perspective for the Campus Ministry*. Richmond and Philadelphia: Department of Campus Christian Life, United Presbyterian Church U.S.A., and Presbyterian Church U.S., 1959.
Coleman, John, *The Task of the Christian in the University*. New York: Association Press, 1947.
Miller, Alexander, *Faith and Learning*. New York: Association Press, 1960.
Moberly, Walter H., *The Crisis in the University*. New York: Macmillan Company, 1949.
Von Greuningen, J. P., ed., *Toward a Christian Philosophy of Higher Education*. Philadelphia: Westminster Press, 1957.
Walter, Erich A., ed., *Religion and the State University*. Ann Arbor: University of Michigan Press, 1958.

326 • THE CAMPUS MINISTRY

Wise, W. Max, *They Come for the Best of Reasons.* Washington: American Council on Education, 1958.

CAMPUS CULTURE

Barney, Jonne, et al. *Profile of a College Student by College Students.* Washington: The American National Red Cross, 1961.

Bender, Richard N., ed., *On the Work of the Ministry in University Communities.* Nashville: Board of Education, The Methodist Church, 1962.

Carpenter, Marjorie, ed., *The Larger Learning: Teaching Values to College Students.* Dubuque: William C. Brown Company, 1960.

Eddy, Edward D., *College Influence on Student Character.* Washington: American Council on Education, 1959.

Goldsen, Rose, et al. *What College Students Think.* Princeton: D. Van Nostrand Co., 1960.

Hamill, Robert H., *Gods of the Campus.* Nashville: Abingdon Press, 1949.

Jacob, Philip E., *Changing Values in College.* New York: Harper & Row, 1958.

Lloyd, Wesley P. *The University in the Changing Community.* Washington: The American National Red Cross, 1961.

Riesman, David, *Constraint and Variety in American Education.* Garden City: Doubleday & Company, 1958.

Sanford, R. Nevitt, *The American College.* New York: John Wiley & Sons, 1962.

Sprague, Hall T., ed., *Research on College Students.* Boulder, Colorado: Western Interstate Commission for Higher Education, 1960.

Walsh, Chad, *Campus Gods on Trial.* New York: Macmillan Company, 1962.

PRAYER AND WORSHIP

Baillie, John, *A Diary of Private Prayer.* New York: Charles Scribner's Sons, 1949.

Bollinger, H. D., ed., *The Student at Prayer.* Nashville: Methodist Student Movement, 1960.

Buttrick, George A., *Prayer.* New York: Abingdon Press, 1942.

Casteel, John, *Rediscovering Prayer.* New York: Association Press, 1955.

Coffin, Henry S., *The Public Worship of God*. Philadelphia: Westminster Press, 1946.

Nelson, John O., ed., *The Student Prayerbook*. New York: Association Press, 1953.

Shepherd, Massey H., ed., *The Liturgical Renewal of the Church*. New York: Oxford University Press, 1960.

EVANGELISM

Bender, Richard N., ed., *Campus Evangelism in Theory and Practice*. Nashville: Methodist Student Movement, 1957.

Maury, Philippe, *Politics and Evangelism*. Garden City: Doubleday & Company, 1959.

McCoy, Charles S. and Neely D. McCarter, *The Gospel on Campus*. Richmond: John Knox Press, 1959.

Niles, Daniel T., *That They May Have Life*. New York: Harper & Row, 1951.

Spike, Robert W., *Safe in Bondage*. New York: Friendship Press, 1960.

THE RACIAL QUESTION

Haselden, Kyle, *The Racial Problem in Christian Perspective*. New York: Harper & Row, 1959.

King, Martin Luther, Jr., *Stride Toward Freedom*. New York: Harper & Row, 1958.

Mays, Benjamin E., *Seeking to Be Christian in Race Relations*. New York: Friendship Press, 1957.

Pope, Liston, *The Kingdom Beyond Caste*. New York: Friendship Press, 1957.

Tilson, C. Everett, *Segregation and the Bible*. New York: Abingdon Press, 1958.

COMMUNISM, POLITICS, AND FOREIGN POLICY

Bennett, John C., *Christianity and Communism Today*. New York: Association Press, 1960.

Bennett, John C., *Christians and the State*. New York: Charles Scribner's Sons, 1958.

Hordern, William, *Christianity and Communism*. New York: Abingdon Press, 1962.

328 · THE CAMPUS MINISTRY

Lazareth, William, *A Theology of Politics.* New York: United
Lutheran Church in America, 1960.

Lefever, Ernest W., *Ethics and U.S. Foreign Policy.* New York: The
World Publishing Company, Meridian Books, 1957.

Miller, Alexander, *The Christian Significance of Karl Marx.* New
York: Macmillan Company, 1947.

Muehl, William, *Mixing Religion and Politics.* New York: Association Press, 1958.

Voorhis, Jerry, *The Christian in Politics.* New York: Association
Press, 1951.

SCIENCE AND THE CHRISTIAN FAITH

Dillenberger, John, *Protestant Thought and Natural Science.*
Garden City: Doubleday & Company, 1960.

Long, Edward LeRoy, Jr., *Science and the Christian Faith.* New
York: Association Press, 1950.

Snow, C. P., *The Two Cultures and the Scientific Revolution.* New
York: Cambridge University Press, 1959.

Shilling, Harold K., *Science and Religion.* New York: Charles Scribner's Sons, 1962.

LOVE AND MARRIAGE

Bainton, Roland H., *What Christianity Says About Sex, Love, and
Marriage.* New York: Association Press, 1957.

Bertocci, Peter, *The Human Venture in Sex, Love, and Marriage.*
New York: Association Press, 1949.

Cole, William G., *Sex and Love in the Bible.* New York: Association
Press, 1959.

Cole, William G., *Sex in Christianity and Psychoanalysis.* New York:
Oxford University Press, 1955.

Hamilton, William, *Faith, Sex and Love.* New York: National Student Council of the YMCA and the YWCA.

Hamilton, William, *The Christian Man.* Philadelphia: Westminster
Press, 1956.

Pemberton, Prentiss L., *Dialogue in Romantic Love.* Valley Forge:
Judson Press, 1961.

COUNSELING THE COLLEGE STUDENT

Arbuckle, Dugald S., *Student Personnel Services in Higher Education*. New York: McGraw-Hill Book Company, 1953.

Cronbach, Lee J., *The Essentials of Psychological Testing*. New York: Harper & Row, 1960.

Froehlich, Clifford P. and J. G. Darley, *Guidance Testing and Other Student Appraisal Procedures for Teachers and Counselors*. Chicago: Science Research Associates, 1959.

Hahn, Milton E. and M. S. MacLean, *General Clinical Counseling in Educational Institutions*. New York: McGraw-Hill Book Company, 1950.

Hoppock, Robert, *Group Guidance*. New York: McGraw-Hill Book Company, 1949.

Jones, Arthur J., *Principles of Guidance and Pupil Personnel Work*. New York: McGraw-Hill Book Company, 1963.

McKinney, Fred, *Counseling for Personal Adjustment in Schools and Colleges*. Boston: Houghton Mifflin Company, 1958.

Merriam, Thornton Ward, *Religious Counseling of Students*. Washington: American Council on Education, 1943.

Robinson, Francis P., *Principles and Procedures in Student Counseling*. New York: Harper & Row, 1950.

Rothney, John W. M., and B. A. Roens, *Counseling the Individual Student*. New York: William Sloane Associates, 1949.

Strang, Ruth, *Counseling Techniques in College and Secondary School*. New York: Harper & Row, 1949.

Strang, Ruth, *Educational Guidance*. New York: Macmillan Company, 1947.

Warters, Jane, *Group Guidance*. New York: McGraw-Hill Book Company, 1960.

Williamson, Edmund G., *Counseling Adolescents*. New York: McGraw-Hill Book Company, 1950.

Williamson, Edmund G., *Student Personnel Services in Colleges and Universities*. New York: McGraw-Hill Book Company, 1961.

Wrenn, Charles G., *Student Personnel Work in College*. New York: Ronald Press Company, 1961.

Woolf, Maurice D., *The Student Personnel Program*. New York: McGraw-Hill Book Company, 1953.